EDUCATION AND SOCIAL MOVEMENTS

EDUCATION & SOCIAL MOVEMENTS 1700-1850

BY

A. E. DOBBS

(Formerly Fellow of King's College, Cambridge)

REPRINTS OF ECONOMIC CLASSICS

AUGUSTUS M. KELLEY · PUBLISHERS
NEW YORK 1969

First Edition 1919

(London: Longmans, Green, and Co.,
39 Paternoster Row, 1919)

Reprinted 1969 by
Augustus M. Kelley · Publishers
New York, New York 10010

Library of Congress Catalogue Card Number
68-55702

PRINTED IN THE UNITED STATES OF AMERICA
by SENTRY PRESS, NEW YORK, N. Y. 10019

TO

ALBERT MANSBRIDGE

FIRST GENERAL SECRETARY OF THE WORKERS'
EDUCATIONAL ASSOCIATION

PREFACE

THE chapters contained in this volume were intended
to form part of a history of English popular education
in modern times, with special reference to movements
of democratic origin or tendency, the significance of
which has received new emphasis in recent years
through the rise of the Workers' Educational Association. They were completed before the outbreak of
the war, when I was compelled by a breakdown in
health and other circumstances to lay aside the task,
having done little more than set in order my materials
for the remaining and, as I hoped, more important
sections. In preparing this part of the work for publication I have thought it best to make few alterations,
adding little in the way of fresh matter beyond what
was required in order to define more clearly the position
reached at the close of the period with which it deals.
In a subsequent volume I hope to complete my original
design, by continuing the narrative down to the present
day.

Though the title may suggest a broader field of
inquiry than is commonly associated with the subject
of education, the matters discussed in certain passages,
especially in the first and third chapters, may be thought
more appropriate to a work on economics. Yet there
is truth in the paradoxical statement of a modern
writer, that progress in English education has owed less

to the zeal of its advocates than to changes in the structure of social life which have often no apparent connection with educational movements. The ideal of universal elementary instruction is at least as old as the Reformation, but the first organised effort to provide schools for the poor of England came at the close of the seventeenth century, when the religious conscience awoke to the problems of social degradation and urban poverty; and the movement which led to the modern system of elementary schools commenced a hundred years later, when society was in the throes of the Industrial Revolution. The sequence of events points clearly to an economic factor underlying the growth of educational demands; and though it is possible to press the analysis too far in assigning motives to the pioneers of popular education, it is both legitimate and necessary to dwell on economic and social tendencies which supplied a practical argument for 'instructing the masses.' From this standpoint one is tempted to define the elementary school as a specialised instrument of training and instruction necessitated by industrial developments which, dissolving the older forms of social life, opened access to a more complex existence along a path beset with difficulties and requiring a higher degree of mental equipment than had sufficed in earlier times.

There are other points of connection between educational and social history. If social changes have given a sanction and impetus to the demand for different forms of instruction, the lines on which their organisation develops are profoundly affected by social tradition. The clue to certain phases of educational controversy must be sought in religious and political divisions which are older than the modern school organisation, and in varieties of social outlook and experience which may be illustrated in some measure by a comparative study of different areas. If some parts of the country have lent themselves more readily than others to democratic experiments, an examination of their past history may throw light on the influences which have made them responsive. The element of education which consists in social experience has an historical interest, not only as illustrating the mental growth of the people in a bygone age when school-attendance was the privilege of a minority, but as shaping the material with which subsequent movements have to deal.

In discussing so wide a theme it is difficult to avoid digressions and an appearance of dogmatism with regard to issues which are often obscure. My hope is that the main drift of the argument is lucid, and that its conclusions are expressed with a caution not unworthy of the eminent authorities to whose labours I am indebted.

The work was commenced at the suggestion of my friend Mr. Albert Mansbridge, to whom I am privileged to dedicate this volume as a small acknowledgment of great obligations. I am also deeply indebted to Mr. R. H. Tawney, who has read these pages with great care in manuscript and in proof, offering much helpful criticism and many valuable suggestions. To others who have assisted me with advice and information, bearing principally on the chapters which remain to be completed, I hope before long to have an opportunity of expressing my gratitude.

November 15, 1918.

CONTENTS

PART I

THE EIGHTEENTH CENTURY

CHAPTER I

THE SOCIAL ENVIRONMENT ON THE EVE OF THE INDUSTRIAL REVOLUTION

xi

CHAPTER II

SCHOOLS AND LITERATURE

CHAPTER III

THE ERA OF REVOLUTIONS

CONTENTS

PART II

THE FIRST HALF OF THE NINETEENTH CENTURY

CHAPTER IV
ELEMENTARY EDUCATION

CHAPTER V
THE MECHANICS' INSTITUTES AND HIGHER EDUCATION

CONTENTS

PART I

THE EIGHTEENTH CENTURY

CHAPTER I

THE SOCIAL ENVIRONMENT ON THE EVE OF THE INDUSTRIAL REVOLUTION

'For it seems to be the ruling maxim of this age and nation that, if our trade and wealth are but increased, we are powerful and happy and secure; and in estimating the real strength of the Kingdom, the sole question for many years hath been " What commerce and riches the nation is possessed of ? " a question which an Ancient Lawgiver would have laughed at '—Browne, *Estimate of the Manners and Principles of the Times* (1757/8).

A century of uninterrupted material progress separates the Restoration of Charles the Second from the age of the Industrial Revolution. The latter half of this period is a time of optimism and internal repose, spanning the interval between great constitutional conflicts and the modern order of social discontents. Its main achievement consists in a steady course of commercial expansion, unaccompanied by any radical change in the social structure or the distribution of wealth. It stands as a type of even prosperity and contentment on the eve of vast revolutions, unprecedented sufferings, and unbounded hopes. Yet it is often in such intervals of tranquil growth that national character is subjected to the most critical tests, and that the frontier is passed which separates one stage of civilisation from another. There are no large alterations in the structure of society or the ideals of government; but there is a profound change in the relative strength of forces which had long been in conflict, and the

3

tendencies which assert their supremacy in different spheres mark the initial stages of a period of transition.

In studying the course of economic change, the crisis of 1688, which is noticed by eighteenth-century writers as a commercial no less than a political landmark, affords in many ways a more convenient starting-point than the date generally assigned for the commencement of the Industrial Revolution. To this earlier period belong one of the most critical phases in the decline of the yeomanry, and the beginnings of a systematic policy of enclosure by Act of Parliament; while in industry some of the problems which were to arise in connection with the factory system cast their shadow back over the intervening years.[1] On the one side, there was an advance of the new agriculture slowly dissolving the older forms of rural life ; on the other, the approach of modern industrialism—a growth of initiative and exploitation, a marked extension of industry in the Midlands and the North, and, in certain districts, a steady movement of population from the country to the town. Not less significant are the modifications which arose almost imperceptibly in the trend of economic thought. The growth of capitalism from the beginning of the eighteenth century was supported, especially in the promotion of agriculture, by a zeal for developing the national resources on scientific lines. In the fiscal policy of the age there was something more than an adoption of new methods for attaining ends already recognised. Over and above the aim of providing employment, there was that of augmenting the sum of national wealth. The mere force of commercial expansion, stimulated by the conquest of foreign markets, was altering the conditions on which national power

[1] Johnson, *Disappearance of the Small Landowner*, 135 *sqq.* ; Webb, *History of Trade Unionism*, 26 *sqq.*

depended ; and social ideals underwent a corresponding transformation.   In the sixteenth century the strength of the nation consisted in its capacity for breeding men ; in the eighteenth, it was measured more generally by the advance of commerce and the production of wealth. In the one case the test of prosperity was a population maintained in undisturbed enjoyment of a decent livelihood ; in the other, it was an ' increase of plenty,' the variety of goods circulating in the market.   The position is reviewed by Arthur Young in the argument of his ' Political Arithmetic,' which turns on the distinction between agriculture as a means of subsistence and agriculture as a trade.   His contention that the same division of land which was in one state of society a political excellence becomes in another a political evil—comparing the position of small farmers under the Roman Republic, when a peasantry subsisting on the soil rendered tribute by military service, with the position of the same class in an age of manufactures and increased taxation—goes to the root of those differences of social outlook which separated his own generation from the age of Elizabeth.   The race of small proprietors are part of a system which has lost its justification from a national standpoint ; they consume the ' earth's produce ' ; they add nothing to the ' national wealth.'   The point to be emphasised is that the conception of a progressive division and redistribution of labour, which underlies the argument, is a conception of social progress.   The process which increases the sum of national wealth involves also a growing interchange of commodities, and opens the door to a continuous rise in the standard of living.[1]

This change of outlook shows one side of the rationalistic movement which asserted its supremacy over

[1] Young, *Political Arithmetic*, 71, 73 *et passim*.

European thought in the seventeenth and eighteenth centuries. The turning point in modern agrarian history, when Parliament began for the first time to assume a decisive attitude on the question of enclosure,[1] came at a moment of profound interest in the growth of the English intellect, when the mental separation between the educated and uneducated classes was approaching a climax. Among the many signs of disillusion and revolt which occur in the middle decades of the seventeenth century, few have a wider significance than the change which took place almost within a single generation in the attitude of the higher ranks to popular beliefs in witchcraft and the supernatural. The same period, also, introduced a phase of social refinement in which the art of the skilled composer lost touch with the music of native growth. Old superstitions and traditional forms of culture and amusement, which had united the sympathies of all classes, were destined gradually, like the husbandry of the open-field, to assume the character of survivals which the enlightened and the busy world had left behind. The development of the press during the early years of the eighteenth century, and the multiplication of treatises on subjects of scientific and general interest, mark the beginnings of a compensatory process by which the fruits of study and criticism were slowly diffused.[2] New standards of comfort found their complement in a new phase of public enlightenment; and both alike pointed forward to a type of civilisation which was to have its centre in the towns.

The chief landmarks of the period are not un-

---

[1] Johnson, *op. cit.*, 85 ; mid-seventeenth century.

[2] Buckle, *Civilisation in England* (*World's Classics*), vol. i. ch. vii. ; Tylor, *Primitive Culture*, i. 125–7 ; Chappell, *Old English Popular Music*, ii. p. vi.

connected with the history of education. The endowment of non-classical schools dates in large measure from the Restoration. The Charity School movement followed the Revolution of 1688. The remainder of the period is filled with sporadic efforts to diffuse instruction and to rescue the young. Viewed from the standpoint of later experience, the growth of philanthropy has a significance outweighing its intentions and its immediate results. It was from rescue-work that later schemes of national education took their rise. Meanwhile it was recognised, first in practice and then in theory, that the problems of progress are problems of education.

Two conflicting emotions are covered by the decent veil of eighteenth century optimism—the enthusiasm of progress, and a growing consciousness of evil which is characteristic of modern thought. The 'better living of every class,' the decent clothing which was itself a ' sign of good feeding,' the general rise of wages, the cheapness of provisions, and the diffusion among the masses of minor comforts which had been a luxury of the rich, were evidences of material welfare constantly adduced during the early half of the century.[1] But the writers who are most confident of progress are alive to impressions of another sort—the disease and profligacy of ' commercial cities,' the demoralised state of large parts of the country-side,[2] and the effects of a mania for gin-drinking which spread through the manufacturing towns during the first years of George the Second, changing the ' very nature of the people ' and threatening the ' very race ' itself.[3] The evil in certain forms was closely related to the general growth

[1] Young, *Political Arithmetic* ; De Saussure, *A Foreign View of England* (engl. trans. 1902), 220, etc. ; Lecky, *History of England*, vi. 204.
[2] *Cf.* Webb, *English Local Government*, i. 69.   Marshall, *Rural Economy of West of England*, i. 107 ; *Midland Counties*, i. 131.
[3] Lecky, i. 479 *sq.* ; *Works of Berkeley* (edited by Fraser), iv. 332.

of prosperity. Different authorities draw a connection between intemperance and increased earnings, between pauperism and the circulation of wealth. Adam Smith, penetrating more deeply and looking back over a longer range of experience, traced a permanent process of moral decay to the influences of an increasing division of labour. On this analysis he founded a plea for organised instruction. The argument in the ' Wealth of Nations ' touches only one aspect of a complex question; but it is sufficient to suggest that, the more closely the connection between civilisation and degeneracy is examined, the more light will be thrown on the nature and origin of educational problems.

One of the attractions of the period for the student of sociology arises from the numerous grades of culture and economic development which are brought simultaneously within the range of inspection. A phrase which has been used of India in recent times, may be applied without undue licence to England on the eve of the Industrial Revolution. ' All the centuries are gathered into one.' From the Northern border, which on the Union of the English and Scottish crowns retained traces of tribal society and of some of the earliest methods of tillage,[1] to the South-Eastern counties, a home of commerce and settled agriculture in days earlier than the Roman Conquest [2] and still in the eighteenth century the garden of England; from Devon and Cornwall, a land of small enclosures but with remnants of the more primitive forms of

---

[1] Slater, *English Peasantry and the Enclosure of Common Fields*, 259. In 1606 a troublesome ' sept of the Grames under their chief ' was transported from Cumberland to Roscommon: Seebohm, *English Village Community*, 219.

[2] Seebohm, 246 *sq.*

husbandry,[1] to the workshops of Birmingham and the extending farm-lands of the Midlands and the East; from the degraded savagery of a lost tribe discovered squatting at the sources of the Tyne,[2] to the broken civilisation of the ' Mud City ' and Seven Dials; from the decayed nature-worship of Somerset and Devon, to the scientific associations of Huguenot weavers in Spitalfields[3]; here a district swept forward on the tide of commercial prosperity, another cherishing traditions of an ancient glory that has passed away, another more wisely husbanding its strength and, like Hythlodaye in the ' Utopia,' ' lefte behynde ' for its ' mynde sake '—the ground traversed offers a wide range of material, illustrating many phases of progress, survival and decline, which have been observed by ethnologists in tracing the ascent from barbarism to the higher levels of civilised life.

Any attempt at comparing different areas raises a number of initial difficulties. To what extent, for instance, are the contrasts which they exhibit to be explained by essential differences of history, race, and environment? To what extent may the characteristics of the more backward and of the more advanced parts of the country be taken to illustrate successive stages of social evolution? Similar questions arise, when an attempt is made to assign to particular types of occupation or social settlement their place in the scale of an advancing civilisation. Certainly, at this period, one of the most potent causes of social variation was the delay with which new ideas and impulses were communicated to the more distant provinces. Defoe's remark

[1] Vinogradoff, *English Society in the Eleventh Century*, 580. (*Cf.* Seebohm, 412 *ad fin.*).

[2] Lockhart, *Life of Scott*, ix. 168 (the reference is probably to some archaic form of the sword dance).

[3] Smiles, *Huguenots in England and Ireland*, 337.

that the country south of the Trent was the 'richest
and most populous' part of the kingdom, acquires a
deeper interest when it is found that the North at this
time, in many aspects of its social and economic life,
presented a picture of conditions which had passed
away elsewhere at an earlier period. In the same
way, some basis on which to found comparisons between
the 'agricultural' and the 'manufacturing life,' or
between town and country, may be gained by following
the slow evolution of specialised industry and the
intermittent process by which villages grew into populous towns, loosening by degrees their connection with
rural pursuits and developing at once new problems
and new forms of practical and mental activity.
Following a series of lines drawn from the more remote
pastoral districts of the North and West and converging
towards the industrial towns of the interior, we pass
gradually within a zone of accelerated progress, in
which mind and character react with increasing rapidity
to the influences of a changing environment and the
growth of human desires is revealed in new standards
of refinement and comfort. We pass also within the
area of social problems, economic helplessness, and
moral relapse. The central districts, including the
metropolis, presented some of the clearest indications
of the lines on which English civilisation was destined
to advance ; and these, too, supplied material to the
critic of moral abuses, and the more obvious examples
of exploitation and distress. Though on a broad view
of history, social, moral and intellectual energies ' are
seen to progress together, . . . they are far from advancing with equal steps,' either as regards a particular
class in society or the community as a whole. As
manufacturers were, as a class, more exposed to certain
demoralising influences than the agricultural peasantry,

as the town life of the period in some phases of its growth resembled a degenerate form of rural civilisation, so we shall find writers recurring to distant parts of the country for examples not only of the primitive virtues, but also of a standard of home life which would seem to have declined among the poor in the more progressive areas.[1]

The tendency which these conditions illustrate is one familiar in educational history. The process which extends social opportunity is continually weakening the forms of discipline handed down from an earlier age, and at the same time, in so far as it intensifies competition or opens new resources, continually increasing the need for mental equipment. This may be illustrated by comparing the effects of social change on the less progressive sections of society with the problems which arise from the contact of advanced and backward races. In either case the final result may be the displacement of a rude manner of life by something higher and more durable ; but the same class of influences which have led to the decay of inferior races in the presence of a higher civilisation, have produced periods of physical and moral decline to which the weaker sections of a civilised people are exposed in the face of changes opening new avenues of culture and increasing the general wealth. In either case the more general causes of decline are economic. They consist partly in the introduction of new articles of consumption and conditions of livelihood which demand a higher degree of knowledge and self-control than the people

---

[1] It is not merely in the North that a superior economy is ascribed to the poor. Eden couples Wales with the North of England and Scotland as affording an example of skilful management, especially in cooking, in the homes of the poor (*State of the Poor*, i. 497). Marshall, advancing from Devon into Cornwall, is agreeably surprised at the social aspect of the country (*Rural Economy of the West of England*, ii. 16).

possess ; partly in privation and oppression, involving a sudden disturbance in their habits of life and sometimes a wholesale removal into uncongenial surroundings, where the arts with which they are familiar are practised with difficulty and they are exposed to new forms of disease and temptation which they are unable to resist.

The analogy cannot be pressed ; but it is useful in helping to connect a number of scattered lines of evidence which bear on this phase of social transition. Important changes occurred in the diet of the poorer classes from the commencement of the eighteenth century, which deserve much closer attention than they have hitherto received. The ' better living ' of the people, says Arthur Young, consists in their ' consuming more food and of a better sort ; eating wheat-bread instead of barley, oats and rye and drinking prodigiously a greater quantity of beer.' At the same time there was an increased consumption of meat and vegetables, balanced by a large expenditure on tea, sugar, and spirits, and in certain districts, it would seem, by a growing scarcity of milk and fuel. The change does not present itself as an unmixed advantage, when we read of the superior health and energy of the Yorkshire labourers who earned phenomenal wages, drank moderately, and kept to the simpler fare of an earlier generation.[1] Young himself has an interesting comment which might have tempered his enthusiasm. The ' increase of national wealth and the superior ease of the poor ' had led to an increased consumption of ' superfluities ' which absorbed an immoderate part of their income, breeding wasteful habits which had already proved disastrous in a season of distress. This applied especially to manufacturers ; ' as to husbandry, they

[1] Marshall, *Rural Economy of Yorkshire* (1788), i. 259.

indulge in all these expenses and yet live well.'[1] Meanwhile a Swedish traveller had observed kindred symptoms in agricultural districts bordering on the Midlands. It was not unusual, in the parts which he visited, for country-folk to spend the entire day at the village ale-house. There was little intoxication; but 'it is not to be wondered at, if many labourers and others, however large the daily wages or profits they can make, can for all that scarcely collect more than what goes from hand to mouth.' This 'custom' he attributed partly to 'the abundance of money in this country and the ease with which a man could in any case have his food if only he was somewhat industrious.'[2] It is a peculiar example of the 'lazy-diligence' which Defoe lamented as a characteristic of these years of comparative ease and prosperity; and it is an element to be considered in judging the criticisms passed by Eden, in the lean years which followed, on the domestic economy of the poor in the South of England.[3] Quite apart from the physiological effects of a new diet,[4] it is seen that an increased command of resources does not necessitate an improvement in the standard of living. Ease of

[1] Young, *Political Arithmetic*, 76.

[2] Kalm, *Visit to England, 1748* (trans. Joseph Lucas, 1892), 333. Young (*Northern Tour*, iii. 248 *sq.*) notices a similar practice among the manufacturing classes of Lancashire in times of prosperity (1770).

[3] Eden, *State of the Poor* (1797), i. 496 etc. ; his general contention is that the domestic management of the poor in the South, as compared with the North, is expensive, wasteful, and relatively unproductive. Hammond (*Village Labourer*, 123 *sqq. et passim*) points out that the resources of the Southern poor had been steadily decreasing. All I wish to suggest, is that the trial of acute distress was preceded by the trial of prosperity; it is this sequence that gives the period its unity from an educational standpoint.

[4] *Cf.* an address by Dr. Leonard Hill, Economics Section of British Association, 1913 (*Times*, Sept. 16). It is a question whether 'wheat bread' was more nourishing than 'barley, oats and rye.' Much would depend on the way in which different articles of diet were combined. If a 'good diet is a necessary part of a good education' (James Mill), it now seems that diet itself is a subject for instruction.

living is useless or pernicious where there is no corresponding moral advancement, no extension of the interests which give to life a purpose and an ideal. But the very changes which increased wealth and brought goods to market, were removing familiar landmarks and casting inexperienced men adrift. In the districts which suffered most under the trial of prosperity, agrarian conditions were changing, and little portions of land were being united into large.[1] Here,

[1] The injury done by the enclosure movement to native instincts, e.g. to the sense of ownership, if it has been denounced somewhat indiscriminately by modern critics, was too little considered by supporters of the change who enlarged on the benefits of regular employment with the prospect of increased wages. Where the social condition of the poor was lowest and the boon offered might appear greatest in proportion, it was less certain that they would stand the test of a more arduous competition than that they would suffer moral and nervous reactions from the upbreak of a system which had moulded their lives.

Arthur Young describes an archaic form of settlement in the Isle of Axholme. ' The inhabitants are collected in villages and hamlets ; and almost every house you see, except very poor cottages on the borders of the common, is inhabited by a farmer, the proprietor of his farm, of from four or five, or even fewer, to 20, 40, and more acres, scattered about the open fields, and cultivated with all the minutiæ of care and anxiety, by the hands of the family, which are found abroad. . . . They are very poor respecting money, but very happy respecting their mode of existence. Contrivance, mutual assistance, by barter and hire, enable them to manage these little farms. . . . A man will keep a pair of horses that has but 3 or 4 acres by means of vast commons and working for hire. . . . Though I have said they are happy, yet I should note that it was remarked to me, that the little proprietors work like negroes, and do not live so well as the inhabitants of the poor-house ; but all is made amends for by possessing land ' (quoted Slater, op. cit., 53 sq.). ' The enclosure of these commons,' he adds, ' will lessen their numbers and vastly increase the quantity of products at market.' It might (for enclosure was resisted) have produced further results. Assuming that for those remaining on the land as labourers an opportunity of increased earnings had made up for the resources lost through enclosure and consolidation, it might (1) have destroyed the sense of ownership which is admitted in this case to have been the fundamental incentive to thrift and exertion ; (2) have weakened their sense of fellowship and co-operation for social purposes (cf. Denson, Peasant's Voice to Landowners (1819), 17–21) ; (3) by rapidly increasing ' wealth ' and producing easy conditions among a people whose standard of living was low, have developed the careless mode of living ' from hand to mouth ' noticed by Kalm. We might arrive perhaps within measurable distance of those Midland labourers whose wages fell short of the Yorkshire rate by about one half—' but a

too, arable was being converted into pasture, and population was drifting towards the towns.

(1) *The Heritage of the Rural Peasantry*

The comparisons between town and country, between the 'agricultural life' and the 'condition of manufacturers,' which occur in the social writings of the period, presuppose generally a degree of economic differentiation which was not realised in practice. At the same time, while emphasising the moral effects of a division of labour in the manufacturing industries, they ignore corresponding changes which affected agriculture, slowly modifying the social environment and transforming the mediaeval peasant into the labourer of modern times. Nevertheless they illustrate a crisis in the general course of social evolution, and incidentally mark the connection between two stages of mental growth—the stage during which education springs naturally from the experiences of daily life, and the stage in which a specialised system of industry demands a special instrument of training and instruction. If in many districts on the eve of the Industrial Revolution it was becoming natural to associate manufactures with urban surroundings and to regard the industries of the town as a refuge for families displaced from agricultural

want of exertion, and an extravagance in keep, especially in *beer*, more than counterbalance the disparity in wages' (Marshall, *Rural Economy of the Midland Counties* (1790), i. 131, an area which had suffered from some of the least social forms of enclosure, see Slater, *op. cit.*, c. x.).

The Axholme settlements, it may be admitted, present some abnormal features and, from a moral standpoint, a favourable example of the open-field system. The worst elements in the labour class at the close of the century cannot be dismissed as a product of recent displacements. One of the arguments for enclosure was found in the existence, under the old system, of a large cottar class who were kept alive in a precarious condition by access to the commons, and whose habits were not above reproach. The question is how far their demoralisation may be explained as a result of eviction and enclosure in other parishes at an earlier period.

employment,[1] it was still reasonable to measure the welfare of urban communities by the standards of country life. Agriculture remained the predominant, and on the whole the most satisfactory, form of occupation ; rural society, in the interval between the decay of mediaeval municipalities and the urban civilisation of a coming age, presented the least disturbed and most organic type of social settlement. In studying different phases of rural organisation, we travel back gradually to the origins of human culture ; following the path of modern industrialism, we discover new processes of education and new types of intelligence.

The school had been, for the most part, an occasional and somewhat irrelevant factor in rural life ; sometimes mainly an instrument of selection, gathering recruits for wider spheres of activity and starting them on the road to preferment. But, although missionary effort had done much to emphasise the need of a school system, its absence would not necessarily entail a state of mental inertia.[2] In those parishes which afford the most complete examples of a social hierarchy, and where agrarian change had not deprived the peasantry of rights on the soil, the life of a labourer might be itself more instructive and intelligible than that of his counterpart, the urban artisan. His work at home and in the field afforded a more varied range of experience, in

[1] Young, *Political Arithmetic*, 71.
[2] Cobbett's argument that a skilled labourer could not be considered an uneducated man, explains some part of the prejudice against schools in the rural districts. Cunningham, *Works of Robert Burns*, 3, remarks— ' The peasantry of Scotland turn their cottages into schools ; and when a father takes his arm-chair by the evening fire, he seldom neglects to communicate to his children whatever knowledge he possesses himself. Nor is this knowledge very limited ; it extends, generally, to the history of Europe, and to the literature of the island ; but more particularly to the divinity, the poetry, and what may be called the traditionary history of Scotland.' It would not be difficult to find parallel instances across the Border, as may appear in the course of our inquiry ; and some form of oral tradition, of more or less educational value, was probably general.

which the relation of means to ends was easily grasped. He saw the nature and meaning of his industry, often the whole of the processes and their connection with social and domestic needs. The open-field system, with its facilities for the hire or purchase of land, secured for the thrifty a means of investment and a prospect in life. To his rights of commonage he might add a share in the arable or a plot to occupy his leisure hours and to afford a subsidiary means of subsistence. His wife span for domestic uses, and trained her children in the household arts. This form of education seems to have been realised, in an exceptional degree, in those self-contained communities where the soil was widely distributed among peasant holders and all articles of common necessity and convenience were supplied by the joint labour of the family ; but considerable remnants of the old scheme of production had survived the influence of a widening market in all parts of the kingdom. And not only was the supply of daily needs a labour which conveyed its own lesson, inspired interests and exercised habits of organisation and self-discipline ; but the intimate relations subsisting between the various functions of a village group, the natural correspondence between the parts of a fabric which was the result of age-long growth, rendered its life in some measure an intelligible whole. The appearance of a self-acting community, developing its own discipline, culture, and outlook on the world, was preserved in the administration of open-field husbandry, and more generally in the round of common amusements and the whole body of rustic traditions and beliefs.

The Church which stood as the symbol of a wider outlook and a higher ideal, and whose discipline of prayer and precept came nearest to a scheme of national education, exercised the main part of her

influence as an institution entwined in the structure
of social life, acting less as an intellectual force than
through her appeal to corporate feeling and the
associations which accumulate round an established
usage. Eighteenth-century worship is, in fact, in its
natural state, a reflex of the prevailing system of husbandry. There is, in both, the same agreeable sloven-
liness of method, the same acceptance of custom, the
same underlying corporate sense, the same hierarchy
of personages and minor officials ; the Church singers
occupying a customary holding in the chancel, so firmly
established by right of inheritance that in many places,
like the yeomanry whom they resembled, they with-
stood the zeal of reforming incumbents and survived
far into the next century. The interest of these phenomena increases when they are studied more closely in
relation to different types of environment. Not only
do we find insulated peasant communities presenting
examples of an archaic organisation, side by side with
parishes in which a high order of capitalistic management has swept away the last traces of communal
custom ; but throughout the country different strata
of civilisation lie exposed on the surface in every department of life. Rural amusement includes ancient
spontaneous forms of rejoicing, bearing in many cases
the marks of a ritual origin and belonging to an order
of folk-culture which may have proceeded ultimately
from the common worship of a primitive village group.
An equal antiquity has been ascribed to those assemblies of the township which survived here and there,
unimpaired by the decay of the manorial system,
administering a complex body of agrarian custom and
exercising rudimentary judicial functions[1] which find

---

[1] ' These ancient sources of the law of villages are still pretty generally
kept open ; even in manors where neither copyhold nor free-rent tenants

their counterpart among Eastern communities at the present day.

It has been necessary to venture on this analysis in order to form some conception of the general problem which a survey of rural conditions presents to the student of educational history. When it is realised that early ideas and customs, which have no intelligible meaning or oppose obstacles to improvement in the age in which they survive, may originally have been shrewd attempts to explain the mysteries of existence or to meet a present need,[1] it is natural to inquire in what sense subsequent progress has been a continuous process of expansion towards a higher culture and a fuller life. The issue does not in practice present itself in so simple a form. A conclusion suggested by the study of primitive races—that 'civilisation is a plant much oftener propagated than developed,' that progress is effected more often 'by foreign than by native action'[2]—would seem to apply with equal force to the history of local groups within a civilised society. The history of mankind may show a continuous stream of evolution connecting the lowest with the highest ranges of culture ; but there are limits to the advance of a small and self-centred community drawing mainly on its native stock of ideas. Improvement

remain. . . . The cleansing of rivulets and common sewers (etc., etc.) . . . are matters which frequently require the interposition of a jury ; who, in places where they are still impanelled, are considered not only as judges of the general welfare of the manor, but are frequently called in as arbiters of private differences '—Marshall, *Rural Economy of Yorkshire*, i. 28 *sq.* (1788), *cf. id. Midland Counties*, i. 15 (1790). The last clause is significant ; *cf.* Maine, *Village Communities*, 71, on the adjustment of civil disputes by the elders of an Indian village ; *cf.* also his remark (*Early Law and Custom*, 170), that ancient Teutonic courts might be properly described as Courts of Arbitration, being unarmed with the power of inflicting penalties.

[1] *Cf.* Tylor, *Primitive Culture*, i. 284 ; ii. 324, 405 ; Seebohm, *English Village Community*, 16.

[2] Tylor, i. 48.

beyond a certain stage will depend increasingly on new combinations, and on the pressure of forces which have been generated in wider fields of social enterprise.   This may be seen by studying the growth of rural communities in England which down to the eighteenth century pursued a solitary course, and the culture which was a product of rural tradition.   Country life is strewn with the remains of successive elements of culture which answered at one time a serious educational purpose, but whose range of growth is set within definite limits. In the same way, a long course of economic reorganisation may proceed with little apparent stimulus from without ; a land of wastes and open-fields may be parcelled out into small enclosures ; but there comes a stage at which the outlook narrows and progress draws to a standstill.[1]   It is partly for these reasons that the life of isolated rural areas is sometimes found relapsing towards a state of savagery.   The influence which corrects these tendencies by promoting wider combinations is in the nature of the case external, and in some sense foreign, to the individual groups which it raises to a higher level.   It proceeds from the growth of a central authority sufficiently elevated to enforce obedience, and from the economic and intellectual forces which its action brings into play.   In the conflict which arises between native and foreign elements, according to the Spanish proverb, ' the more there is of the more, the less there is of the less.'   The rise of a central power exercising discipline over local groups entails the restriction of their sphere of independence and, sooner or later, the disintegration of their corporate life.   Larger political and economic combinations dissolve the framework of custom in smaller units which

[1] *Cf.* Marshall, *Rural Economy of Yorkshire*, i. 52–6, 255 ; *West of England*, i. 25 *sq.*, 104 *sqq.*

they link together and absorb. As the intellectual horizon expands, earlier forms of culture reach the limits of their natural growth and undergo a decline both in quality and significance. That which had once a serious purpose and marked an advance in thought or art, tends to degenerate in tone or to survive mainly as a source of harmless amusement.[1] As the higher civilisation advances, the lower begins to recede and dissolve.

It does not follow that the gain will be evenly distributed. The process which forms a nation tends to replace the vertical division between self-centred communities by a horizontal cleavage between class and class. It may happen that a change which brings civilisation to one part of society will bring ruin to another. There is a definite connection, at different periods, between freedom and pauperism; and the principle applies as much to mental as to material progress. It is unlikely that the concerns of a large political unit will occupy the same place in the consciousness of the masses as those of the local group whose corporate life is falling into decay; or that the decline of a lower culture will be readily compensated by access to a higher. Where the distance between the educated and uneducated classes becomes great, the latter not only reap no immediate benefit, but may experience an actual loss. It is plain, however, that the forces which assist national progress operate on the framework of rural life in different combinations, and with different degrees of intensity, in successive epochs; and in so far as they include institutions, they include agencies whose

---

[1] Proverbs and riddles, once important factors in education (Tylor, i. 81 *sq.*); balladry, once a serious source of history; compare the decay in the significance of myth, legend and rustic rites, etc. Sometimes the decay in significance is followed by a decay in quality, as in certain forms of folk-music and dance.

work may be submitted to an educational test.   The
study of rural education in some of its broader aspects
is a study of successive forms of organised discipline
following one another in a definite sequence.   With
the national awakening in the fifteenth and sixteenth
centuries, the *régime* of feudalism ends and is replaced
gradually by the paternal rule of a governing class.   The
tests which may be applied at each phase of transformation are those outlined in Mill's definition of the ideal
of government.   A system of government should give
the people ' that for want of which they cannot advance,
or advance only in a lame and lopsided manner ' ;   in
carrying them through one stage of progress, it should
not ' unfit them for the step next beyond ' ;   and its
success in this respect will depend on the extent to
which, ' in seeking the good which is needed, no damage,
or as little as possible, be done to that already
possessed.' [1]

Feudalism has been represented as a connecting link
between two very different forms or conceptions of freedom—the freedom of early times, implying membership
of a free group, having its roots in military organisation
and in a network of provincial institutions, ultimately
of tribal origin ;   and the freedom which emerged on
the ruins of status and privilege, deriving its strength
from economic achievement and from the increasing
authority of the central government and of national law.[2]
As the growth of the manorial system foreshadows
in certain respects an advance in the conception of
individual ownership, so from an early period the

[1] Mill, *Representative Government*, 40.   'The one indispensable merit of
a government, in favour of which it may be forgiven almost any amount
of other demerit compatible with progress, is that its operation on the
people is favourable, or not unfavourable, to the next step which it
is necessary for them to take, in order to raise themselves to a higher
level '—36.

[2] Vinogradoff, *op. cit.*, 213.

growing power of an aristocratic element in public assemblies, and the surrender of territorial jurisdiction to feudal potentates, may point forward dimly to the monarchic rule of a landed aristocracy acting in their magisterial capacity as organs of the central government. But what is, at first, most striking in this intermediate stage of organisation, is the relation which it bears to a past order of things. The fabric of early custom is not superseded so much as incorporated in a new structure, and, as it were, placed under control. The feudal courts embody fragments of an antecedent judicial and administrative system which have been subordinated to the authority of powerful lords. The manorial organisation is largely a natural growth, enshrining a traditional form of rural economy, and leaving room for a complex body of mutual restrictions and customary rights. A parallel may be found in the history of the Mediaeval Church. The parish priest whose virgate-holding lay scattered among the strips of the villagers in the open-fields, is a type of the intimate relations maintained between religion and custom during the Catholic period. If feudal arrangements show everywhere underlying traces of an earlier scheme of government, still less is there any sudden break of continuity between the forms under which the new religion was introduced to the barbarous races of Northern Europe and the pagan worship which it was intended to supersede. The Village Feast is one of many surviving examples of an attempt to consecrate to Christian uses an ancient custom, which may yet in its later developments preserve an element of primitive barbarism. The ceremonial of the Holy Well, which has retained a place in public worship in certain localities down to modern times, presents yet more remarkable instances of a cult redeemed by Christian influence and infused gradually with a higher spiritual meaning. As in the age of the Reformation, so in that which followed the introduction of Christianity into England we find in statements of ecclesiastical policy a clue to the educational tendencies of the social system as a whole. 'Because,' wrote Gregory the Great, 'they have been used to slaughter many oxen in the sacrifice to devils, some solemnity must be exchanged for them on this account, as that on the day of dedication . . . they may build themselves huts of the boughs of trees, about those churches which have been turned to that use from temples, and celebrate the solemnity with religious feasting . . . because he who tries to rise to the highest place rises by degrees and steps, and not by leaps.' [1]

Whatever may be said of the darker side of manorial serfdom and its spiritual counterpart, they were at least free from those elements of disturbance which have rendered the discipline of freedom in many ways more perilous than the most despotic rule—the destruction of inherited instincts, the spiritual conflict between tradition and enlightenment, between custom and progress. Judged with reference to the psychological conditions of the period, the system conforms to a sound principle of education. New influences were brought to bear on the peasantry, without crushing their sense of security and of a life peculiarly their own. Circumstances set a limit to exploitation and to oppressive interference with their economic arrangements ; while the lord's enclosure, standing side by side with the land of the tenants, gave an example whose

---

[1] Seebohm, 72 *sq.* For the Holy Well ritual at Tissington (Derbyshire) on Holy Thursday, see Sydney, *England and the English in the Eighteenth Century,* ii. 246 ; the wells, five in number, were decorated with flowers, and after a service in church, a procession visited each well in turn, at which the psalms and epistle and gospel for the day were read, the service concluding with a hymn accompanied by a band of music ; the rest of the day was given to rustic sports.

influence became effective as manorial custom fell into decay. A somewhat analogous instance is presented by an important vehicle of the Church's teaching. The Morality plays gave exercise to traditional dramatic instincts ; and they were carried on and developed, after the decline of ecclesiastical authority, by the amateurs of town and gild, giving birth in turn to the interlude and the secular drama.

Both the advantages and the limitations of this stage of discipline are suggested by the phase of rural prosperity which followed at its close. The most recent research has discovered, in the interval between the decay of the manorial system and the agrarian changes of the sixteenth century, all the signs of a ' continuous improvement in the condition of the peasantry ' : a ' keen competition for the use of land,' increasing enterprise, individualism and mobility, and a gradual process of exchange and enclosure, in all of which the small man played a predominant part.[1] The account may be supplemented by evidence drawn from another source. The economic revival, which led to the formation of a prosperous middle class among the rural peasantry, seems to have been accompanied by a parallel advance in culture. Balladry and folk-music felt the influence of new literary and artistic standards, and there was a considerable outburst of popular drama in which the sympathies of all ranks were for a time united. The advantage, however, in either case depended on a peculiar balance of conflicting elements which rendered it essentially insecure ; in the economic sphere, on a balance between the forces of custom and competition ; [2]

[1] Tawney, *The Agrarian Problem in the Sixteenth Century*, 97, 114 *sq.*, 178, etc.

[2] ' In that happy balance between the forces of custom and the forces of economic enterprise, custom is powerful, yet not so powerful that men cannot evade it when evasion is desired ; enterprise is growing, yet it

in the sphere of culture, on the mutual proximity of popular and skilled art at a time when the former was approaching the climax of its development and the latter was entering on its career. The economic position of the peasantry was too much indebted to the safeguards of custom not to be imperilled by changes in which they took the lead, and from which they derived at the time no small advantage. Their culture was too limited in its range and too dependent on conformity to a traditional type not to suffer indirectly from the general progress of refinement which may at first have supplied new sources of inspiration. The growing disrepute of popular verse in the presence of a higher form of poetic achievement, and the encroachments of the large farmer on his less fortunate neighbours, were in different ways a sign that influences which for a time enriched and elevated the poor might work their ruin. The same causes which produced a prosperous middle class prepared the way for the labour problems of the sixteenth century.[1]

The fifteenth century, and the early part of the eighteenth, are known as periods of rural well-being ; and both were followed by times of revolution and distress. But the two phases of prosperity seem essentially distinct. The former, as has been seen, includes

has not grown to such lengths as to undermine the security which the small man finds in the established relationships and immemorial routine of communal agriculture '—*Ibid.*, 136.   *Cf.* the relation at this period between folk poetry and polite verse, skilled and popular music (*Cambridge History of English Literature*, ii. 375 *sq.* ; Chappell, *Old English Popular Music*, ii. preface).

[1] It is possible that an element of demoralisation which runs through subsequent stages of rural development, may be traced to the demand which arises in all large agricultural organisations for occasional labour, and the consequent growth, from early times, of a cottar class, occupying a precarious position on the outskirts of village life, who were likely to suffer morally from the loosening of manorial discipline and to have their numbers increased by successive evictions from the ranks above them. *Cf.* Vinogradoff, *op. cit.*, 458 *sqq.*

an advance in culture; in the latter, so far as
the poor are concerned, progress is measured in terms
of employment and material benefits. There is something more than a vision of comfort in the gardens
encircling the cottage homes which remained one of
the glories of the English country-side,[1] but the old
culture of song and dance and pageantry had lost much
of its vigour, and nothing as yet had appeared to take
its place. The difference is reflected in contemporary
impressions of peasant life. The traveller in the sixteenth century might remember the ' dancing, singing
English '; in the eighteenth, he carried away reports
of their food and clothing. A change in the quality
of rural life was accompanied by essential modifications in its structure and organisation. In the fifteenth
century progress is almost synonymous with the growth
of peasant properties; in the eighteenth, it is achieved
almost continuously at the expense of the small freeholder class. Meanwhile old institutions which had
given the villagers in some degree a law of their own
and a management of their common affairs fade
imperceptibly from the landscape until their place is
forgotten and their meaning lost. No element in rural
life is completely obliterated. The country fellow in
' Sir Roger de Coverley ' discussed the parish politics on
Sunday, distinguishing himself ' as much in the Church-
yard as a citizen does upon the 'Change.' But the days
of a ' bold peasantry ' were drawing to a close, and
' independency ' was already passing into a term of
abuse. Addison's sketch of the villagers in a Wiltshire
parish is not an ungenerous conception of social contentment, during the transition period, under a kindly
paternal rule; but it misses some of that indefinable

---

[1] Young, *Eastern Tour*, iii. 124 *sq*; Cobbett, *Rural Rides*, June 24,
1822, etc.

spiritual force which is the characteristic mark of a peasantry ; it is not a picture of peasant life as it appeared in glimpses of Elizabethan England, and as it still existed in more remote parts of the country. As the century advanced, the peasant was gradually lost in the labourer, and a low estimate of his mental capacity became part of the accepted order of things. No features of the age are more clearly marked than the growing wealth of the nation and the slow growth of educational ideas.

A particular crisis may be as much an index, as a cause, of fundamental changes in the life of a people. The upheaval which occurred towards the close of the eighteenth century is seen in a wrong perspective, unless attention is paid to the gradual course of economic reorganisation which connects the great enclosures of the period with the agrarian revolution of an earlier age, and to the less direct, and often unperceived, influences of altered surroundings which reacted on every phase of rural life. It is this pervasive change of environment which gives unity and significance to the long period of transition from mediaeval to modern methods of agriculture. At the outset, a crisis in rural affairs is connected with movements which embraced the whole range of national thought and enterprise. A revival of learning and a change in the religious order coincide approximately with the downfall of feudalism which altered the relations of landlord and tenant and enhanced the economic value of land ; with the growth of commercial capital which led to a continuous influx of new elements into the landlord class ; and with the progress of political reconstruction under the Tudor monarchy, which found a counterpart in the reorganisation of local government under Justices of the Peace. Such combinations generally end in some conspiracy to elevate the masses. It was no accident that the two great phases of economic re-organisation—the one in the sixteenth, the other in the latter half of the eighteenth century—were attended by movements which aimed at a ' reformation of manners ' and a restatement of religious responsibility. Between the commercial spirit, the magisterial instinct for order and efficiency, and the spirit of religious reform, there was an underlying connection both in the circumstances of their origin and in the mental bias which they introduced.

To assume that these movements created a uniform and sudden change in rural conditions, would involve a misconception of the problems which they produced. They represent rather the growth of a new social order, acting intermittently and from without on the fabric of rural custom, and gradually dissolving the ideas and social forms beneath it. The old order passes, partly as a result of encroachment and repression, partly by a process of insensible decay. The disciplinary powers of the manorial courts were already falling into decrepitude when a position of supremacy was assigned to Justices of the Peace.[1] The systematic enclosures which later on altered the face of rural society seem to have been preceded by a gradual decay of the open-field system, which may be connected, at least indirectly, with the general reactions of commerce on agriculture during the intervening period.[2]

[1] Even down to the commencement of the nineteenth century, manorial courts were characteristic organs of local government; but many of their powers were falling into decay in the fourteenth, and in the sixteenth they were overshadowed by Justices of the Peace.

[2] ' When we read of the condition of those parishes which at the beginning of the eighteenth century were still unenclosed, we are astonished, not that enclosure came when it did, but that it had been delayed so long '—Johnson, Disappearance of the Small Landowner, 97. The argument against the manner in which enclosures were carried out, is not assisted by neglecting evidence of the overcrowding of commons and the precarious state of a large part of the poor who maintained themselves

Similarly, while emphasis may be laid on the repression of popular amusements which followed at different stages in the course of religious and moral reform, it is of more importance to observe the general tendency of social change to dispel the atmosphere in which these activities flourished.

Both sides of the process must be considered, if the period is to convey a lesson of more than transitory importance.   One of the first points to arrest attention is that developments which showed little regard for the feelings and instincts of the peasantry, were welcomed at the time almost without reserve by disinterested reformers, and were attended by a rising sense of responsibility in the governing class.[1]   The history of enclosures, and of a simultaneous movement for the reform of popular morals,[2] at the end of the eighteenth century, affords examples of this seeming paradox ; but the tendency is one that extends back over the period as a whole.   The argument for enclosure as a means of elevating the poor in an age of competition recalls unmistakably the attitude of sixteenth-century puritans, who suppressed local drama and pageantry as no longer edifying in ' this happie time of the Gospell.' [3] There is a sense in which the Reformation itself finds a counterpart in agrarian reform.[4]   The common aim which underlay them both may be described as a process

by the exercise of common rights, etc. ; the growth of this class may be explained, to some extent, by competitive influences displacing the small landholder, and by the influx of squatters displaced by enclosure in neighbouring parishes, and by the general growth of population.

[1] Webb, *English Local Government*, i. 377 *sq.*

[2] *Ibid.*, i. 356 *sqq.*

[3] The ' quiet but persistent suppression by bishop, preacher and zealous mayor, of local plays and pageants throughout England during the middle years of the sixteenth century '—*Cambridge History of English Literature*, vi. 378.

[4] I do not wish to suggest that any connection was claimed or admitted to exist between the Reformation and the sixteenth-century agrarian revolution, which was in fact denounced by many religious reformers.

of simplification, sweeping aside the encumbrances of an obsolete system, and preparing the way in the one case for a more rational worship, in the other for a more efficient use of material resources. Both too, though in varying degrees, involved a removal of ancient landmarks and of elements which lay near the roots of social life. Further analysis carries us within the range of those intellectualist fallacies which are familiar in the economic writings of a later age. Certain essentials of progress are defined with a latent assumption that the minds of the people will respond to the same train of motives and ideas that has governed the aims of the reformer; and reform comes to be identified with a change of system which eliminates the source of existing abuses. It is less clearly seen that the removal of elements which may be turned to a wrong use may mean the loss of elements of potential value; that a change of system may mean the destruction of an order of things which possessed for the uneducated a meaning and value of its own, and the substitution of new standards of thought and conduct too remote from their experience to exercise an effective influence on their lives.

Some such analysis is necessary to a full understanding of the demoralisation which seems in many cases to have followed the course of the enclosure movement, and of the religious state of the poor in the eighteenth century. In one respect the history of social reconstruction is a record of lost opportunities, of a sacrifice of ethical principle in the interests of efficiency. The old religious order had exercised social faculties whose growth was checked with the progress of reform; the open-field system contained elements of permanent social worth, which disappeared more or less gradually in the enclosed parish; and it may be suggested that the faculty of self-government exercised in a rudimentary form in the old manorial assemblies found no legitimate expansion under the new phase of paternal autocracy. In another respect a study of social history shows the necessity of continually adjusting the means of education to new social conditions, if progress is to be more than a surface movement. It may be seen, on an inquiry into the sources of improvement, that progress, whether religious or economic, is as much an effect as a cause of advance in civilisation. The new religion follows the new learning; the new agriculture proceeds from the influences of commerce and a growing intercourse of the landlord class with the outer world.[1] It is a legitimate inference that, as the leaders of reform have passed through a phase of mental preparation, so the masses in their turn, if they are to participate actively in the scheme of progress, must be raised to a new level of intelligence. The most direct illustrations of this principle are found in the history of religion. Educational effort among the poor in the eighteenth century was awakening to the truth, imperfectly realised at the time of the Reformation, that, before new forms of worship or opinion can obtain a vital hold on the minds of the people, ' some intellectual change must first have taken place.' Later on, when the results of previous discipline came to be tested by the removal of population into urban areas, there is evidence which suggests that the strongest instances of religious attachment among the industrial classes were found in the Roman Church which had adhered

---

[1] We may note during the seventeenth century the influx of commercial elements into the landlord class, and the necessity which impelled the older families to increase their income ' by marriage or trade ' as a means of maintaining their position—Johnson, *op. cit.*, 77 *sq.* A writer in 1667 notices a change in the outlook of the country gentry; ' more of them have seen the use and manners of men, and more apply themselves to traffic and business than ever '—quoted Sydney, *Social Life in England, 1660-90*, 158 *sq.*

to the older forms of spiritual appeal, and in denomina-
tions of recent growth where religious revival had been
accompanied by a zeal for education.[1]

The reforms of the period have never been sufficiently
examined in their bearing on the mental growth of
the peasantry. Belonging, as they do, in a special
sense to the history of another class, they come of a
wider range of social evolution than is covered by the
growth of rural communities, and are ultimately a product
of forces acting from without on the structure of rural
life, breaking the continuity of its traditions, and imposing on the masses a form of discipline more or less
disconnected with the antecedent stages of their growth.
We see here the beginnings of a process familiar in the
later history of education, and exemplified in recent
times in the manifold reactions of urban on rural life
and the application to the country of policies primarily
designed to suit the needs of the town. There is also
some indication of general causes which contribute to
the result. Defective reform seems closely related to a
defective conservatism ; the dangers of oppressive interference from without to the absence or impracticability of a gradual reconstruction from within. The

---

[1] *Cf.* Kay-Shuttleworth, *Social Condition of the People* (1850), i. 593,
contrasting the adaptation of Roman Catholic worship to the needs of the
poor with Protestant services which he regards as too intellectual ; the
educational influences of Methodism I have discussed elsewhere. There
is a good deal in the history of this period to support Buckle's argument that
the ' religion of mankind is the effect of their improvement, not the cause
of it.' Mandeville's protest that the Church service and catechising should
meet the spiritual needs of the poor ' without the assistance of reading and
writing ' (*Essay on Charity and Charity Schools*, 352 *sq.*) is an indirect
testimony to the fact that his opponents, in founding schools, had come
to realise the need of some leverage in the way of general education to
raise the labouring class to the level of religious instruction. This is
more directly suggested by an account of the weekday schools established
by Griffith Jones in Wales in the eighteenth century, with the object of
preparing the poor by reading and Bible study for the Sunday worship
and catechetical instruction—Phillips, *Wales, Social Condition, etc.*, 296 *sq.*

displacements which accompanied enclosure at the end of the eighteenth century were the nemesis of a long period of inaction which had suffered abuses to accumulate in a system fraught with decay.   The suppression of amusements, which formed part of the programme of moral reform, was a reaction from the lax discipline which had spread demoralisation in earlier years.[1]   The defects of paternal government will be found to consist much less in acts of repression than in failure to reconstruct.[2]

The study of education cannot be divorced from that of the social system in which it arises.   One of the reasons which have been assigned for the growth in Scotland of a democratic scheme of education, is that a strong educational tradition had been established there before society was divided by the influx of wealth.   One of the reasons for its absence in England has been traced to the decay of the small freeholder class, commencing at the time when sixteenth-century endowments were affording a wider access to liberal studies.   In Scotland, again, the Reformation produced a relatively democratic form of Church Government, from which liberal traditions derived support.   In England the course of religious, as of political, reconstruction moved in a different direction.

Attention has been drawn to a central fact in the social history of the period—the growing ascendancy

---

[1] Webb, *English Local Government*, i. 69, 398, 356 *sq.*

[2] It is much easier to note the absence of a rural policy than to discuss the extent to which remedies were available.   But it is legitimate to mention a group of proposals which bear on the issues raised in the text, and might, if advanced earlier, have formed the nucleus of a broad conception of rural reform ;   (1) the allotment schemes of Arthur Young and others which aimed at retaining, after enclosure, some of the social benefits of the open-field system ;   (2) the plea for instruction, and Eden's ideal of a higher recreation, as a means of raising the level of social life (*State of the Poor*, i. 446) ;   (3) a passage in Marshall's *Rural Economy of Yorkshire* (1788 ; i. 28 *sq.*), which foreshadows a scheme of parish councils suggested by certain surviving examples of the manorial court.

and prestige of an order which, deriving regular powers of jurisdiction from the Crown, gradually absorbed the functions of earlier quasi-judicial assemblies and exercised an increasing control over local affairs. The ideal squire became the pivot of rural society, the ' regulator of manners,' the ' settler of disputes,' the supreme guardian of the poor, the leader of religion and social life, the pioneer of agrarian reforms ; as a magistrate, he took over many of the disciplinary powers of the manorial court, a process which finds a parallel in the frequent substitution of close for open vestries during the period immediately following the Reformation ;[1] and there is a further example of the same monarchic tendency in the consolidation of landed estates which was at once the basis and the most visible sign of political power. It is, here, instructive to turn to a group of communities whose social order presented a striking contrast to the normal type ; an example of which, possessing certain features of special interest, may be taken from Marshall's account of the township of Pickering in the North Riding of Yorkshire. The district is occupied by a multitude of small freeholders, many of them holding estates which ' have fallen, by lineal descent, from the original purchasers.' ' No great man, nor scarcely an esquire, has yet been able to get a footing in the parish ; or, if any one has, *the custom of portioning younger sons and daughters by a division of lands* has reduced to its original atoms the estate which may have been accumulated.' Its affairs are administered by a jury of the township, which not only attends to the public concerns of the community, but acts also as arbiter in private disputes.[2] A similar

---

[1] Webb, *op. cit.*, i. 91, 182. *Cf.* Hammond, *Village Labourer*, 16–18.
[2] Marshall, *Rural Economy of Yorkshire* (1788), i. 20–29 ; the italics are mine.

social formation was observed by Arthur Young in the Isle of Axholme. It meets us again in societies of ' statesmen ' in the Lake District, which had known neither esquire nor pauper ' within the memory of man,' and which were found recruiting their own clergy and sustaining their social life without the intervention of any higher rank. The case of Pickering is peculiarly instructive. The subdivision of the soil is here definitely connected with a rule of succession more ancient than that generally upheld by English Law ; and there is external evidence suggesting a descent from one of those settlements of small freemen which had come to occupy the position of ' self-governing townships ' within some of the larger manorial combinations of the feudal period. One of the marks which distinguish these townships is the absence of hall and demesne, indicating a relatively independent group of tenants, often farming their own dues and free from the incidents of personal servitude. In any case their dependence would be in the main tributary ; and there is in many instances a direct transition ' from the rendering of produce to payment in money, without the intermediate stage of labour arrangements which were the most usual and important expression of the manorial system in other places.' Their history illustrates the evolution of a social unit, not only antecedent to the manor, but capable of developing without the direct interference of the manorial authority in its internal affairs. It represents, as nearly as possible, the natural growth of the village community when the causes are absent which convert it into the manorial group.[1]

[1] Vinogradoff, op. cit., 395–8, 328, 322, 136. He remarks that, what he defines as the characteristics of the ' self-governing township,' are found especially in the case of communities of sokemen, ' that is of organisations of tenants emphatically free ' (136) ; the description seems to apply to Pickering (436, n. 1), where the course of development into a

It is difficult, in criticising these communities, to improve on the language suggested by a comparatively recent observation of analogous groups in British India. It is contended 'that they secure a large amount of comfort and happiness for the families included within them, that their industry is generally, and that their skill is occasionally, meritorious'; but 'their admirers certainly do not claim for them that they readily adopt new crops and new modes of tillage, and it is often admitted that they are grudging and improvident owners of their waste land.'[1] Another and kindred defect was their failure to deal with a problem which was, in fact, never adequately solved by Teutonic townships— that of preserving a balance between 'landholding and population.' A normal result of economic progress was the concentration of shares in the hands of a dominant minority. Even where a more regular distribution was secured by equal inheritance, there was a tendency for

community of freeholders was probably much the same as in the Soke of Rothley (*cf.* 135-7).

To appreciate the force of these examples, one must go back to Maine's distinction between 'the tribe and the tribal chief as distinct sources of positive institutions,' 'property in land' having arisen 'partly from the disentanglement of the individual rights of the kindred or tribesmen from the collective rights of the family or tribe, and partly from the growth and transmutation of the sovereignty of the tribal chief'; and to his further generalisation that, whereas in France the 'land-law of the people' triumphed ultimately (at the Revolution) over the 'land-law of the nobles,' in England the converse process has taken place—the 'system of the nobles has become in all essential particulars the system of the people' (*Early History of Institutions*, 120 *sq.*, 124): In the case of Pickering there are still clear traces of the 'land-law of the people,' e.g. in the custom of gavelkind (*cf. ibid.*, 124 *sq.*), while Marshall's description of the gradual division of its common fields and meadows '*by commission*' suggests a final stage in the growth of several ownership (arising 'from the disentanglement of the individual rights of the kindred or tribesmen from the collective rights of the family or tribe').

[1] Maine, *Village Communities*, 162 *sqq.* Marshall suggests this limitation: it is the large landholder (whose advent leads to the transformation of the community) who makes improvements. His account of the enclosure of commons in Pickering seems to point especially to the neglect of waste-lands by the landholders of the township (*op. cit.*, i. 54).

the group, as it lost its power of absorption, to develop
the characteristics of a close corporation.   It would
seem, indeed, that many of these 'free communities'
were composed, from an early period, of aristocracies
of the conquering race and subordinate groups of cottars
or *bordarii*, who, as their name implies, stood in some
measure outside the commonwealth of the township.
It is possible that the picture of such a society in the
last stage of dissolution is to be found among those
derelict and anarchic types, not uncommon at the close
of the eighteenth century, where a small clique of
well-to-do farmers are discovered exercising an uncontrolled tyranny over a mass of poverty-stricken and
brutalised dependents.[1]   But, while these societies may
illustrate by their defects the advantages of paternal
government, they suggest also an alternative to what in
England was the normal course of social evolution.   Their
dissolution came of a combination of forces which are
found everywhere disintegrating the old economic order
and the social life connected with it ; but it is not unimportant that in distant parts of the country these
influences were delayed.   Marshall's account of the township of Pickering—with its numerous yeomanry who
have recently dissolved the partnership of the open-field
by mutual agreement, while retaining a consistent control
of their common affairs—is the picture of a community
which comes within measurable distance of reorganisation on modern co-operative principles.   In different
parts of the North at this period we seem to find the
materials which formed the basis of rural co-operation

---

[1] *Cf.* Hannah More's account of Cheddar (Somerset) and adjoining
parishes (*Letters to Wilberforce*, in *Life of H. More* (anonymous)).   Maine,
op. cit., 201, has some interesting remarks on the growth of close corpora-
tions in open-field settlements in New England.

in Denmark in later years, in a society similarly constituted and among men of the same northern breed.
We shall discover, too, the germ of intellectual interests,
which might have found expression in something akin to
the Danish Folk-Colleges. But English energy was to
be diverted into another channel ; the idea of a new
rural civilisation was to be indefinitely postponed.

(2) *The Growth of Industrialism, Manufacturing Towns and Mining Settlements*

A ' plain country fellow ' might answer the description of the old satirist—as one that ' manures his ground
well but lets himself lye fallow and untilled '—and yet
fulfil that which was expected of him, keeping a good
home, living decently in health and moderate comfort,
and rearing hardy and courageous sons for the service
of their country. It was in these respects that, towards
the close of the eighteenth century, the ' agricultural
life ' was held to compare most favourably with the
' condition of manufacturers.' Eden asks whether
' application to a few mechanical processes which an
improved state of manufactures usually requires ' was
not a cause of the disorderly living prevalent among
highly paid artisans ; and he proceeds to assert, as an
accepted commonplace, the superiority enjoyed by one
engaged in the ' varying operations of husbandry,' ' in
domestic comfort . . . in certainty of work and consequent independence,' and in a life ' favourable to health,
to morals and to religion.' [1] The verdict of Adam Smith
is even more decided. ' Not only the art of the farmer
. . . but many inferior branches of country labour ' are

---

[1] *State of the Poor*, i. 440.

more conducive to breadth of mind than 'the greater part of the mechanic trades.'[1]

In such estimates there is an element which requires little corroboration. That the agricultural were normally superior to the manufacturing classes in domestic virtue and contentment, is attested by cumulative evidence from many quarters. Nor is there any doubt that quality of occupation was an important factor in the difference. The tailoring trade had already supplied a striking instance of the demoralising effects of seasonal employment coupled with a degree of specialisation which degraded workmanship from an art to a routine ;[2] and the effects of physical and mental strain were no less apparent in ' mechanic ' industries demanding a higher type of skill and intelligence. ' Joseph,' writes Watt, of one of the few mechanics who gave him satisfaction, ' has pursued his old habit of drinking in a scandalous manner, until the very enginemen turned him to ridicule,' . . . but ' he has done much good at his leisure hours. . . . He has had some hard and long jobs, and consequently merits some indulgence for his foibles.'[3] The emphasis which is laid on the evils of specialisation, is partly accounted for by the transition through which industry and social thought were passing at the period. Considering the place which craftsmanship had occupied in English educational tradition, it was natural to assume that an ever-growing division of labour meant an inevitable decay of character and intelligence. The modern view of specialisation, which sees in it a means of economising the time and energy

---

[1] The labourer's ' understanding . . . being accustomed to consider a greater variety of subjects, is generally much superior to that of the other (i.e. the town mechanic), whose whole attention . . . is commonly occupied in performing one or two very simple operations '—*Wealth of Nations*, bk. i. ch. x. pt. 2.

[2] Webb, *Trade Unionism*, 26.

[3] Smiles, *Lives of the Engineers : Boulton and Watt*, 196.

of the worker and thereby affording him a fuller share
of culture and social life, is based on the experience
that a process which has become purely mechanical
may be performed by machinery. To say that a particular employment had ceased to educate might mean
that human energy had been set free, which would
produce good or evil results according to the nature
of the pursuits in which it found an outlet. The poor
stocking-weavers composing the Methodist circle at
Nottingham, who showed an ' uncommon gentleness
and sweetness in their temper and something of elegance in their behaviour,' [1] supplied an answer to many
fatalistic assumptions ; and against the dissipation
engendered by monotonous and exacting toil must be
set examples of a higher culture which were found
chiefly among the manufacturing classes, and the habit
of reading which was characteristic of certain sedentary
employments. On the other hand, a further stage
of economic progress might redress the balance, by
placing employment on a new intellectual footing.
The darker side of industrial evolution appears in the
subordination of the worker to the machine ; but a
comparison of field-labour with the ' mechanic trades '
suggests also a contrast between two types of intelligence—between the wisdom of tradition and experience,
of which husbandry and the old order of craftsmanship
illustrated different aspects,[2] and the talent shown

[1] Wesley, *Journal*, June 18, 1777.

[2] ' Most of the labourers employed (in the construction of the Bridgewater Canal) were of a superior class, and some of them were " wise " or
" cunning " men, blood-stoppers, herb-doctors, and planet-rulers, such as
are still to be found in the neighbourhood of Manchester. Their very
superstitions . . . made them thinkers and calculators. The foreman
bricklayer, for instance, as his son used afterwards to relate, always
" ruled the planets to find out the lucky days on which to commence any
important work," and, he added, " none of our work ever gave way." The
skilled men had their trade secrets, in which the unskilled were duly
initiated—simple matters in themselves, but not without their uses '—
Smiles, *Brindley*, 210–212.

in a combination of manual dexterity with a knowledge
of scientific principles. Side by side with the vision
of unthinking drudgery, rendered more thoughtless and
monotonous by a progressive division of labour, came an
increasing demand for intelligent workmanship. The
incompetence which baffled a generation of inventors
at an early stage of the Industrial Revolution, affords
some measure of the scope for mental expansion which
new forms of industry were destined to create.

The influence of urban surroundings is a factor
which enters more and more into these comparisons. A
formula describing the rural districts as ' more ignorant,
contented and happy, than enlightened, industrious and
ambitious,' may be taken as the starting point of a
controversy which reveals, perhaps more clearly than
any other example, the differences of temperament
underlying all sectarian disputes. One writer has a
vision of ' villages abounding with health ; commercial
cities with disease ' and intoxication. Another contrasts the freedom and business energy of Birmingham
with the dreariness of his native village and the
behaviour which he witnessed on a visit to Bosworth,
where the inhabitants set ' their dogs at us in the streets,
merely because we were strangers.' ' Human figures, not
their own, are seldom seen in those inhospitable regions :
surrounded with impassable roads, no intercourse with
man to humanize the mind, no commerce to smooth their
rugged manners, they continue the boors of nature.' [1]
Assertions of this kind, from either side, are not likely
to stand the test of criticism. It is not difficult, in
the eighteenth century, to discover rural slums whose
social condition seems to exaggerate the worst features
of the manufacturing town. A decayed rural civilisation wears an appearance more ghastly than the

[1] Hutton, *History of Birmingham*, 63 *sq.*

chaotic beginnings of urban life. The triumph of barbarism and a collapse of civil and religious discipline are found alike in the crowded thoroughfare and over the secluded country-side. But rural society is not to be judged by its worst examples ; and, in following the course of urban development, it is legitimate to distinguish the case of newly developed districts,[1] where towns were a sign of industrial activity and the demand for labour kept pace with an increase in the supply, from the purlieus of older cities where an influx of population added to the turmoil of a community already suffering from the evils of overcrowding and misgovernment. Too much importance may be attached to descriptions of the Metropolis. Then, as now, it constituted a special problem, and from the time of Elizabeth had been developing characteristics the legacy of which remains to the present day.

It is necessary to bear in mind the twofold nature of the transition through which England was passing, and which was destined to convert a predominantly rural and agricultural into a predominantly urban and manufacturing community. Town life was awakening new energies which carried special problems and dangers in their train. It was evoking the humanising influences of a wider life, but a life of surpassing difficulty which required to be learnt. Just as the division of labour created a mental void which was to be filled by the call of wider interests, so nothing less than a new form of social organisation was demanded by the en-

---

[1] Smiles, *Brindley*, 272–4, refers to the opening-up of the Pottery districts of Staffordshire after the construction of the Grand Trunk Canal. Its effect was ' not only to employ but actually to civilise the people.' He quotes Wesley—' I returned to Burslem : how is the whole face of the country changed in about twenty years ! Since which, inhabitants have continually flowed in from every side. Hence the wilderness is literally become a fruitful field. Houses, villages, towns, have sprung up, and the country is not more improved than the people.'

vironment in which an increasing part of the community were to pass their days. The interest of this phase of urban growth lies in the impression which it conveys of a gradual differentiation of one form of social settlement from another, of the emerging of a new order of social life from the ruins of the old. As manufacture and husbandry were still in the process of dissolving partnership, so the town continued to maintain a struggling connection with the life and habits of the country-side. Down to the early years of the nineteenth century the weavers of Spitalfields had gardens in the neighbourhood of Bethnal Green ; the artisans of Birmingham, on the outskirts of the town.[1]   On the other hand, many of the darker aspects of urban life may be explained by the decay of institutions which, however suitable to the needs of a rural parish, broke down rapidly under the pressure of a growing population and unprecedented demands,[2] and by the survival of rustic pastimes in an atmosphere which led to their corruption and debasement. But this is not the sum of the difference. That which distinguishes a growing town from an overgrown village is a sense of building on new foundations, the forming of new social groups, the slow awakening of corporate consciousness, the yearning for self-realisation on a higher social and intellectual level. Already

[1] *Select Committee on Public Libraries*, 1849, Q. 2732 ; Langford, *Century of Birmingham Life*, ii. 283, 314, 440.

[2] Webb, *English Local Government*, i. 69–91, 207, 233–45. The purlieus of growing cities were the special resort of the ' Trading Justices ' (328–33) ; the magistrates of Middlesex were the worst of their order. The most notorious specimen was Joseph Merceron, who obtained an ascendancy in Bethnal Green by tolerating dog-fighting and bullock-hunting in the streets and allowing unlimited license in the liquor trade ; on his fall in 1818 the Rector set up a school, which had been previously prevented, and some measure of order was restored by the enrolment of special constables (*ibid.*, i. 83–7). This helps to explain the extraordinary state of affairs described by the Rector in 1816 ; *Select Committee on Education* (1816), 209, 234.

the elements of a new order were crystallising into some definite shape. Its beginnings may be traced, partly in the gradual process of reorganisation which here and there transformed a tumultuous vestry into an effective instrument of popular government,[1] partly also in the sporadic growth of institutions which were to give an intellectual background to social life—the theatre, the museum, the musical society and the debating club, and the more remarkable scientific and naturalist associations which were formed among the Huguenot silk-weavers of Spitalfields.[2]

If the growth of manufacturing communities marked a new stage in the process of economic differentiation, opening access, in spite of many initial disadvantages, to a higher level of social opportunity, the mining settlements arose under conditions which seemed to combine the evils of town and country life without any of their refinements—one of those products of industrial development which appear like a survival of organised savagery in the heart of a modern civilisation. The population employed in mines and collieries formed no inconsiderable part of the labouring classes of Great Britain, though the assertion that they numbered in 1756 upwards of a hundred thousand is little more than rhetorical guesswork.[3] The peculiar conditions of their employment, and of an existence at once gregarious and secluded, had set a stamp on their character and physique which marked them off, in general, from the rest of the community almost as a distinct race. They had a dress, manners and speech of their own, and were sometimes of a different stock from

---

[1] Webb, *op. cit.*, i. 134.

[2] Smiles, *Huguenots in England and Ireland*, 336 *sq.* ; Sydney, *England and the English in the Eighteenth Century*, i. 61.

[3] *Vindication of Natural Society*, quoted Eden, *op. cit.*, i. 416.

the surrounding peasantry.[1] In the records of the
eighteenth century they stand as a type of ignorance,
roughness, and irregular living, and as a type of misery
and exceptional privation. They came to occupy, in
some degree, the same place in the public imagination
that was afterwards assigned to the factory operatives.
The long hours of confinement in an unhealthy atmosphere, the absence of supervision, the constant separation of parent and child, and the general disturbance of
family life, foreshadowed many of the problems which
were to arise in connection with the factory system ;
and it is in the mining colonies that we find some of the
earliest examples of those organised schemes of social
betterment which have developed with the growth of
large industrial establishments.[2] If we except certain
sketches of rural society, they are perhaps the only
group among the labouring class of whom any vivid
impressions are to be derived from eighteenth-century
literature, thanks to their backward condition, which
brought them under the notice of one of those simple
enthusiasts in whom sympathy has developed some of
the qualities of a great artist. Wesley was the first
to appreciate the Titanic element in their life and character—a life of colossal immoderation in weird harmony
with the wildness of nature, and yet, in a sense, essentially innocent and unspoiled ; a wildness broken by
strange silences ; a boisterous humour that melted

[1] Knight's *Quarterly Magazine*, 1823, art. 'Staffordshire Collieries.'

[2] E.g. Duke of Bridgewater's Model Village with Sunday Schools
and a scheme for controlling debt ; the Duke's colliers ' soon held a higher
character for sobriety, intelligence and good conduct than the weavers
and other workpeople of the adjacent country '—Smiles, *Brindley*, 231.
Young (*Northern Tour*, ii. 288 *sqq.*) notices that a large proprietor at
Swinton had presented each of the colliers on his estate with an allotment,
on the condition of their cultivating the ground in their leisure hours.
Cf. Reports of the Society for Bettering the Condition of the Poor, vol. i.
app. i. (1798).

suddenly in large and simple emotions when the magic chord was touched. He had the merit of recording those minor episodes which disclose at a glance the individuality of a people or neighbourhood and give the atmosphere of a dramatic scene. He tells us of the old collier, ' not much accustomed to things of this kind,' who shouted ' for mere satisfaction and joy of heart '; how at a vast gathering from the lead mines about Newcastle he noticed a row of children ' under the opposite wall, all quiet and still '; and of the tribute paid by a small colliery town in Cumberland, where ' the poor people had prepared a kind of pulpit for me, covered at the top and on both sides, and had placed a cushion to kneel upon of the greenest turf in the country.'

The refining of this raw material, which forms one of the most attractive episodes in educational history, may be said to commence with the Methodist Revival. In Cornwall, one of the strongholds of the movement, there is a unique example of the change which may be wrought in the character and outlook of a people, where education is combined with a steady advance of economic opportunity. The Cornish miners enjoyed a relatively independent status owing to the custom of joint-venture and profit-sharing peculiar to the district. This arrangement made it necessary for them to reckon possibilities and to acquaint themselves with the mechanism of their trade, and developed a degree of mental energy which came to distinguish them from the mass of workers throughout the country.[1] The system had,

---

[1] ' In Cornwall the mines are worked strictly on the system of joint adventure; gangs of miners contracting with the agent, who represents the owner of the mine, to execute a certain portion of a vein and fit the ore for market, at the price of so much in the pound of the sum for which the ore is sold,' etc.—J. S. Mill, *Political Economy* (ed. Ashley), 765. *Cf.* Warner, *Tour through Cornwall* (1809), 297 *sqq.*

also, the disadvantages inherent in all forms of speculation, and demanded a sense of responsibility and self-restraint which did not exist at the outset.   Social history presents few phenomena more striking and well attested than the contrast between the riotous life which during the early years of the century plunged the whole neighbourhood in debt and degradation, and the improved state of manners and intelligence which is discovered at its close.   The change may be fairly ascribed to two forces working together on a temperament naturally susceptible and alert.   Methodism, by its civilising influence, prepared the way for economic improvement ;   the advance of industry, producing steadier conditions of employment, encouraged a higher standard of living and removed obstacles to spiritual growth.   Both influences wrought through educational channels, and combined in developing a more complete type of personality.   If Methodism deepened the spiritual consciousness of the people and made them responsible for the religious training of their children, economic progress helped to enforce the claims of secular knowledge.   By the close of the century there were said to be few miners in the district unacquainted ' with the lower branches of arithmetic ' ; and, owing to the attention paid to improvements in machinery and technique, a good miner had generally some knowledge of practical geometry.[1]

(3) *Regional Survey ; Historic Factors in the Social Evolution of Different Areas*

A study of social life in different parts of England is continually revealing characteristics which appear to have no immediate or necessary connection with local

---

[1] Warner, *loc. cit.*

surroundings and to be explained most easily by the intrusion of some foreign influence. It is difficult to avoid connecting some of the customs ascribed to the weavers of Spitalfields in the early years of the last century with the traditions of an old Huguenot settlement; and the same stream of immigration may help to explain certain forms of culture which flourished among kindred groups in the manufacturing districts of the North.[1] But the growth of the French quarter in London, and the dispersion of Huguenot settlers throughout the country, have an historical interest far outweighing their direct contribution to national industry and social progress. They illustrate, in a comparatively recent example, the effects of a long process of conflict and assimilation which has been the making of England, extending back beyond the period of the Norman Conquest to those more remote ages of colonisation when the island was a battle-ground of races and a network of loosely organised states.

The history of this process may be read in place-names, dialects, and monumental remains, and no less in local diversities of character and custom. Ethical peculiarities are attributed to different districts by a consensus of eighteenth-century evidence, which preserve the traces of earlier divisions of nationality and race. The same strenuous, self-reliant qualities, persisting through every change of circumstance, distinguish the

[1] The Spitalfields weavers, in the early half of the nineteenth century, were classed among the poorest and most ignorant of the population; yet they displayed a love of birds and flowers (*Committee on Public Libraries*, 1849, Q. 2731 *sq.*), and formed libraries (*ibid.*, Q. 2709). Smiles (*Huguenots in England and Ireland*, 335–7) mentions the love of flowers among examples of the culture which he ascribes to the original members of the French colony in this district. 'Others of the immigrants,' he says, 'who settled in Manchester and Macclesfield, carried thither the same love of flowers and botany which still continues to characterise their descendants.'

areas to North and East which had been replenished by a
strong admixture of Germanic and Scandinavian stocks;
while the far West, which had been the chief strong-
hold of Celtic resistance, presents an equally marked and,
in many ways, a complementary group of characteristics,
essentially the same as those ascribed to its population
in Roman times.[1] A further source of evidence has
been opened by economic research. ' One is inclined
to suppose,' says a modern writer, ' that the introduction
of each new element in the population of a village—
Saxon, Angle, Dane and, in a less degree, Norman—
profoundly modified earlier customs, and that in each
part of Britain a local type of village community resulted
from the blending of different racial traditions. This
hypothesis is directly suggested by the evidence of
recent economic survivals. The most familiar type of
village community is characteristic of the Midlands. . . .
It is most easily conceived as a compound of the pure
Keltic system, known in the Highlands and Ireland as
Run-rig or Rundale, and the North German system
traditional among the Angles, in which the two elements
in equal strength are very perfectly blended together.
In the South of England we find a different type . . .
in which the influence of Keltic tradition is more
strongly seen. The village community in Norfolk and
the adjoining parts of Suffolk shows some remarkable
special features . . . which appear to be easily accounted for as a result of the later intrusion of Scandinavian tradition. Further, throughout the West
of England, from Cumberland to Devon and Cornwall,
we find evidence that the primitive type of village

---

[1] *Cf.* Warner, *Walk through Wales* (1797), 178–84, and *Tour through
Cornwall* (1809), 348–59 ; also Marshall's accounts of the labouring classes
in his works on the *Rural Economy of Yorkshire,* of *Norfolk,* and of the
West of England.

community approximated very closely to the Keltic Run-rig.'[1]

It becomes evident, as we pursue this line of inquiry, that racial influence is crossed by another group of forces equally potent as a cause of differentiation. The qualities and traditions which each new element in the population imports, are modified by fusion with other elements and by the pressure of physical surroundings. Much, again, that has been attributed to racial habit, may be traced more generally to geographical and political causes which favoured in each case a particular form of settlement.[2] This leads back to an inquiry which has been already outlined. Must we assume, at the outset, an essential separation between the races predominating in different parts of the country ? Or are alleged ' differences in kind ' in reality little more than differences ' in degree of development ' ? How far, for example, may conditions which survived in the Celtic West be taken as characteristic of a society still continuing in the tribal and pastoral stage, from which other races have already emerged at the time of their settlement on English soil ? The conception here suggested postulates a normal course of evolution through which different areas advance successively towards a common level of civilised life, differing from one another meanwhile in social characteristics according to the stages which they have reached at a given period. It may be seen, at any rate, that the groups formed during the initial periods of colonisation fell continuously under the sway of forces which moulded the framework of national life. As the country became more settled, the influences which originally separated the

---

[1] Slater, *English Peasantry and the Enclosure of Common Fields*, 5 *sq.* ; *cf.* ch. xv.

[2] Vinogradoff, *op. cit.*, 263–303.

local units diminished, while the unifying forces, arising from a wider range of political and economic development, increased in importance. Differentiation would come to depend less on local peculiarities of race and environment, and more on the rate at which the new influences travelled.

It may be admitted that this conception is most easily illustrated by comparing large tracts of territory which were conquered and peopled by closely allied branches of the Teutonic race. The North, down to the time of the Industrial Revolution, is continually reproducing social phenomena which are found in the South at an earlier epoch. Its condition at the period of the Norman Conquest betrays evidence of a more recent influx of colonists, and it succumbed less readily than the South to feudal organisation.[1] In the sixteenth century, when the feudal order was rapidly breaking down under the pressure of a powerful central government, it retained a foothold in the northern shires ;[2] their agrarian arrangements being of the rigid type that had once prevailed in the South and East and had there yielded to the dissolving influences of industry and commerce.[3] The same phenomenon recurs at a later period. In descriptions of Lancashire and Yorkshire on the very eve of the Industrial Revolution we find rural communities still passing through the phase of peasant proprietorship which had reached its zenith in more advanced agricultural districts two centuries

[1] *Cf.* Vinogradoff's remarks on the contrast between the ' strongly manorialised South ' and the North with its ' heterogeneous mass of tenures in which the small freemen still play a great part ' (*op. cit.*, 57 *sq.*), and on survivals of the ' soke ' side by side with the ' manor ' in the North (322 etc.) ; also his general conclusion that ' the Saxon South had gone through approximately the same stages as the Scandinavian North, but had already arrived in the eleventh century at the goal reached by the northern districts only in the twelfth and thirteenth centuries, under the influence of the Normans ' (134, *cf.* 441).

[2] Tawney, *Agrarian Problem in the Sixteenth Century*, 189 *sq.*

[3] *Ibid.*, 57, 64–66.

earlier ;[1] a system of trade and industry in which economic functions are less clearly differentiated than in the older manufacturing centres of the South and West ;[2] and a social life which is correspondingly frugal and self-contained. Nor, if we consider the wider reactions of a social order at this stage of transition, is it fanciful to compare the spread of Methodism among the Yorkshire peasantry with the effects of Wycliffite tradition in the villages of the South at an earlier epoch, or to see in the north-country grammar schools down to the close of this period the signs of a desire for education among the poorer classes, recalling the traditional England of the fifteenth century when a prosperous yeomanry had ' put their sons to school.'[3] But there is clearly more to be said of the history of different areas than is contained in the conception of social change extending gradually from the centre to the circumference. To illustrate successive stages of economic evolution, it is necessary to pass continually from one neighbourhood to another. The antecedents of the factory system must be sought rather among the exploited industries of the South-West than in the

[1] Mr. Tawney's account of the growth of peasant prosperity between the first decay of the manorial system and the agrarian revolution of the sixteenth century may be paralleled in many essential points by Marshall's survey of East Yorkshire in 1782 (*Rural Economy of Yorkshire*): e.g. such incidents as the numerous small owners, the active manorial courts dealing with the corporate interests of the community (Marshall, i. 28 *sq.*), the open land-market dealing in small estates (Marshall, i. 30 ; *cf.* Tawney, 60), the protective custom of tenant right (Marshall, i. 24 ; *cf.* Tawney 136), the gradual re-allotment and enclosure of holdings and the colonisation of waste lands by peasants (Marshall, i. 52 ; *cf.* Slater, *op. cit.*, 230 ; Tawney, 70, 157, 165 *sq.*).

[2] The Yorkshire woollen industry remained in the hands of small craftsmen marketing their produce, down to the rise of the factory system, whereas the woollen manufacture in the South-West had long been conducted on a specialised system of wage labour—Webb, *Trade Unionism*, 28–30 ; *cf.* Smiles' description of the Manchester manufacturer of the early eighteenth century : ' part shopman, part weaver and part merchant, working hard, living frugally, principally on oatmeal, and usually contriving to save a little money ' (Smiles, *Lives of the Engineers ; Brindley*, 160).

[3] *Cf.* Tawney, 134.

simpler conditions which prevailed in the North down
to the latter half of the eighteenth century.   Norfolk
loses its supremacy as an industrial centre only to
become a pioneer of capitalist agriculture.   The South-
West, losing its manufactures, relapses into a position
of relative obscurity.   Wales, with her prolonged
independence terminated abruptly by the English
conquest, has a history of her own.   The same sequences
of cause and effect are very far from being repeated in
different parts of the country ; nor is there any exact
resemblance between corresponding stages of their
growth.   The mass of detail which is lost in contempla-
ting from a distance the march of civilisation becomes
all important in an assessment of educational values.
Between two districts equally backward in outward
appearances there may be the vast difference which
separates an arrest of progress from a slow advance to
maturity.

Though it is legitimate to lay stress on the action
of centralising forces, political and economic, which
made for national unity and a common civilisation,
to assume that the areas affected by these influences
passed through the same course of social experience
is to suppose not only that physical resources were
equally distributed, but also that the materials cast
into a common mould were homogeneous or at least
uniformly plastic.   It is seen, on closer inspection,
that the local units, which gradually coalesced to form
a national community, exhibited important varieties
of structure and contained the seeds of different
social formations.   One group of factors, differentiating
local characteristics, must have exercised a paramount
influence from the earliest times.   It would make a
considerable difference to the outlook and habits of a
community, whether the conditions of soil and situation

gave a bias towards pastoral or agricultural pursuits; whether they encouraged a compact or a scattered mode of settlement; whether there was much or little room for expansion; whether the 'farmer has to perform his task in an isolated homestead' or 'joins in a vast agricultural undertaking where a definite place and share are assigned to him on condition of his following the rules and customs adopted by the community.' Another group consists in the survival and interaction of racial habits and ideas.

Both factors helped to determine the original form of settlement, and, through the bias which they gave to its subsequent expansion, exercised an important influence on character and social habits. The gradual process of enclosure, which is characteristic of the West and some parts of the North from an early period, may be connected with certain incidents arising from the pastoral character of these districts.[1] Early enclosure is also likely to arise from some peculiarity in the original forms of tenure or distribution of the soil. There is an antecedent probability that one of the main factors in the economic organisation of the West must be sought in the legacy of customs derived from

---

[1] *Cf.* Slater, *op. cit.*, 159 *sq.* Dr. Slater refers to Cornwall and Devon and the north-western shires as typical of those parts of the country where the 'division of intermixed arable and meadow land took place early and gradually, and in subordination to the reclamation of the waste': the result being a 'creation of numberless small holdings and properties' and the opening of a career to the 'enterprising and laborious.' He adds the significant comment that some explanation of the great part played by the men of Devon in the Elizabethan age may be found in the stiffening influence of this discipline, in the 'reaction upon the character of the people' of a hard-won triumph over 'rocky soil, woodland and moor' (261). Substantially the same course of gradual enclosure and colonisation of the waste land seems to have been pursued widely through the West and North; it appears in the North and West Ridings of Yorkshire from the middle of the sixteenth century, in Durham about a hundred years later—the movement gradually extending towards the Scottish border as the country was pacified (226, 230, 260).

Celtic tradition.[1]   Here it is to be observed that national systems of law, which developed with the growth of a central governing power, covered only a part, though an increasing part, of the field of economic and social relations and were themselves largely derived from earlier local usage.   In the struggle between custom and national law, the former gradually sank into a subordinate position ; but there remained continuous traces of a network of provincial and local institutions over which the central power extended its control, and for an indefinite period what most intimately concerned the mass of the population in the affairs of daily life was not the law of the land, but the customs of the township or manor in which their lot was cast.   The process, moreover, by which a common law was defined in the Royal Courts, was anticipated in the systematisation of provincial usage in the pre-feudal assemblies of the shire.   In this way important varieties of custom were established over definite areas, whose influence may be traced in certain cases through the feudal period and into later times.   The numerous and independent yeomanry who survived in Kent in the eighteenth century were the product of a land law firmly rooted before the Norman Conquest.[2]

[1] Dr. Slater is inclined to attribute the ' priority of enclosure ' in the West partly to Celtic influence (*op. cit.*, 162) ; he remarks that ' fluidity in the tenure of the soil, which is one of the characteristics of the Celtic run-rig as compared with the Anglo-Saxon common-field system, favours the separation of properties and holdings at the time when co-aration ceases to be practised ' (243), also that the absence of rights of common-age over the arable, which presented obstacles to enclosure and are absent from open arable fields through the West and North-West, is apparently a characteristic of run-rig (178, 255).   Vinogradoff, *op. cit.*, 267, attributes the ' single farm and hamlet arrangement ' on the Welsh border to the ' tribal habits of the Celts, subjected to Norman sway, but still keeping to their customs,' including the ' rearrangement and scattering of homesteads in consequence of divisions and re-divisions among heirs.'

[2] ' Not only is the system of agrarian measures quite peculiar there (Kent) . . . but, not long after the Conquest we find a whole body of

ₗThe historic division between the ' Anglo-Saxon '
and the ' Anglo-Danish ' halves of the kingdom is
marked by two broad varieties of law at one time in
concurrent use. The two systems, however, were nearly
allied ; and the phenomenon to be observed in this
case is not so much the continued influence of Scandinavian institutions in the North Eastern areas as the
persistence of ideas and elements of organisation which
may be paralleled in the condition of the South at an
earlier period.[1] The North throughout its history never
loses the shadow of that older Teutonic society which
' might have resulted in something more akin to the
formation of Denmark or Norway than to that of
England as it has come to be.'

It is clear that the social structure reared after the
Norman Conquest had to embrace societies at very
different stages of development. In the districts to
North and East, covering frontier territories recently
settled by hosts of warlike freemen, the new order
found materials less prepared than in the South, where
the differentiation between warriors and labourers, and
the process of rounding off estates under separate
landlords, had already matured. There is evidence,
in fact, in the Domesday inquest, of a transitional

---

customary rules in force in the county which are directly opposed to
those prevailing in the rest of England. Socially, the most important
of these is the famous rule of Gafolcund (gavelkind), succession demanding
equal division among heirs . . . and, needless to say, the enforcement
of this rule produced a very different system of holdings from that
commonly prevailing in feudalised counties. . . . With all its accompanying circumstances, it accounts probably for the startling fact recognised
by exponents of Common Law in the thirteenth century, namely that
there was no villeinage in Kent in the later legal sense, that is, no servile
population holding at the will of the lord. . . . Customs similar to gavelkind may be noticed in this or the other place outside Kent, but these
would be rooted in manorial usage and not in county law, whereas the
rules enumerated in the Kentish custumal may be considered, if one may
use the expression, as the Common Law of the shire '—Vinogradoff, 92-4.
[1] Vinogradoff, *Introduction*.

stage in the growth of the manorial system, brought about by the extension of the lord's jurisdiction over settlements of free tenants and others formerly answerable to the hundred and the shire. The groups thus formed are said to be ' under soke ' or ' in the soke of ' their lord ; the ' soke ' as a territorial division being in the nature of a jurisdictional district added to an estate.[1] To such the manorial court is primarily a centre of civil jurisdiction and political authority. Economic subjection comes as an adjunct to political dependence ; but the burden is fixed and in the nature of a contract ;[2] nor is there much scope or necessity for manorial interference in the internal management of these subject communities.[3] These features may be observed, to a great extent, in all large manorial combinations, where the authority of the hall as an administrative centre extends over a number of scattered settlements. It is to be noticed that ' socmen as members of jurisdictional sokes ' have a special prominence in the counties of the Danelaw, particularly in Lincolnshire, but also ' in Nottinghamshire, Yorkshire, Norfolk, and Suffolk.'[4] In the North, including the East Anglian shires, the soke survives as a distinct institution, ' side by side with the manor and in combination with it,' ' a piece of public administration broken off from the hundred and granted to a private lord, but still retaining its public features ' ; in the South, it is ' almost entirely merged into the manor, while socmen and freemen appear only exceptionally and the court of the manor has to attend to all jurisdictional business.'[5] Corresponding differences are seen in the growth of

---

[1] Vinogradoff, 135.　　　[2] Ibid., 133 sq., 322, 436.
[3] Ibid., 136 ; cf. 328 sq. (with special reference to manors of the North and East).
[4] Ibid., 436.　　　[5] Ibid., 134, 322.

the feudal military system. In the North it is based rather on a ' regular repartition of service ' between agrarian groups than on ' a selection of particular estates ' for military obligation. In some cases the fees have to be ' taken over . . . by entire communities of sokemen,' an arrangement which at once approximates to earlier conditions of service in the pre-feudal levies and deprives the feudal service of its most characteristic feature, a ' personal contract of vassalage.' [1]

Now there is no à priori ground for assuming that these distinctions, and the social contrasts which they imply, continued without modification through the feudal age ; still less, that the position of the socman, or of the freeman under soke, necessarily corresponded to that of the freeholder of later times. Political subjection was a step towards economic dependence, and the contrast between the Danelaw and other parts of the country was continually reduced by a gradual assimilation of the free with the servile elements on an estate and by the fusion of the soke and the manor. [2] Nevertheless, there are features in the later history of these districts which refer back to the contrasts suggested in the Domesday record. The large proportion of freeholders which is found on manors of Norfolk and Suffolk in the sixteenth century has plainly some connection with the exceptional independence which the free tenants and socmen of this neighbourhood had been able to assert after the Conquest ; [3] and perhaps similar historical causes may explain the ' independency ' which characterised parts of Yorkshire at a still later period. [4] The territory which, in Domes-

---

[1] Vinogradoff, 57 sq. ; cf. 85 sq.   [2] Ibid., 134 sq.
[3] Ibid., 105, 331 ; Tawney, op. cit., 26 sq.
[4] Marshall, Rural Economy of Yorkshire, i. 257 sq.

day, is the chief centre of jurisdictional sokes, includes areas which in the eighteenth century are occupied by settlements of small proprietors [1] and where the democratic element in rural institutions is exceptionally strong. [2] Another line of evidence is suggested by the evolution of tenant-right on the northern border. Though the general history of the North shows that the vast majority of small landholders passed into the position of customary tenants, it does not follow that those who fell within this category formed a homogeneous class, as regards social status or security of tenure. The border warfare had filled Cumberland and Westmoreland and parts of the adjoining shires with a mass of small occupiers, holding their land, as was generally supposed, on the condition of providing contingents for service against the Scots. [3] Its cessation after the union of the English and Scottish Crowns, gave rise to a struggle between landlord and tenant, extending over a long period and bearing some analogy to the social conflicts which occurred in the Danelaw in the eleventh century. In many cases the tenants relapsed into a rightless condition ; in others, especially in the Lake District, they emerged as freeholders. But the immediate issues of the struggle are of less significance than the state of society which it exhibits and the spirit which it evoked. Some importance must be attached to the tradition preserved among the Cumberland ' statesmen ' that they had inherited their land from pre-Norman times ; [4] and to the plea advanced during the struggle, and apparently substantiated in one case by a judicial verdict, that ' though the tenants had been undoubtedly liable to border service, it was

---

[1] *Cf.* Slater, *op. cit.*, 53.   [2] *Ibid.*, 85.
[3] Ferguson, *History of Westmoreland*, 128.
[4] Kitchin, *Ruskin at Oxford and other Studies*, 63.

no part of the service of their estates, nor done by order or direction of their lords, but was part of their general allegiance and subjection, and done by order of the lord warden of those parts.' [1] It would seem that in these troubled warlike regions, where the fighting farmer was bound to the king's service and to the defence of his homestead, the social order had perpetuated traditions of citizenship, at once older and in a sense more democratic, than those which developed normally under feudal influences—the immemorial heritage of a colonising race. Nor is it merely in scattered instances that this continuity is suggested. The North, as a whole, down to the Industrial Revolution, retains many of the characteristics of a frontier state, a land of colonists and adventurers, with vast undeveloped resources and great tracts of untenanted soil. What followed, marks the concluding phase in a long process of colonisation extending back to the dawn of history. The frontier spirit is manifest—both for good and evil—in those who led the way to untold labours and unmeasured wealth.

(4) *North and West*

The neighbourhood of the English Lakes, extending northwards to the border and back towards Lonsdale and the Yorkshire moors, was a region at this time comparatively unknown; a land peopled in the main by descendants of a powerful Norse colony with remnants of an earlier Celtic stock; little affected by the stream of immigration which had followed the growth of commerce around its borders; and yet, by reason of its seclusion, possessing a peculiar interest as a storehouse of racial energies, of materials of which the

[1] Ferguson, 136.

Northern character was formed.[1] Nowhere, in the districts reached by the Scandinavian inroads, had there been precisely the same combination of circumstances strengthening the individuality of the early settlers and the social habits in which it found expression. They came, it would seem, to a land much resembling their original home in climate and physical characteristics : from the mountains of the Hardanger to the desolate fells and hill-sides of Cumberland, from the Norwegian fjord to the English dale. They were born of a good fighting stock and settled in a territory which lay exposed for centuries to the dangers of attack. A vigorous climate ; a hard life rewarded by simple plenty for all ; the secluded dale nestling in the shelter of the mountains ; the challenge of a common danger from without, with its continuous lesson in self-reliance and hardy comradeship—these influences go far to explain the type of character, at once so limited and so complete, which survived in the Cumberland ' statesmen ' of the eighteenth century. The social order harmonised with these rude, wholesome surroundings. There were numerous parishes where wealth and destitution were alike unknown ; and where the place of an upper class was filled by the ' priest ' and the schoolmaster—the former being little removed in social position from his flock, the son of a ' statesman,' living a statesman's life, tilling his glebe, knitting his stockings, and in addition writing his parishioners' letters and instructing their children from within the chancel rails. There were, here, few of those characteristic amenities which excited the wonder of continental visitors in the home

[1] *Cf.* Robert Ferguson, *Northmen in Cumberland and Westmoreland ; Dialect of Cumberland.* Richard Ferguson, *History of Westmoreland.* Collingwood, *Scandinavian Britain.* Kitchin, *Ruskin at Oxford and other Studies* (ch. ii. *The Statesmen of West Cumberland*). Hutchinson, *History of Cumberland.* Jollie, *Sketch of Cumberland Manners and Customs.*

counties, from which foreign impressions of England were chiefly derived. The hard, penurious life of the small proprietors has been compared to that of the French peasantry ;[1] the dress and diet of all ranks, from the farmer to the humblest labourer or artificer, betrayed few of the external marks of refinement ; and an exaggerated routine was relieved by an elaborate observance of feast-days and rustic traditions, less akin to the measured rejoicings of the South than to the custom of other lands, where mediaeval influences had never relaxed their hold. And yet the life of these border districts had advantages in the breeding of men, a continuity of purpose not lightly to be exchanged for the hazard of speedier progress, smoother manners, and greater ease of living. The same impression of maturing strength is conveyed in a report sent home by a court emissary in the reign of Elizabeth, and in an account of the rural parts of Northumberland returned by a royal commission three centuries later. ' These people,' wrote Burleigh's informant, ' situate among wild mountains and savage fells, are generally affected to religion, quiet and industrious, equall to Hallyfax in this, excelling them in civility and temper of lyfe, as well as in abstaining from drink as from other excesses.' Their history during the intervening period might be used to illustrate, by force of contrast, precisely those respects in which the experience of the poorer classes was defective in other parts of the country. They were left to plan their own lives, unaided and unrepressed ; they enjoyed a plenteous supply of material for the household arts ; and they were untouched by that rapid change from comparative ease to acute privation which

---

[1] Kitchin, 66. Eden, *op. cit.*, i. p. vii, notices the wearing of ' clogs ' instead of shoes ; the contrary practice in the South of England being a point on which foreign observers insisted as a sign of English prosperity.

was one of the main causes of demoralisation among
the poor in the latter half of the eighteenth century.
The reason is, partly that the influences of social
change were slow to penetrate the extreme North, partly
that the course of economic development, in its effect
on the resources of the labourer and the relation between
effort and opportunity, was essentially different in a
remote pastoral country and in the well-populated arable
districts of the Midlands and the South.   The advantage
possessed by the northern peasantry in an abundant
supply of milk and fuel became increasingly important
as the century advanced ;   and it is a fact of no less
significance that, while in the Midlands arable land was
being converted rapidly to pasture, the general effect
of enclosure in the North and West was to extend the
area for tillage and with it the means of constant
employment.[1]   Left to themselves, with ' difficulties to
overcome and freedom to overcome them,' their advance,
if slow, was certain and continuous, proportionate to
an increase of skill and exertion.   There was neither
the slackening influence of premature prosperity, nor
the sudden disturbance which was a normal result of
economic progress where the system of husbandry was
rapidly changed.

The memorials of life in these remote districts may,
at first, remind one of those speculations on a natural
state of society which engaged the philosophers of the
period.   On the one side is a vision of endless drudgery
and mean contentment ;   on the other, an almost
idyllic peace, approaching as near to the essentials of
happiness as the conditions of human life permit.   The
next impression is perhaps that of an exuberant medley
of traditions, a genial confusion of ill-assorted types

---

[1] Slater, 104 *sq.*

blending together on the distant landscape. Much is heard of the 'sameness of disposition' engendered by ancient pedigree and long sojourning on the same plot of ground ; of generous, solid, peaceful qualities, relieved on occasion by bursts of extravagance and savage force ; of a liking for pugilism and athletic exercise ; of a football match played annually at Workington with goals a mile apart and no rules ; much, again, of the romance of a mountain country, and of an occasional respect for learning that is not infrequently the guerdon of solitude and the heritage of long descent. And over all there is a glow of sunset, the mystery of a departing age—the ancient merriment of Christmas and Twelfth Night ; the lilt of the minstrel's song ; some quiet gathering at the Holy Well, seeking the spirit of 'temperance, cleanliness, simplicity and love ' ; and the solemn sound of the mourners following in long procession over hill and dale, as one of the brotherhood is borne to his last resting-place, with a sad melody of psalms and dirges wafted on the northern breeze.

To those who viewed their life at close quarters and in its quieter moods, the picture might unfold a clearer meaning, an underlying consistency of aim. Eden was drawing mainly on his knowledge of this neighbourhood, when he maintained that the poorer classes in the less developed regions of the North and West made up for an apparent backwardness in outlook and material achievement by a superior capacity for organisation and an intelligent thrift in the management of simple resources. The life of the Cumberland peasantry, as he saw it, was more concentrated and self-dependent than that of their countrymen in the South. Despite its rude exterior it was essentially richer and more of an art. Its roots lay in an intense attachment of the family to the soil, which rendered the home a centre of absorbing interests—and here, again, we may find a closer parallel in the attitude and ideals of the French peasantry than in the prevailing traditions of the Midlands and the South. The cottage hearth is an altar on which the fire burns without ceasing, day and night, a symbol of the unity and permanence of family life, of the wisdom handed down through many generations, of the pride which educates and keeps the affections pure. Housekeeping is carried on in the patriarchal fashion, with much simple skill in ' culinary preparations,' and at a great saving of expense ; everything nearly, in the way of dress, being a home product, except hats and clogs for outdoor wear.[1] Under these conditions men might drudge to any extent without serious damage or loss of temper, partly because thrift was practised as an art, partly because the affections extended naturally beyond the homestead. The intense sentiment which united the members of a domestic circle overflowed in reunions of friends and relatives in joy or sorrow and at festive seasons of the year. The same natural co-operation that rendered the home self-sufficient appeared at christenings and at the marriage feast, when the neighbours, high and low, brought contributions in kind to a revelry which was not disgraced by ' drunkenness and riot,' nor was it costly, ' as is, alas, so commonly the case in more favoured regions.' [2] Thus family life expands easily into that of the larger family ; and in the interests which spring from well-ordered affections there is a guiding influence which will lead on to higher purposes, however slow the ascent. To those who dwell

---

[1] Eden, i. p. vii *sq.*, 496, 525, 542, 554. He refers to the superior skill in cookery of the peasantry of the North, Scotland and Wales : the cheapness of fuel and the use of barley in making soups being among the reasons ' why the culinary preparations of the Northern peasant are so much diversified and his table so often supplied with hot dishes.'

[2] *Ibid.*, i. 598 *sq.*

with fondness on the small beginnings from which movements arise, there is some significance in an account of the homely gatherings of countrywomen in the valley of Dent—of the company engaging in a knitting contest with much talk and laughter, till one is asked to read and gives them page on page of Robinson Crusoe or the Pilgrim's Progress, after which they fall to discussing what they have heard or resume ' the interesting threads of local gossip.'

It has been observed that the eighteenth century, a period during which the right of the poorer classes to education was seldom mentioned, was remarkable for the number of poor men who rose to high positions in Church and State and in the world of letters. Though examples may be drawn from all parts of the country, there is a mass of evidence ascribing to the northern counties, especially as they approach the Scottish border, a special pre-eminence, and revealing traces of a widespread belief in education, even in learning for its own sake, that had no parallel in the South. In Cumberland and Westmoreland at the close of the century there were few illiterates; and the superiority of the northern peasant in general knowledge was a common observation in diaries of travel. The writers allude, more precisely, to the ' superior arithmetical and literary knowledge ' to be remarked ' in the middling and lower classes,' among whom were men tolerably acquainted with the classics and ' more than tolerable mathematicians.' At a much later date, well on into the second half of the nineteenth century, a government report refers to men of humble station who spoke with pride of their recollection of classical authors. Probably no single explanation is sufficient to account for a phenomenon so striking and so well attested. Special influences may be adduced in particular cases : an element of Presbyterian tradition on the Northumberland border, in Westmoreland a multi-plicity of endowed schools. But undoubtedly the more general causes which gave freedom and stimulus to the native genius must be sought in the social environment : in the absence of conditions which elsewhere erected commercial standards, raised the cost of education, and discountenanced the poor, and in the survival of a social order led by the yeoman class—the class that had given to mediaeval universities their democratic character, and whose presence had once supplied the most effective link between the peasantry and the means of higher education. One way in which this influence reacted on educational opportunity was re-marked as specially characteristic of the Lake District. The practice of recruiting the clergy from yeoman families made it necessary that the village school should combine, in some measure, the function of an academy with that of a place of elementary instruction for the poor ; among whom, in turn, some ' love of Greek and Latin ' was found to diffuse itself after the disorderly fashion of that time and place.[1]

[1] *Schools Inquiry Commission*, 1868, ix. 903 *sq.*   On the state of educa-tion, see Clarke, *Survey of the Lakes of Cumberland, Westmoreland and Lancashire* (1787), p. xxiii. ' Few possess more native genius [than the inhabitants of this district] : among the most unpolished of them are . . . men who are tolerable proficients of the classics and who are more than tolerable mathematicians ; even among the poor artificers, such as tailors and shoemakers, may be found some tolerable poets '—*ibid.*, 36. ' Much more general knowledge may be found [in Cumberland] than is to be met with among people of their class in the southern counties '—Houseman's Tour (1797), *Monthly Review*, iv. 448. ' In different parts of my tour, I frequently heard of north-country curates and excisemen, and in London the compting houses are much supplied with country lads from Cumber-land and Westmoreland, who exchange the plow and flail for the pen and prove as expert with the one as the other.   Whether it be owing to the keen and pure air of these counties, which sharpens the genius of their inhabitants, or the ease and small expense with which education is acquired there, or to what other cause we ought to attribute the superior arith-metical and literary knowledge, etc., observable in the middling and lower classes in the North, I shall not attempt to determine ; however, the fact, in my opinion, is indisputable '—*ibid.*, v. 108.   The *Schools Inquiry*

A time of change was approaching. Broad distinctions were drawn, among the Cumberland peasantry, between the dwellers on the central plains, the shepherds who passed a peaceful, secluded existence in the mountainous districts, and the rough borderers of the far North. Manufacturing centres at Kendal and Carlisle opened new sources of employment to the surrounding hamlets. Agriculture made a gradual, steady progress ; the use of broadcloth in place of homespun, for Sunday wear, being one of the innovations

Commission (*l.c.*) notices that men ' in the humbler walks of life ' might still be met with, who spoke ' with pride of their recollection of Homer and Virgil ' ; *cf.* the account given by Moritz (*Travels in England in* 1782, Eng. ed. 1886, 149) of his meeting with a saddler from Matlock who conversed of Homer, Horace and Virgil, with quotations, ' pronouncing the words and laying his emphasis with as much propriety as I could possibly have expected, had he been educated at Cambridge or at Oxford,' and who had, moreover, the good taste to pay the reckoning at the inn where they halted ' to drink and talk, . . . because, as he said, he had brought me thither.'

Heath, *English Peasantry* (1871), 85–7, refers to the Presbyterian influence on education in Northumberland : in another passage, he cites the case of a Cheviot shepherd, father of eleven children, who ' twenty years ago ' hired a schoolmaster at his own expense. ' After a year or two, he took his master and two other shepherds into partnership . . . the schoolmaster moves about from house to house among his four employers, receiving board and lodging during the fourteen days for each scholar. . . . In the winter time the parents will send the bigger boys into lodgings at Wooler, that they may have further advantages in the way of education. In the school belonging to the English Presbyterians, the master speaks of having two sons of shepherds, one learning Latin, the other French and Euclid '—*ibid.*, 214. The practice, here noticed, of supplying the schoolmaster with board and lodging is probably of some antiquity. It was the recognised method of supporting and rewarding the schoolmaster in the hedge schools of Kerry, a county where, seventy years ago, according to Hall's account, it was ' by no means rare to find among the humblest of the peasants, who have no prospect but that of existing by daily labour, men who can converse fluently in Latin and have a good knowledge of Greek,' and where a century earlier ' classical reading ' was said to extend ' even to a fault among the lower and poorer kind in this country '—Hall, *Ireland*, i. 258–68. The same authority tells how a wild mountain tribe, being unable to induce a schoolmaster to venture among them, waited for the next moonless night and proceeded to capture one. A safer parallel to the state of education in the Lake District may be found in a description of two wayside schools in Antrim, one elementary and the other classical, given in Porter's *Life of Dr. Cooke*, 3 *sqq.*

which marked the growing wealth and changing manners
of the farming class.[1] And with progress came the
familiar signs of disintegration. The quiet, self-contained
life of the country-side became slowly entangled in the
traffic of the great world beyond its borders, losing in
the process much of its native strength and compactness,
and ere long falling a victim to the giant forces which
it had nourished. The general result was everywhere
much the same. The crisis following the Napoleonic
wars, which brought final ruin to the yeomanry of the
South after a period of inflated prosperity, swept away
the old race of Cumberland ' statesmen.' But at such
times of transition the result by itself is often a matter
relatively insignificant and even ambiguous. Social
dissolution may be the climax of a long decay, of a
series of displacements cutting the ground beneath
a population for the most part passively resistant to
change. Or it may be, in the main, a sign of energy
breaking from within, of a people advancing to meet the
destinies which await them. It is the latter simile
that seems to describe the progress of the North at
this critical epoch. A series of inventions added
enormously to the productive power of certain districts,
which became the centre of new economic and social
formations ; and the movement as a whole in its constructive aspects was an expression of the character
which had been slowly maturing. The peculiar combination of shrewd conservatism with a stubborn spirit
of adventure, which has enabled the manufacturing
districts to take the lead in so many directions during
the past century, had already revealed itself in
parts of the North which were least affected by the
stimulus of economic change. There is, at first sight,
nothing so inconsistent with the quiet life of the northern

[1] Eden, i. 554 sq.

dalesmen as the country lad who worked his way to the University at Edinburgh,[1] or the continuous stream of emigrants who filled the counting-houses in London or found a career in the Church and the lower ranks of the public service. Yet there is nothing, in reality, so characteristic of the stock from which they sprang. The spirit of Viking ancestors was ever stirring in this northern race, breaking forth with the same deliberate strength that drove the routine of daily life. A steady concentration on the task nearest to hand generated a surplus energy, which found a vent, as opportunity offered, in low extravagance or in the conquest of the world. It is the same type of manhood that drudges contentedly on a northern homestead, that drinks with stolid zest on festive occasions, and that effects revolutions in the social system. A people so constituted are normally slow to change their course, little affected by impulse, but ever seeking an outlet for the energy which has been accumulated in plodding forward on the beaten track. A change of objective is the fruit of no sudden emotion, but of the steady pressure of stored force bursting deliberately into new fields of action as the horizon expands. Such, too, is the impression conveyed by the manufacturing districts on the eve of the Industrial Revolution. It is a land whose people have advanced slowly, accumulating the strength and traditions of many centuries, and now at length as in the fresh vigour of manhood entering on a new career ; a land of old loyalties and new adventures, the past and the future blending into one. Marshall's survey of rural Yorkshire, Defoe's passages on the woollen industry, and an account of the manufacturers about Manchester before the days of the power-loom, all

---

[1] Kitchin, 89 *sq.*

convey the same record of thrift, energy, and personal
independence which had no parallel in other parts of
England. They leave also another impression—that
industry in these parts was still passing through a
phase of development in which the man of small means
was able to hold his own, gradually emancipating
himself from the shackles of custom without falling
a prey to commercial oppressions. Change in the
industrial order comes at a moment when older forms
of industry exert their greatest stimulus on character ;
the factory system rises against a background of old
traditions, whose strength had departed long since in
commercial centres of earlier growth.[1] It is the
same with mental progress. The culture and wisdom
of earlier days maintained a vigorous existence side
by side with the first-fruits of science and speculation
which were to lay the groundwork of a new social
life. In the Yorkshire dales there were wizards who
detected crime ; the minstrel who was no ' scholard '
but a man of native wit, a welcome guest in tavern
and hall ; and poor men who had taught themselves
mathematics and gave their leisure to mechanical
inventions. The country round Manchester was still
famous for its skilled labourers of the old school,
' cunning ' men who were also herb doctors and would

---

[1] The character of the change, as an outburst of latent enterprise,
is seen in the rise of the early Lancashire manufacturers who ' for the
most part . . . started nearly equal in point of worldly circumstances,
men originally of the smallest means often coming to the front—workmen, weavers, mechanics, pedlars, farmers or labourers—in the course
of time rearing immense manufacturing concerns by sheer force of industry, energy, and personal ability ' (Smiles, *Industrial Biography*, 317).
Holt (1795) attributes the decrease of yeomanry in the County of
Lancaster not to misfortune, but to the attraction of a new career in
business ; he adds that the farmers who are ' mostly sprung from the
industrious labourers place their children in the manufacturing line '
(quoted by Johnson, *op. cit.*, 141, who remarks, p. 146, that for the small
owner to sell out in good times and take to trade was abnormal).

'rule the planets' before engaging on any important
task; and a disreputable company of boggarts and
clap-clans haunted the way at nightfall to the quiet
hamlet where a circle of Methodists were studying the
'Age of Reason' and the 'Rights of Man.'

Marshall commences his study of rural conditions
with his native county of Yorkshire, and concludes with
Devon and the adjoining neighbourhood. In Yorkshire he notices the 'spirit of improvement which has
lately diffused itself among all ranks'; there is no
district 'where industry and economy are more conspicuous, or where a personal independency is so
strongly rooted among men in middle life.' In Devon
these progressive qualities are lacking; nowhere 'of
late years' has the 'spirit of improvement . . .
slumbered more composedly.' There can be no doubt
as to the acuteness of the conclusion to which his
inquiry leads. He has travelled from a country
which is entering on a new career, to one from which
an old supremacy has departed; from the land of
the future to the land with a great past. This description applies very generally to the Western districts.
Devon in its mighty days had been the cradle of national
enterprise; Wales and Cornwall had long preserved
in their language and traditions the remains of an old
Celtic civilisation; and to this day the West country
is a repository of folk-lore and the peasant culture of
a bygone age. But the distinction between North
and West towards the close of the eighteenth century
is not summed up in any simple antithesis of progress
and decline. If Devon showed signs of an exhaustion
of energy, Cornwall and Wales were awakening under
the influence of a spiritual revival which in the history
of the latter is a landmark of equal importance with

the economic revolution in the manufacturing districts. Between the Celtic West and a large area of the North there were, in fact, sufficient points of resemblance and analogy to render their differences peculiarly instructive. Both shared in the characteristics of a remote rural life. Both had the same types of superstition and ritual, the same vein of poetry and romance. In both, the peasantry were characterised by a native intelligence which was often contrasted with the torpor of the labouring class elsewhere. Both were powerfully influenced by the Methodist movement. In both a strong sense of local patriotism was combined with conservative instincts and a respect for the past; and both Wales and the North in later times have supplied striking examples of the democratic spirit. Many of the contrasts revealed in their later history point back to a fundamental difference in the changes which passed over them at this critical epoch. If the North has been described as entering on a phase of accelerated expansion after a long period of quiet growth, Wales may be said to awaken from the sleep of centuries after an age of arrested development. The Industrial Revolution commenced a new stage in a career of progress; the Welsh revival was nothing less than the re-birth of a race, destined to recover the threads of its history and to consecrate to a higher purpose qualities which had for long lain dormant and unperceived.

Of the Welsh people it is pre-eminently true that the strength and weakness of the race may be read in their culture and educational achievements. A great wave of enthusiasm passed over the community during the Methodist revival, and again in the development of intermediate and higher education a century later. For some time the instruction of the people was carried on mainly by their own efforts in the peculiarly democratic system of Sunday Schools connected with their chapels. Their literature consisted chiefly of religious periodicals, to which the peasantry were almost the sole contributors.[1] Later on, they subscribed large sums towards the College at Aberystwyth,[2] and many had been accustomed to save money for such opportunities of higher instruction as came within their reach. It was not uncommon for the younger generation to leave farm and quarry for a year's additional schooling during early manhood ; and it is remarkable that self-sacrifice in these matters was shown rather by the children than by their parents.[3] The characteristic which requires explanation is a want of proportion between enthusiasm and the range of mental achievement. In eighteenth-century writers, the intelligence of the Northern peasantry is proved by the extent of their general knowledge ; the intelligence of the Welsh is seen in contrast to their state of culture. At a later period, evidence of an ' exceptional desire ' for education has to be reconciled with the confinement of their intellectual outlook. Thought and feeling flowed with abnormal energy within certain channels. In the eighteenth century, men in the prime of life would learn to read and write, in order to obtain copies of their native songs ;[4] their descendants composed essays

[1] Rhys and Jones, *The Welsh People* (3rd ed.), 534.

[2] *Committee on Intermediate and Higher Education in Wales, 1880* ; *Report*, p. 89.

[3] *Ibid.*, pp. 20, 27 ; *Evidence*, Q. 3620 *sq.* Schools Inquiry Commission, *1868*, viii. 6.

[4] I am indebted to Mr. David Thomas of Tal-y-Sarn, near Caernarvon, for some notes on education in that neighbourhood, which he procured for me from Mr. W. G. Williams, one of the excellent band of schoolmasters who are also antiquarians and take an interest in the history of their native places. The following is an extract. Before the spread of Methodism ' into these parts, the bards occupied a respectable position in the esteem of the rural population, and these bards not only produced

and poems for the local Eisteddfods.[1] The religious revival revealed a delight in language and in discussion among the common people, which recalls the atmosphere of ancient Greek democracies. The humblest cottagers became connoisseurs of pulpit eloquence, and debated abstruse points in theology.

Such intensity is not generally consistent with breadth of outlook. The Welsh peasantry were preserved from the baser literature which circulated among

songs (of varying excellence) for the people, but also instructed many of the younger men in the rules of poetry and in the simpler but more useful arts of reading and writing. The cobbler's workshop, the village smithy and the weaver's hut became the rendezvous of men eager to overcome the difficulties of the arts of reading and writing. As these men were mainly of the labouring class and consequently of poor circumstances, it is highly probable that they never received any schooling beyond that obtained from the village poetaster and rhymester. . . . I learned from two old workmen who had cultured their minds to a greater degree than most of their fellows, that the tavern connected with the parish church in many places (Ty'n llam = church-house) was nightly patronised by two classes of men—those that came for drinking purposes and those that gathered thither to meet the village sage who led them along the fields of mental culture with which he was acquainted. Most of the young men seem to have been filled with a desire to possess copies of the songs of their own days as well as those of former times. Tragic occurrences and awkward events were readily rendered into songs and satires by the poetasters; love-songs were in common and in high favour; carols were popular especially in the " Plygain " (Christmas meetings, held some time after 3 a.m.). All kinds of songs were transcribed into convenient manuscript books, and the desire to obtain a copy seems to have been the chief inducement for young men to endeavour to master the art of writing. The segregation of men in barns and stable-lofts during the long and inclement winter evenings seems also to have been the means of the further dissemination of knowledge, and it was not uncommon for the farmer's son who had received some town education to become the tutor among his father's employés.'

I take this opportunity of recalling the courtesy with which I was received by those whose acquaintance I made during a short stay at Caernarvon. I regret that a change in the plan of my book has prevented me from making more use of the help received from these and other Welsh friends. After collecting materials for a study of Welsh education, I came to the conclusion that the subject requires separate treatment and had better be left to those who are more competent to do it justice.

[1] *Schools Inquiry Commission, l.c.*—'It is quite usual for servants and labourers to compose essays and poems for the various eisteddfods.' *Cf.* Sadler, *Moral Instruction and Training in Schools*, 439 *sq.*

the English masses; but there were large numbers whose reading was confined to the publications of their religious sect. The native literature was rich in poetry and sectarian metaphysics; it remained deficient in all branches of secular knowledge.[1] In the North a different state of things was observed. There, the native intellect showed a distinct bias towards mathematical and scientific studies;[2] the pursuit of knowledge, never far divorced from a practical outlook on life, became subordinated gradually to industrial and political ends. There could be no clearer indication of the differences of ideal and impulse which separated the two peoples at this stage of their evolution. In the North the supremacy of a scientific practical spirit was connected with a type of conservatism which easily discarded its impedimenta and answered the call of progress. Among the Welsh an abnormal growth of the imaginative and poetic faculties was bound up with a pronounced attachment to the past, a conservatism which never yielded its possessions or acknowledged defeat. That which constituted their strength was also their weakness, rendering them the more liable to sudden reactions and the slower to attain harmony in the expansion of thought and character.

To ascribe the difference to racial influences is to say at once too much and too little. The essential fact in the history of the Welsh at this stage of transition is a reawakening, under peculiar circumstances, of energies which had been submerged at an earlier period.

---

[1] Welsh Education Commission, 1846, pt. iii., pp. 59 sqq., and App. F. and H. Southall, Wales and her Language, 96. Committee on Intermediate Education, 1880, QQ. 6247 sqq., showing a considerable progress.

[2] I do not overlook the strong romantic element in the Northern character; but, so far as I can judge from the evidence at my disposal, it was in mathematical and scientific studies (including nature study) that the Northern intellect excelled.

From the thirteenth to the eighteenth century the intellectual condition of Wales is the fate of a people who, having reached a degree of mental culture in advance of their social organisation, became subject to a different race at a much higher level of political development. Welsh society at the time of the English Conquest retained in all essentials its old tribal structure, although the germs of a broader national life may be seen in the literary and religious movements which were inspired by the struggle for independence. It is useless to imagine the transformation which might have occurred, had independence been prolonged under a native aristocracy. The immediate effect of the Conquest was a profound discouragement, from which the people were slow to recover. The growth of native culture was arrested. The masses were shut off from English civilisation by barriers of language and geography ; and their isolation was intensified by the inevitable apostasy of their natural leaders and by a policy of repression. These conditions remained after the revival in the eighteenth century, and explain the narrowness of its intellectual results. Meanwhile it is not suggested that the Conquest was without positive moral effect. Political and social reorganisation quashed disorder and prepared the way for a new outlook and a sense of purpose. But the imagination of the people was little affected by the changes of this intervening period. They remained, as it were, passive under an operation ; and, when consciousness returned, they had a memory of far-off things. Nor, again, was the awakening so sudden and unprepared as is sometimes suggested by historians who accept the language of revivalists; for, from the sixteenth century to the eighteenth, there was a succession of educational and religious movements gradually drawing into closer sympathy with the spirit and needs of the masses. It was sudden as an explosion is sudden, though the train has been carefully laid; and, when it came, it showed how little had been lost or learned during a long period of quiescence.

The Welsh Revival has been accurately described as a Renaissance; for it was a modified reassertion of native instincts which had lain dormant since the days of tribal independence. Much, indeed, of the old culture had remained throughout. In the eighteenth century, verse-making was still in certain localities a cardinal part of education; reading and writing were ancillary arts. In the village bard may be seen the descendant of a race of schoolmasters, probably as old as the Druidic order.[1] The religious movement, which discredited this ancient frivolity, was as truly a native product and had its roots in the past. Methodism, both in its austerity and in the services which it rendered to the national language, followed in the path of the monastic revival of the twelfth century. The taste which it developed for oratory and discussion recalls the literary awakening of the same period.[2] Its sectarian animosities are venerable as a relic of tribal warfare. Tribal instinct may be discerned also in the facility with which the population crystallised, as by some natural impulse, into self-governing groups. The religious congregation became a compact social unit, the centre from which a new intellectual life gradually extended.[3]

---

[1] v. *supra*, p. 75, *n.* 4.

[2] Lloyd, *History of Wales*, ii. 529 *sqq.*, 595 *sqq.*

[3] *Cf.* account of Welsh Sunday Schools in Phillips, *Wales, the Language, Social Condition*, etc. (1849), 55 *sq.* The growth of the Eisteddfod, with its national gathering and tributary local meetings, expresses most clearly the old conception of Welsh nationality—a spiritual federation of tribal groups. Whatever the defects of this movement, there can be no doubt as to its spontaneity, its wide influence, and its democratic character. The local meetings are a source of education, whose value and possibilities of extension are probably only realised by those who have an inner knowledge of Welsh life. *Cf.* Sadler, *l.c.*

CHAPTER II

(1) *Schools*

WE are concerned with the early growth of educational institutions only in so far as it illustrates the lines on which an educational system gradually developed. In this connection the rise of the older Universities stands out unquestionably as the most conspicuous event in the Middle Ages; the growth, or reorganisation, of Grammar Schools as the achievement of the sixteenth and early seventeenth centuries. Later on, we trace the beginnings of an organised movement which offered elementary education to the masses. But even if we disregard a number of simultaneous developments which are excluded in this general survey, the paradox which asserts that the fabric of national education has been constructed at intervals from the top storey downwards remains, as an historical statement, only partially true. Time was when the University of Oxford might be described as the 'chief Charity School of the poor and the chief Grammar School in England, as well as the great place of education for students of theology, of law and of medicine.' [1] The process of differentiation

---

[1] *Oxford Commission*, 1852, *Report*, p. 19 : the reference is to the reign of Henry III. For an account of the pre-Reformation schools and foundations (including Grammar Schools), see Foster Watson, *English Grammar Schools* (1908) ; Leach, *English Schools of the Reformation* ; also a memorandum on the history of Endowed Schools by the same author, printed by the *Secondary Education Commission* (1895), v. 57 *sqq.*

and exclusion which gradually established her modern social characteristics, raised the age of admission, and marked out for her the province of higher studies, had only commenced, when the basis of a secondary system was being laid afresh in the endowed foundations of the sixteenth century. Similarly it was not until the kingdom had been covered from end to end with elementary schools, that the Grammar Schools came to be regarded exclusively as centres of secondary education.

It has been claimed that the ' ecclesiastical organisation of the Middle Ages . . . established a school system both on the secondary and elementary planes of a far more extensive kind than historians have ordinarily supposed.' How far, it may be asked, did the disendowment of the old religion in the sixteenth century displace opportunities of instruction, for which no sufficient substitute was afterwards provided ? How far, again, did the social effects of the Reformation, and the economic forces which accompanied it, tend to institute class-barriers in the higher branches of the educational system ? [1] Of conscious change in policy there is little

---

[1] Huber makes the extreme statement that the Reformation inflicted on both Universities ' only injury both outward and inward ' ; *cf.* Mullinger, *History of Cambridge University*, 101–4 (abridged edition). The disruption of the monastic orders and various changes in the position of Church and Clergy led to an immediate falling off of the poorer students ; a tendency which was increased by the economic decline of the yeomanry and the growth of commerce under Elizabeth. What effect this social transformation had on the standard of scholarship and the intellectual atmosphere of the Universities in the sixteenth century, is not immediately clear ; but even if we discount the continual complaints made—during the latter half of the century—of the growth of luxury and the vagaries of royal patronage, it is probable that something was lost through the influx of a new class of students who had on the whole less incentive to laborious study than their predecessors, at a time when the initial opportunities of rich and poor students were not so dissimilar as at the present day. See Brodrick, *University of Oxford*, 82 *sqq.* ; Mullinger, *op. cit.*, 93–104 ; Maxwell Lyte, *University of Oxford*.

One pretext for the dissolution of the monasteries being their neglect of education, Henry VIII appears to have founded the meagre sum of ten Grammar Schools out of the proceeds of this transaction. The majority

evidence. The ostensible aim of reform in the educational, as in the economic, sphere was to secure greater efficiency in the application of traditional methods and ideas. The reorganised Grammar School, connected with the universities and developing an accepted form of liberal culture, found its complement in the apprenticeship system and the catechetical teaching of the national Church. The parish remained a centre of spiritual discipline for the people at large, and its organisation was not complete without a school of some description.

The Grammar Schools, according to a Commission of Inquiry which reported in 1868, had been intended ' as a means of bringing a higher culture within the reach of all, and raising from among the poorest, as well as the richest, those who should thereby be able to serve in larger measure the Church and Commonwealth '[1]— a conclusion which is borne out in the main by an analysis of the trust-deeds appended to the report. The object of the Manchester endowment (1515) was to bring up boys, without restriction, in good learning and manners, especially in the ' liberal science and art of Grammar as the ground and foundation of all other liberal arts and sciences.' Elsewhere Grammar is variously defined to include a study of the ' learned languages,' ' Latin,' or ' Greek and Latin,' to which ' Hebrew ' is occasionally added. In some cases candidates were to be refused admission until they could read and write English or read Latin; or there was a specific arrangement for elementary instruction in addition to, and in preparation for, the teaching of Grammar. There appears, also, to be little reason to

of the older Grammar Schools, being attached to Collegiate Churches, Chantries and Gilds, were dissolved under the Chantries Act in the next reign. Leach, Memorandum, *Secondary Education Commission* (1895), v. 72.

[1] *Schools Inquiry Commission*, i. 120 (1868).

doubt that from a social standpoint the aim of these foundations was on the whole as comprehensive as the report of the commissioners would lead us to suppose. Generally, where instruction was not gratuitous throughout the school, some arrangement was made, by means of a graduated scale of admission fees and quarterages and a system of maintenance, to bring the benefits of the institution within reach of the poorest. It is true that the term 'poor,' as employed in connection with educational trusts of this and later periods, does not necessarily carry the same significance that it has acquired in more recent times ; but, as a rule, the object of Grammar School endowments was defined in terms sufficiently broad to comprehend all ranks of society, and in certain instances the possibility of admitting scholars from the labouring class was definitely raised.[1]

The verdict of history is contained in a sentence of the report referring to a process which had been for some time at work. ' A free Grammar School is an anachronism. If the school be free, it is filled with a class of children who do not learn grammar ; and

---

[1] *Cf.* Cranmer's reply to the Commissioners in 1541 who proposed to confine the Canterbury Grammar School to the sons and younger brothers of gentry on the ground that the sons of husbandmen, for instance, were not called to learning, that their labour was needed, and that ' all sorts of men may not go to school '—' I grant much of your meaning herein as needful in a commonwealth : but yet utterly to exclude the ploughman's son, and the poor man's son from the benefits of learning . . . is as much to say, as that Almighty God should not be at liberty to bestow His great gifts of grace upon any person, nor nowhere else, but as we and other men shall appoint them to be employed, according to our fancy and not according to His most Godly Will and pleasure, who giveth His gifts both of learning, and other perfections in all sciences, unto all kinds and states of people indifferently . . . wherefore, if the gentleman's son be apt to learning, let him be admitted ; if not apt, let the poor man's child that is apt, enter his room '—Strype, *Cranmer*, i. 127. The scale of admission fees at Llanrwst is of interest in this connection—' 1, every knight sonne, 2s. 6d. ; 2, every doctor or esq. sonne, 2s. ; 3, every gentl. or minister sonne of 50 li. p. annum, 1s. ; 4, every yeomane sonne of 20 li. p. annum and rich tenants, 9d. ; 5, poorer and meaner men's sonne to pay 6d. ; 6, but poore indeed, *gratis.*'

if the classics are sedulously taught, the schools soon cease to be free ' or sufficiently inexpensive to remain within reach of other than well-to-do parents. Here and there might be found an establishment, relatively well endowed, which had been able to afford free education and at the same time, having a satisfactory local connection, to maintain a reasonable standard of scholarship ; [1] but in most cases the only way in which a school could be made to render effective service or even to continue in operation, was by minimising one or other of the objects which the founder had in view. In the great majority of endowed schools which remained open to the ' lower section of the middle class and the upper section of the artisans,' the classics were taught, if at all, to a very small proportion of the scholars ; and although in this way some tradition of culture had been kept alive where it would otherwise have been obliterated, the arrangement entailed a conflict of interest between two separate groups of scholars, both of which in an under-staffed school were unlikely to receive adequate attention.

The fate of a school would depend, to a great extent, on the situation in which it was founded, and on the

[1] Thus the Commissioners in 1867 found the Manchester Grammar School giving free instruction, and sending about eight scholars to the Universities per annum ; classics preponderate ; entrance by competition owing to the number of applicants ; third boy in the school the son of an artisan. It is noted that a reform had been initiated in 1849 under a scheme ordering (1) the teaching of modern languages, arts and sciences ; (2) the provision of necessary apparatus and increase of the teaching staff ; (3) purchase of books, provision of new premiums, University Exhibitions, etc. The position of the school at the close of the eighteenth century may be estimated to some extent from the narrative of Samuel Bamford, who on first entering began with spelling and rose to be ' first scholar in the first Bible class ' and might have proceeded to Latin with the chance of eventually reaching the University, had not his father removed him—Bamford, *Early Days*, 68 *sqq.* (new ed., 1893). On the foundation of the school in 1515 it had been laid down that the master should every year appoint one of his ' scollers ' to teach the infants ' their ABC primer and forthe till they begin Grammar.'

financial provision made for its upkeep. In the course of time the cost of a classical education increased, generally 'in far greater ratio than the value of property' with which the endowment was connected; nor was there any guarantee, especially where the school did not constitute the sole charge on the property, that the trustees would be disposed to pay 'in the double proportion of the depreciation of the value of money and the increase of that of the funds.' It often happened that schools which were founded by the Government after the dissolution of the Chantries received their endowment in the form of a fixed annuity, which became sooner or later inadequate to the purpose. Under these circumstances there was a plain inducement to charge fees or to admit a certain number of stipendiary pupils; the free scholars and those unable to pay more than a nominal sum being gradually excluded or placed in an unfavourable position as recipients of charity.[1] On the other hand, where the regulations prohibiting fees or limiting the scale of payments were scrupulously observed, difficulty might be experienced in securing the

---

[1] With the change of social ideas and of class relations, the same kind of stigma would come to be attached to free scholars entering the Grammar School on a poverty qualification that is found in the case of servitorships at the University, and especially so where the scale of payments for fee-paying scholars was raised. Thus the Commissioners found twelve foundation scholars at the Bromsgrove Grammar School, the sons of artisans and small tradesmen, wearing a special dress and despised by the rest of the school, who were the sons of well-to-do parents paying a high fee; and there was an intermittent feud between the two classes. Similarly at the Alton Grammar School, boarders and free boys played at different ends of a small playground, with severe penalties for transgressing the line of division. Apart, moreover, from the difficulty which arose, in such cases, of admitting the poor free scholars and the well-to-do fee-paying scholars on the same footing, there had been growing up distinctions in education corresponding to distinctions in social life. It is not surprising, for instance, that Edward Cave, the son of a local shoemaker, found himself out of his element at the Rugby Grammar School in the early part of the eighteenth century—Knight, *Shadows of Old Booksellers*, 172.

services of a master competent to teach the classics.[1]
Up to a certain point, these considerations are sufficient
to explain the tendency of the Grammar Schools to
develop, on the one hand, into secondary schools for
the rich, and, on the other, into elementary schools
for the poorer classes ; but administrative difficulties
might have been diminished, if a more far-sighted
policy had been conceived at the outset. As often
happens in the history of popular education, a
relatively advanced system of instruction had been
established without adequate attention being paid to
the preliminary stages, the substructure on which its
efficiency depended.[2]   This neglect, which may have
been unimportant so long as the desire for education
could be generally taken as evidence of more than
average ability, became a source of serious inconvenience
as soon as the demand for elementary instruction in
the vernacular began to develop out of all proportion
to the demand for ' grammar ' and the higher branches
of learning. It meant that in many schools, which made
provision for the poorer classes and where the teaching of subjects other than grammar was not actually
prohibited in the trust deeds, there was a tendency for
elementary instruction to predominate, to the exclusion
of everything else. It is possible that an opportunity
for constructing a continuous system of instruction,
which might have anticipated some of the work done

[1] See generally, *Schools Inquiry Commission*, ix. 152 *sq.* ; Memorandum
by Mr. A. F. Leach, *Secondary Education Commission* (1895), v. 73 ; M.N.
(Marchamont Needham), *A Discourse on Schools and Schoolmasters*, 1663 ;
Letter to Henry Brougham (1818), 9, 23.

[2] To underestimate the difficulties of the ascent to higher education
may be described as the besetting sin of pioneers in popular education,
of which the nineteenth century affords numerous examples : *cf.* the
history of the Mechanics' Institutes, of Welsh University Colleges before
the Welsh Intermediate Education Act, and the difficulty experienced
in persuading public opinion that a sound secondary education is a
necessary preparation for the higher branches of technical instruction.

during the past fifty years, was suffered to pass. Had elementary and secondary education been more liberally provided as distinct grades—after the manner of Archbishop Harsnett who established at Chigwell in 1629 'two large and fair schoolhouses,' an English and a Latin school, side by side—it would have been easier to regulate the 'rush on the Grammar Schools,' by selecting those who had passed through the elementary departments; while the coexistence of two separate, yet connected, grades of school would have kept alive the idea of a continuous course.[1]

[1] Comenius in his *Didactica Magna* (*circa* 1630) sketches a scheme of State education including (1) Public Vernacular Schools (ages 6–12), (2) Gymnasia or Latin Schools (12–18), in every city for those who qualify from the Vernacular School; (3) Academies (18–24). The Vernacular Schools 'contain the whole school population up to the age of twelve, without respect to rank, wealth or sex. The Vernacular School is the common school; all there pass through the common minimum curriculum . . . out of which all advanced studies spring. Class distinctions must not be encouraged, and at the early age of six it is impossible to say whether a particular boy is better fitted for manual labour or for a learned profession' (Adamson, *Pioneers of Modern Education*, 62).

Comenius attracted the notice of the English Parliament and was apparently invited to join a proposed Commission for the reform of the existing system, 1641 (De Montmorency, *State Intervention in English Education*, 100). Attention is thus drawn to the general movement for extending and reorganising education, of which traces are found during the Cromwellian period ; and it is possible to regard the Puritan movement as the common ancestor of educational systems which subsequently developed in the American Colonies, and of certain forms of educational propaganda in England during recent years in which the democratic features of American Education are cited with approval (*cf.* R. E. Hughes, *The Democratic Ideal in Education*). Throughout this period, the idea of equalising opportunity and discriminating between different kinds of talent seems to have occupied the minds of reformers. Thus Hartlib's proposal for the education of pauper children in London (1650) compares advantageously with later Charity School schemes in discriminating the 'quick-witted,' who after the common grounding are to be made 'scholars, or accomptants, or what they delight in,' from the common sort who are to be apprenticed (Adamson, *op. cit.*, 111 *sq.*). Again Hoole, in his *New Discovery* (1660), seems to anticipate the modern Higher Elementary School; his 'Petty School' teaching children (5–8) to read English in preparation for the Grammar School, 'is also a place " wherein children for whom the Latin tongue is thought to be unnecessary, are to be employed after they can read English." *Instead of dismissing*

As Latin gradually lost its position as the language of learning, a reaction commenced—which had been foreshadowed by Mulcaster—in favour of education in the vernacular; and, connected with it, we trace the growth of a demand for universal instruction. From the commencement of the seventeenth century, and in a few foundations even at an earlier date, there is evidence of a deliberate effort to develop elementary education, adapting it to the requirements of a class who had no prospect of proceeding to grammar.[1] After the Restoration it became more common to endow a distinct class of schools for elementary instruction only, Latin being admitted in some cases as a possible extra.

It may be submitted, with some justification, that the founders of Grammar Schools relied in many cases on the possibility of the demand for elementary or preparatory training being met by tuition at the hands of the clergy, or through various unendowed agencies which must have existed in one form or another from a very early period. Elementary Schools were

such as " incapable of learning," the Petty School is to give them still more practice in reading English, and to add writing and arithmetic. . . . While the other children are to learn the accidence, these Latin-less youngsters are to " be benefited in reading orthodox catechisms and other books that may instruct them in the duties of a Christian, . . . and ever afterwards in other delightful books of English History, as the *History of Queen Elizabeth*, or poetry, as *Herbert's Poems, Quarles' Emblems*; and by this means they will gain such a habit and delight in reading as to make it their chief recreation when liberty is afforded them. And their acquaintance with good books will (with God's blessing) be a means to sweeten their (otherwise) sour natures, that they may live comfortably towards themselves, and amiably converse with other persons." ' There was to be one such school in every town and large village, apparently no fees, and classes not to exceed 40 (*ibid.*, 162 *sq.*).

[1] See *Encyclopædia Britannica* (11th ed.), 958. 'We have here a great number of poor people in our parish who are not able to keep their children at grammar. But we are desirous to have them taught the principles of the Christian Religion and to write, read and cast accounts, and so to put them forth to prentice '—Foster Watson, *op. cit.*, 150 (*re* St. Olave's Southwark, 1561).

established from time to time in connection with the
parochial organisation, being instituted or at any rate
supervised by the clergy and carrying on a practice
common in the Middle Ages, when the parish clerk,
' often a beneficed cleric,' held the position of schoolmaster.[1]   Moreover a growing demand had encouraged
the development of private enterprise in teaching as
a commercial speculation.[2]   In some cases the parish
clerk would, on his own initiative, open a road-side
establishment and undertake to ground the children
of the village in spelling, reading, ciphering, and pot-
hooks for a small payment ; or a tradesman who
had come to grief would try his hand at teaching and
travel from place to place in search of pupils, old and
young.   But the type of ' adventure school ' with which
tradition has rendered us most familiar was held under
the auspices of the village dame.

Of the character of these institutions it is difficult
to speak in general terms.   That a satisfactory standard
was often reached, may be reasonably assumed, especially in parish schools falling under the first category,
where the clergy interested in their welfare were men
of sympathy and intelligence.[3]   The merits of the
private adventure schools varied probably to a greater
extent, according to the nature of the local demand

---

[1] Foster Watson, op. cit., 153.

[2] Private adventure schools in the sixteenth century, ibid., 156 sq.

[3] The ' religious societies,' which developed during the last quarter of
the seventeenth century, helped to awaken opinion and activity among
the clergy and others, before the work of promoting Charity Schools was
taken up by the S.P.C.K.—Holman, English National Education, 28 sq. ;
cf. the case of five village schools founded by Archdeacon Sharp, Rector
of Rothbury, Northumberland, in the next century—' In a long course of
years there were very few to be found in the parish who could not write,
if not retain also some knowledge of figures ; and no people could be
more remarkable for industrious exertion in humble labour, and at the
same time for modesty and good behaviour, than the parishioners of
Rothbury in general '—Overton and Relton, English Church, 1714-1800,
274.

and the personality of the individual who assumed the functions of teacher. 'A dark room, a dame, a horn-book and a good birchen rod '—a congested troop of infants droning in an oppressive atmosphere—a stray hen scouring for scraps on the threshold—and the mistress attending intermittently to her domestic affairs : such, in the main, is the prose version of the celebrated stanzas of Shenstone popularised by Royal Commissioners in a later and more fastidious age. But it is conceivable that during the period of their ascendancy, and in the rude surroundings which gave them birth, the dame-schools answered a definite, though humble, purpose ; and in the urban districts, where a superior demand existed, there were many instances of exceptional success. Thomas Cooper at least had reason to recall with gratitude the memory of an 'expert and laborious teacher of the art of spelling and reading,' whose ' knitting too (for she taught girls as well as boys) was the wonder of the town.' The confession elicited from the dames at a later date—' it's little they pays us, and it's little we teaches them '—is the perennial murmur of protectionists in the declining years of an industry whose profits and whose fame are gone.

Discontinuity, lack of organisation, and the absence of a reliable system of management are defects common to the various forms of experiment which have been reviewed. Even in Endowed Schools, resting on a permanent basis and with a scheme of government prescribed in the trust deeds, the administrative machinery was often signally defective. The state of the law and other circumstances were such as to render the trustees practically irresponsible and, at the same time, to restrict their power of carrying out necessary reforms and exercising an effective control over the masters whom they appointed. Thus it happened that innumerable abuses, both serious and amusing, made their way into the schools, in addition to defects which an able management would have found it difficult to remedy.[1] To the latter half of the seventeenth century belong the beginnings of a far-reaching change. New fields were opened to educational enterprise, and the time had arrived when the efforts of individual benefactors began to yield place to organised movements dependent on public support and subject proportionately to the control of public opinion.

It is customary to contrast the foundations of the sixteenth century with the Charity Schools for the poor which sprang into existence a hundred years later. The essence of the contrast is not to be found in a difference of curriculum. There might be little difference between the subjects taught in a decayed Grammar School and the curriculum of a Charity School, and yet a prodigious change in tone, associations, and social outlook. While mention of the poor in connection with the older foundations might refer generally to those who were not rich enough to obtain advantages elsewhere, the ' poor ' of the Charity Schools are a distinct social class. The aim of the Grammar Schools was selective : to work beneath social distinctions and to open access to the higher walks of life. The aim of the Charity Schools was disciplinary : to rescue the masses and to ensure their obedience.

Yet it may be said that the indiscriminate censure passed on the system by modern critics has had an unfortunate result in diverting attention from experiments

---

[1] At a village Grammar School in Yorkshire, almost within living memory, there was a holiday whenever the master desired to go fishing, and the school prizes were ' tossed for ' at the end of term amid universal merriment—Speight, *Craven and N. W. Yorks. Highlands,* 197 *sq.*

in industrial training and in the development of relations between the school and practical life, and also from an important advance in methods of organisation. An attempt has been made, with very plausible reasoning, to establish a connection between simultaneous movements in philanthropy and commerce which occur during the latter half of the seventeenth, and the earlier decades of the eighteenth, century.[1] It may be shown, at any rate, that the spirit of association developed in both spheres during this period ; and that, about the same time that the possibilities of joint-stock began to create a sensation in business circles, the idea of organising the superfluous wealth of the community for philanthropic purposes, by methods analogous in many respects to those which obtained in commerce, took shape in a number of suggestive experiments. Thus an administrative system was called into being which has formed in the main the basis of voluntary organisation ever since. A movement in 'associated philanthropy' would generally originate among a group of active supporters prepared in varying degrees to render personal service. Sooner or later it would be found advisable to appoint a permanent committee to direct operations at headquarters. And at the same time there would be an attempt to elicit financial support from the general public, who might acquire in many cases certain rights of control and a position somewhat analogous to that of shareholders in a business concern.

This form of organisation, which dealt more or less effectively with the financial difficulty and marked at the time a distinct advance towards effective and responsible management, was adopted, first, in the foundation of large boarding institutions in the Metro-

[1] Kirkman Gray, *History of English Philanthropy*, ch. iv., v.

polis for the rescue and upbringing of children actually destitute of the means of subsistence, and secondly, in the development of societies for the spread of education and religious knowledge among the poor in different parts of the kingdom. It was in the latter case, where organisation extended over a wide area, that the possibilities of ' associated philanthropy ' were most apparent. The services which may be performed by an intelligent central body with funds at their disposal—by stimulating and assisting local initiative, by forming a point of connection between institutions at work in different areas, and by undertaking in the interests of the movement as a whole the direct performance of certain functions which require organisation on a large scale carried out in the light of a wide experience—are now so generally admitted that it seems almost pedantic to inquire when the idea was first introduced. Yet in this connection the part played by the Society for Promoting Christian Knowledge in the formation of Charity Schools is of special interest, and demands at least a passing notice. The Society undertook to defend and popularise the principles of the movement. It aided in the establishment of schools throughout the kingdom, and periodically issued instructions and advice as to their management and the art of teaching. It appointed an inspector to visit schools in the Metropolitan area. By a resolution passed in 1703 it condemned classes in excess of fifty scholars ; and there were a series of proposals with regard to the training of teachers, which prove the trustees of the Society to have been at least a hundred years in advance of their time.[1] We may

---

[1] A minute of 1710 refers to the ' expediency of establishing a Grammar School, to which boys of great talent and merit should be transferred from the Charity Schools that they might be prepared for situations as masters.' In 1723 Dr. Waterland, preaching before the Society, announced

note, also—to illustrate the tendency of educational organisations to develop beyond their original sphere— that the formation of night classes for adults in connection with the day schools is recommended in some of the earlier minutes.

The Canons of 1604 had placed the control of education in the hands of the Church. No schoolmaster was to teach in ' public school or private house ' unless approved by the ordinary as a man of learning, apt for the office and of sound doctrine.[1] When the Puritans gained the ascendancy, the one thing certain was that this settlement would be undermined. The confiscation of Church property placed a fund at the disposal of Parliament, and it had been resolved in 1641 that it should be devoted to the ' advancement of learning and piety.' It soon transpired that reform would mean something more than a change of patronage, and in the ensuing years drastic proposals made their appearance. Milton's tractate, advocating a new model of secondary and higher education, was published in 1644. Petty followed in 1649 with his plan for elementary trade schools. Others approached the legislature, recognising the State for the first time as the official agent of education. Comenius, who came to England in 1641, was the advocate of a graduated scheme of public instruction based on a universal system of vernacular schools. Six years later, in a treatise addressed to Parliament, Hartlib made the far-reaching proposal that the ' magistrate should see schools opened,

---

that the trustees thought of founding a superior school for training school-masters and mistresses. Unhappily nothing came of these proposals ; but apparently prospective teachers were enabled to visit the best managed Metropolitan schools (the principle of the model school). Phillips, *Wales, Social Condition, etc.* (1849), 266 *sq.*

[1] Canons 77–79 ; Cardwell, *Synodalia,* i. 291.

provided with teachers, endowed with maintenance, regulated with constitutions, and . . . have instructors and overseers to the observance of good order in this business.'[1]

There is evidence that the subject interested the legislature or certain of its members, and some important measures were passed. Under the Propagation Act of 1649 commissioners were appointed who laid the basis of a general school system in Wales.[2] This was followed by a measure allocating a portion of the Crown revenues to the payment of approved schoolmasters and preachers. In the same year there was a proposal to found a University at Durham, by diverting part of the cathedral property. Lastly in 1653 Parliament appointed a Committee for the Advancement of Learn-

[1] *Considerations tending to the Happy Accomplishment of England's Reformation in Church and State : Humbly presented to the Piety and Wisdome of the High and Honorable Court of Parliament.* See Adamson, *Pioneers of Modern Education, 1600–1700,* 108.

[2] They were authorised to provide for the 'keeping of schools' with 'fitting yearly maintenance' and the 'education of children in piety and good literature'; the funds to be provided by a charge on 'ecclesiastical livings in the hands of Parliament,' and the yearly stipend not to exceed forty pounds (*cf.* Adamson, 98 *sq.*). Mr. Shankland describes the measure as 'in the broadest sense an Education Act for Wales '—' Under this Act the Commissioners [1650–1653] provided the thirteen counties of Wales with a well-organised system of schools, staffed with the best-equipped schoolmasters that they could command. The Trustees [under a separate Act of 1649 for the maintenance of 'Preaching Ministers or Schoolmasters or others in England and Wales, settled or confirmed by Ordinance or Order of Parliament'] maintained and perfected the system from 1653 to 1660. Free schools were established in every market town of any importance throughout Wales, and in many other towns and villages convenient to the children. In most of the great towns two able, learned, and University men were appointed to prepare children for the Universities if desired. A sixth of the tithes of Wales was devoted to the maintenance of these schools ; . . their curricula provided for the teaching of reading, writing and ciphering, and in the large towns they prepared for the Universities. . . . The question of a Welsh University College was also mooted by the Puritans. . . . The Restoration nearly paralysed the whole organisation, many of the schoolmasters were deprived for nonconformity, but a number remained at their work '—*Sir John Philipps and the Charity School Movement in Wales,* by the Rev. Thomas Shankland (*Transactions of the Hon. Society of Cymmrodorion, 1904–5,* 132 *sqq.*).

ing, which included men in the first rank of public life.[1] Yet the total achievement was small, the subject of education being continually postponed under the pressure of more urgent business and overwhelmed by political issues. Reform meant in the first instance the removal of hostile elements, and part of the work was founded on spoliation. The Welsh Act, which achieved the most solid results, was an undisguised political move. The wider schemes, involving a complete change in method and organisation, had not time to mature before political reaction intervened, sweeping away a fabric of good intentions partially carried out.

The century following the Restoration is important, however, for the assertion of administrative principles which underlie the growth of State interference within the past eighty years : the principle of rate-maintenance and local public control, the principle of grants-in-aid, and the principle involved in the extension of public control over voluntary institutions. The State recognised a direct responsibility for education in connection with the Poor Law. There was an Act passed in 1662 ' for the better Reliefe of the Poore of this Kingdom,' in consequence of which the Common Council of London, some years later, decided to give a number of poor children the benefits of an elementary and industrial education ; and this was followed, after a long interval, by a private Bill of 1769 enabling the parochial poor of London to be educated out of the rates. The Workhouse Act of 1723 and numerous private Bills of the period contained provisions to the same intent. The principle of grants-in-aid was recognised in the case of the Foundling Hospital, which

[1] Adamson, *op. cit.*, 103.

received at one time substantial assistance from the national exchequer. Meanwhile, in 1716, the Commons had passed a drastic measure for the reform of close vestries in the Metropolitan area, which would have had the effect of transferring to an elective body the ' sole right of appointing masters and mistresses of any voluntary Charity School that might be carried on within its parish, and of selecting the children to be admitted to such schools.' Against this the ' trustees of the Charity Schools, in which nearly 5000 poor children were being educated and clothed, represented forcibly that these schools were not maintained by the parishes, but were " chiefly supported by voluntary subscriptions," and that the greater part of the subscribers contributed because they thereby secured the right of appointing schoolmasters and nominating the children to be admitted. To hand these powers over to an elective body would certainly check the flow of subscriptions, and would, in fact, " tend to discourage, if not totally dissolve, the said schools." ' [1]

(2) *Literature*

There was in the eighteenth century no general and organised system of popular education, but there were a variety of schools to which different classes in the community might obtain access. Similarly, there was no systematic supply of cheap literature, but a certain amount of printed matter lay within reach of the poorest. The interval between the close of the seventeenth century and the accession of George the Third witnessed a considerable extension of the book trade. Printers and booksellers, a class formerly almost unknown outside the Metropolis, began to set up in the provincial

[1] Webb, *English Local Government,* i. 255 *sq.*

towns,[1] and fed a subordinate army of hawkers and travellers who canvassed the neighbourhood far and wide. Number-men, or itinerant booksellers, passed from village to village, leaving samples, and erected their stalls wherever a suitable market could be found. Pedlars and fortune-tellers carried odd volumes in their packs to remote parts of the kingdom. Old women, vending sweetmeats, kept a corner of their boards for the Illustrated Bible, the Pilgrim's Progress, and an assortment of chap-books.[2] The proprietor of the *Sherborne Mercury*, established in 1736, had relays of messengers travelling on horseback to Penzance and branching off the main road into the surrounding country, who delivered his journal and took orders for books.[3] From these and similar sources, by begging and borrowing, by saving pence and cajoling shopkeepers, or by loitering over a bookstall, such of the poorer classes as had a taste for reading might with good fortune find the material of which they were in quest, and often managed to scrape together the nucleus of an incongruous library.[4] Except, however, in cases where a generous patron placed himself at their service, the choice and acquisition of good literature were matters of some difficulty. There is a sad story of Samuel Drew— a Cornish shoemaker of some repute—journeying one day to a bookshop at Truro and demanding ' Plato on the Soul.' Standard works of the best authors might be obtained in London readily enough and at a cheap

[1] Buckle, *Civilisation in England,* i. ch. vii. *n.* 395. In 1693 the Act of 1662 restricting the number of master-printers was repealed ; see W. H. Allnutt, *Notes on Printers and Printing in the Provincial Towns of England and Wales* (read before the Library Association of the United Kingdom, 1878).

[2] Knight, *Memories of a Working Man* (by a tailor), 20.

[3] *Life of Samuel Drew* (by his son), 40 *sq.*

[4] Knight, *Pursuit of Knowledge under Difficulties,* i. 88 *sqq.,* ii. 92. Wallas, *Life of Place,* 17.

rate. 'At stalls and in the streets,' says a traveller of the period, 'you every now and then meet with a sort of antiquarians, who sell single or odd volumes; sometimes, perhaps, of Shakespeare etc., so low as a penny; nay, even sometimes for a halfpenny a piece. Of one of these itinerant antiquarians I bought the two volumes of the "Vicar of Wakefield" for sixpence.'[1] In the provinces—even in the larger towns—there was a great scarcity of first-rate literature, a disproportionate amount of space being occupied by tales of magic and adventure, lives of highwaymen, ephemeral histories, love stories, valentines, prophetic almanacks, 'godly and other patters,' slip-songs, children's books, and antiquated treatises on various subjects sold in numbers, four sheets for a penny.[2]

It is clear that, while the student laboured at a disadvantage, there existed in some sense a literature for the masses, whose history bears on the transition from mediaeval to modern methods of instruction and enter-

[1] Moritz, *Travels in England in 1782* (English ed. 1886), 35 *sq.* Stephen Duck (1700–1756), an agricultural labourer of parts, commissioned a friend visiting London to bring him books; he received a selection of ancient and modern poets and Seneca's *Morals*—Knight, *Pursuit of Knowledge under Difficulties*, iii. 84; *cf.* Smiles, *Industrial Biography*, 237 *sq.*

[2] 'Shopkeepers and travellers may at all times be supplied on the most reasonable terms, with all kinds of Histories, Godly and other Patters, slip-songs, carols, etc., etc., at J. Turner's, Printer' (Coventry advertisement)—Knight, *Shadows of the Old Booksellers*, 239. The Sheffield press issued (1736–1745) 'all sorts of new songs and penny histories,' a 'new historical catechism by W. L.,' and ballads such as 'The Golden Bull, or the Crafty Princess, in four parts'—Leader, *Reminiscences of Old Sheffield*, 107.

Lackington in his tours (1787 and 1790) found that the bookshops in large towns between Edinburgh and London, with the possible exception of Leeds and York, contained very few first-rate books and a deal of trash. Knight, *ib.*, 294 *sq.* Samuel Bamford's account of books read during his schooldays gives an excellent idea of the literature obtainable in Manchester and the neighbourhood, about 1800. Bamford, *Early Days*, 87, 102; see also Knight, *The Old Printer and the Modern Press*, and *Passages in a Working Life*, i. 226 *sq.*; Thomas Cooper, *Autobiography*.

tainment. The oral teaching of the Church continued, but was supplemented by the dissemination of Bibles, and of religious tracts which date back to the close of the seventeenth century. Elements of the miracle play survived in rustic drama and puppet-shows; but the modern counterpart of religious drama, once a mighty instrument of spiritual instruction, might be found perhaps in such works as the Pilgrim's Progress, which occupied the window-ledge in many a religious household. Songs and ballads and romances were still preserved among the peasantry by oral tradition; but, since the sixteenth century, the practice of recording old English song had increased, and new compositions were commonly issued in the form of broadsheets.[1] It is during the Tudor period that we find the first traces of a form of criticism which cheap literature has aroused at many stages of its development. Mary issued a Royal injunction against ' books, ballads, rhymes and treatises . . . set out by printers and stationers of an evil desire for lucre and covetous of vile gain '; and the rapid multiplication of ballads and ' lewd ' songs in succeeding years was repeatedly denounced in much the same terms as the inferior products of the cheap press at the present day.[2] It is doubtful, however, whether this form of literature in its earlier phases can be seriously compared with the type of pasquinade which came in with the growth of large towns, and the demoralisation of popular taste, in the eighteenth century.

[1] Ballads often adorned the walls of cottages and inns, along with King Charles' Golden Rules, and religious and patriotic prints. ' The prints and pictures which I have seen at these inns are, I think, almost always prints of the royal family . . . or else I have found a map of London and not seldom the portrait of the King of Prussia. . . . You also sometimes see some of the droll prints of Hogarth '—Moritz, *op. cit.*, 144.

[2] Chappell, *Old English Popular Music*, i. 54 *sqq.*

The chap-book, which appears to have been the chief reading-book of the masses, drew its material from every available source. These publications were sold up and down the country at a farthing or a half-penny each, and consisted of sheets folded into sixteen or twenty-four pages, adorned with rough woodcuts and covering a wide range of subject-matter, from episodes in sacred and profane history to the lives of devils, highwaymen, and clowns. Tradition tells of one Stephen Knowles, a miner dwelling at Grassington somewhere in the earlier half of last century, a collector of chap-books, who believed what he read. ' It is not likely,' he argued, ' that anyone would go to the expense of printing lies.' Baron Münchausen was a special favourite and a sore point. Once a weather-beaten seaman from Greenwich, who had come north on a visit, ventured to approach the matter in a spirit of criticism ; but Stephen was equal to the occasion. ' A fool,' he said, ' comprehendeth not the profound sayings of the wise, and it ill becometh an ignorant tar and out-pensioner of Greenwich Hospital to ridicule the surprising and truthful narrative of a German Peer ! ' [1]

A very different kind of importance attaches to the periodical literature which had been spreading, in the form of newspapers and magazines, with increasing velocity since the last years of William the Third. ' Not many years ago,' wrote Dr. Johnson in 1758, ' the nation was content with one *gazette* ; but now we have not only in the Metropolis papers every morning and

[1] Dixon, *Chronicles of the Craven Dales*, 425 *sqq.* See generally, *Life of Holcroft*, i. 135 ; Crabbe, *Parish Register*, pt. i ; Bowles, *Days Departed* ; Sydney, *England and the English in the Eighteenth Century*, ii. 141 *sq.* ; *id.*, *England and the English in the Nineteenth Century*, i. 238, *cf.* Place, *Add. MSS.* 27825, p. 79 (B.M.) ; *Select Committee on Education* (1835), Q. 800 ; J. H. Dixon, *Ancient Poems, Ballads and Songs of the Peasantry of England* (1846) ; Ashton, *Chap-books of the Eighteenth Century*.

every evening, but almost every large town has its weekly historian who regularly circulates his periodical intelligence and fills the villages of his district with conjectures on the events of the war.' ' All foreigners,' he adds, ' remark that the knowledge of the common people of England is greater than that of any other vulgar. This superiority we undoubtedly owe to the rivulets of intelligence which are continually trickling among us, which anyone may catch.'[1] More than one authority has recorded the intense excitement which prevailed among all classes during the campaign of that year ; the eagerness with which small knots collected in the streets to hear the proud possessor of an Observator or a Review declaim its smattering of news and comment. At an earlier crisis a traveller had remarked, with mingled amusement and surprise, during a visit to London, that ' workmen habitually begin the day by going to the coffee-house in order to read the latest news. I have often seen shoeblacks and other persons of that class club together to purchase ' a journal.[2] It was not the least significant of the many portents which were gathering on the horizon of English life.

[1] *Idler,* Nos. 7 and 30.
[2] *A Foreign View of England in the Reigns of George I and II ; Letters of M. de Saussure, tr. Madame van Muyden* (1902), 162.

CHAPTER III

A TENDENCY to differentiate educational methods in accordance with the supposed requirements of different classes was, in some ways, an inevitable incident in the advance towards a policy of universal instruction. The contrast which is commonly drawn between the Grammar Schools of the sixteenth century and the Charity Schools of the eighteenth—to the disadvantage of the latter —involves, to a large extent, the fallacy of comparing institutions which had different functions to perform, and of reading into the theory of an earlier age ideas which belong to modern democracy. The Charity School movement may, at any rate, be explained with reference to social preconceptions which influenced Elizabethan statesmanship and have their roots in earlier usage and tradition.

The nucleus of conservative tradition may be traced in the mediaeval conception of society as consisting of a series of classes, each with its appointed status in the commonwealth, its customary scale of income and expenditure, its round of duty which ranked almost as a public trust. Each commodity had its 'just price'; to each class there was a fair reward for labour which was relative to its customary standard of living. To lower this standard was an act of oppression; to better it might be tantamount to an encroachment. It was the business of government to see that each group fulfilled its allotted rôle and, by striking a balance between conflicting interests, to secure for each its proper livelihood.

The inference that each class had its appropriate standard of culture, and that the prospects of the individual which depend on instruction should be determined by the rank of his parents, was not part of the mediaeval theory. The impulse to education was religious, not economic. The question of educating the masses had not arisen, but to the individual belonged God-sent talents which it was a duty to cultivate. Schools existed for the *élite*, but not an *élite* of wealth. The same statute that debarred villeins from apprenticing their children confirmed their right of access to places of instruction.[1] A change occurred in the sixteenth century. The measure of instruction prescribed by the Apprentice Laws was governed by an economic motive ; its aim being to secure that idle and vagabond children should be trained for industry on conditions defined by the State.[2] When the Grammar Schools were reorganised, the old ideals were maintained, but it was necessary to combat an objection that the son of a ploughman was not called to learning, and that his labour was as important to society as functions which belonged to a higher rank.[3] But the most

---

[1] ' No one shall put their child apprentice within any city or borough, unless they have land or rent of 20 shillings per annum ; but they shall be put to such labour as their fathers or mothers use, or as their estates require. But any persons may send their children to school to learn Literature '—7 Henry IV, c. 17 (Raithby, *Statutes at Large*, i. 561).

[2] Craik, *State in its Relation to Education* (*English Citizen Series*), 6 *sq.*

[3] It was ' meet for the ploughman's son to go to the plough, and the artificer's son to apply the trade of his parents' vocation ; and the gentlemen's children are meet to have the knowledge of government and rule in the Commonwealth. For we have as much need of ploughmen as any other State : and all sorts of men may not go to school '—Strype, *Cranmer*, i. 127.

striking illustration of the turn given to mediaeval theory in dealing with a new instrument of popular instruction is found in a statute passed during the last years of Henry the Eighth. To allay certain symptoms of disorder occasioned by a free use of the Scriptures, it was enacted that the English Bible should not be read in churches. The right of private reading was granted to nobles, gentry, and merchants that were householders, but was expressly denied to artificers' prentices, to journeymen and serving men 'of the degree of yeomen or under,' to husbandmen and labourers.[1] It was left to a later generation to draw from sage premises absurd conclusions. The old social theory is expressed in a saying of Edward the Sixth— ' this country can bear . . . no husbandman or farmer worth above £100 to £200 ; no artificer above 100 marc ; no labourer much more than he spendeth.' Nearly two centuries later, the satirist produced a scheme of municipal 'nurseries,' to prepare children for 'such a condition of life as befits the rank of their parents and their own capacities as well as inclinations'—the offspring of gentry, merchants, traders and handicraftsmen receiving appropriate degrees of culture, whilst the ' cottagers and labourers keep their children at home, their business being only to till and cultivate the earth, and therefore their education is of little consequence to the Publick.'[2]

A mistrust of independent action on the part of individuals or sections of society had followed from the

---

[1] 34 & 35 Henry VIII, c. 1 (Raithby, ii. 201). Burnet, *History of the Reformation*, i. 517.

[2] *Gulliver's Travels*, pt. i, ch. vi. Contrast the genuine mediaeval attitude as shown in Henry VIII's instructions to the clergy to exhort parents, masters and governors of youth to ' bestow their children and servants, even from their childhood, *either to learning, or to some other honest exercise, occupation or husbandry* '—Burnet, iv. 91 (the italics are mine).

premises on which the mediaeval theory of social equilibrium rested. A maximum, no less than a minimum, of opportunity had been implied in the doctrine of 'just price.' The persistent efforts of government in the Middle Ages to control capitalist enterprise, to manipulate the labour market, to fix the limits of remuneration and profit, above all to prohibit collective bargaining, were an essential part of the policy which aimed at protecting the standard of living through all grades of society. Within these limits the course of Tudor statesmanship suggests little more than an extended application to the nation as a whole, of 'ideas which had been implicit in the local organisation of earlier times'; but the reorganisation which it involved has an important bearing on the political growth of the nation, and marks a dividing point in its economic history. It is difficult to find any metaphor adequate to express the process of national consolidation that reached a climax during these years of transition. Broadly it may be said that a number of individual organisms, exhibiting various degrees of structural complexity, have coalesced to form a larger and more complex unit co-extensive with the nation. Underlying the process is the conception that society as a whole, and each of the units composing it, is a corporate structure subject to some form of organised control. Its starting point is the clustering together of members of a social or economic group for the protection or advancement of their common interests. As society becomes more complex with the differentiation of economic functions, each new group tends to associate in self-defence, until it is incorporated as part of a larger unit.

Some such course of evolution may be traced in the growth of the gilds during the later Middle Ages. The town has already emerged as a self-governing community, with its methodic organisation of commerce and production in the interest of its members. The rise of the craft-gilds marks an advance in economic complexity and a corresponding differentiation in the structure of local government. The burgess body is thus reorganised in a number of constituent associations, standing sever-ally in the same relation to the municipal authority, and forming together the 'subordinate mechanism of self-government' and the instruments by which the town carries out its system of economic regulation. It is characteristic of this phase of urban life—so long as the market is essentially local and there is a substantial equality among those enjoying the privi-leges of burgess-ship—that municipal self-government is broadly representative of the main body of the towns-folk and relatively free from outside interference, and that each subordinate group retains a large measure of self-determination subject to the control of the municipal authority which is in turn responsive to the corporate will of the community. Meanwhile forces which were destroying the economic isolation of town and manor, worked with disintegrating effect on the old forms of communal life. The whole structure of trade and industry reacted to the influences of a widening market and the growing importance of capitalist enterprise. Capitalism brought new problems—the growth of wage-labour, a redistribution of functions, a new rivalry of interests, the economic and political subjection of class to class. The movement affected not only the organisation of the crafts, but also the balance of town government. Power concentrated in the hands of oligarchies; self-government became less a reality; and the gild-organisation entered 'into a smaller part of the daily life of the members.' The same tendency may be traced in the process by

which associations originating among the new journeyman class were gradually divested of every semblance
of spontaneity, and became instruments whereby a
trading corporation provided for the relief of its
dependants. With these internal changes in town life
were connected the spread of industries over the rural
districts and the increased intervention of the central
authority. As industry extended beyond the sphere
of local regulation, as local institutions fell short of the
requirements of discipline and justice, there commenced
a process of reconstruction in which the lines of national
policy were marked out by the central government
and local organisation was enwrapped in a framework
of national control. National legislation encroached
more and more on the sphere of the municipality and
superseded the custom of the manorial courts ; the
task of supervising the gilds, together with a part
of their administrative functions, was gradually transferred to magistrates controlled by the central executive.

A definite drift of political tendency underlies the
course of economic development. There is an intelligible
transition from the forms of association and self-
government which may be studied in the earlier stages of
town life, to the urban oligarchies of the fifteenth century,
and to the centralised paternalism of the Elizabethan
age. The central government, working for national
ends, asserted its control over a form of association which
had drifted from its original intention, and a quasi-
representative system which had fallen into decay ; and,
in doing so, it tended to supersede them both. The process of national consolidation was a gradual movement
towards the stage at which policies were designed and
executed from above. The tendency reappears beyond
the sphere of economic regulation. In the religious
movements of the period there is the same element of

emancipation as in other phases of national development, but the prevailing note is a renewal of discipline. The conception of national religion as an instrument for enforcing the duties and positions of the social system comes out in the language of the Church Catechism, and in the special prayers for landlord and labourer which were formulated by royal command.[1] The Church service finds its place in the same comprehensive scheme of delegated responsibility that entrusted magistrates with the assessment of wages and a general supervision of popular morals. At the same time, with the passing away of the old order, important social influences may have fallen into decay. The effect of the disendowment of religious fraternities depends not merely on the quantitative loss or gain which accrued from the reapplication of their funds to various objects, but also on the extent to which it crushed a habit of voluntary co-operation whose loss was not to be compensated by any increase of efficiency.[2]

The situation at the close of the Tudor period illustrates the truism that, while it is easy to formulate

---

[1] *Cf.* Heath, *English Peasant*, 20. Compare Henry VIII's Instructions to the Clergy, describing the Bible as ' the Spiritual Food of man's soul, whereby they [his subjects] may the better know the Dutys to God, to their Sovereign Lord the King and their neighbour '—Burnet, *History of the Reformation*, iv. 91. Mr. R. H. Tawney has sent me an extract from a document (*Considerations delivered to the Parliament, 1559*, preparatory to the Statute of Artificers, 1563), preserved among the Burleigh MSS., which throws light on the connection between religious and social discipline as conceived by the Government. It is recommended (*inter alia*) that ' no man hereafter receive into service any servant without a testimonial from the master he last dwelt with, sealed with a Parish seal kept by the constable or churchwarden witnessing he left with the free license of his master, penalty £10. So by the need of the masters servants may be reduced to obedience, which shall reduce obedience to the prince and to God also ; by the looseness of the time no other remedy is left but by awe of the law to acquaint men with virtue again ; whereby the Reformation of religion may be brought in credit, with the amendment of manners, the want whereof has been as a thing grown by the liberty of the Gospel.'

[2] The same remark applies to the suppression of local drama, etc., which took place in certain districts, under Puritanical influences.

schemes of social equilibrium, it is difficult to control the material forces by which the course of social development, and ultimately of social thought, is actually determined. Though in the sixteenth century property was widely distributed and persons dependent entirely on wages formed perhaps a minority of the whole population, the ' two nations ' were already emerging from the wreck of feudal society—on the one side, ' the classes enjoying a large common measure of economic freedom ' ; on the other, the wage-earners who were to become the ' masses,' ' in whose position, as defined by the law, there is an element of mediaeval serfdom, an element of freedom, an element of protection and guarantee.' [1] The position of the latter had been accepted, rather than modified, by national legislation. Their status was most easily controlled and apparently most in need of regulation. Their power of initiative and constructive action was little developed, and upon them restrictions on personal freedom fell most heavily. They were a class, as it seemed, marked out by circumstance for protection and control. This actual cleavage necessarily tended to weaken that sentiment of social solidarity which had been enforced by Tudor despotism in the face of economic change ; an effect which became more apparent in the next century, as political predominance shifted from the crown to the governing classes, and as with the decay of personal monarchy there passed away some part of the idealism which its prestige had sheltered.

If the constitutional conflicts of the Puritan era weakened the machinery for enforcing Elizabethan policies and loosened the conceptions on which they rested, the Restoration and the Revolution of 1688

---

[1] Meredith, *Economic History of England*, 86.

revealed with growing emphasis the strength of those interests which became a dominant influence in eighteenth-century politics. Attempts to define the position of the masses assumed an altered complexion, when they were conceived no longer as part of a general scheme of subordination embracing society as a whole, but reflected primarily the opinion of one section of society as to how another should live ; and the confusion was increased by a blending of feudal tradition with the maxims of commerce. In the plea for cheap labour which influenced both supporters and opponents of the Charity Schools, there is at once an echo of the old social theory which imposed a customary restraint on the class standard of living, and a foretaste of the attitude of later economists who treated labour as an item in the costs of production.[1] Meanwhile complementary sides of economic thought were slow to develop. While the protective system of the Elizabethan age gradually lost its warmth and vigour, the independence of the wage-earning classes was hardly more intelligible to eighteenth-century conservatism than the ' masterless man ' to the Tudor statesman. The judicial assessment of wages was abandoned as a general practice, and unions of employers tacitly admitted, some time before the labourers were granted a legal right of combining to protect themselves. If certain lines of economic advance during this period illustrate the danger to be apprehended when national welfare is estimated in terms of rent and profit, the measures introduced at the close of the century show yet more plainly, not only how far paternal rule had receded in practice from the tradition of a fair wage, but also the confusion bound up with a system of government which was yielding to a new economic principle

[1] Cf. Mandeville, *Essay on Charity and Charity Schools*.

without admitting its corollaries. In the interval there appeared the writings of Mandeville, in part a caricature of the Elizabethan ideal, in part a shrewd assertion of fact, in part an anticipation of individualism in its cruder forms. The welfare of the masses is subordinated to the liberties of a successful minority ; [1] and they are consoled with the thought that individuals may rise to positions of comfort by virtue of self-discipline and the love of money. His tract on the Charity Schools was publicly burnt. He was both behind, and in advance of, his age. He had outraged genuine instincts of duty and benevolence ; he had stated difficulties which were more easily ignored than solved ; he had also held up the mirror to social snobbery.

Yet the change of sentiment may be easily exaggerated. Criticism did not crystallise into a reasoned body of thought before the coming of Bentham and Adam Smith. The ægis of paternalism had passed from the Privy Council to the governing class which had been educated under its control, and social effort continued to be inspired and biassed by tradition. While the main part of the controversy concerning Charity Schools turned on the expediency of instructing the lower grades of labour in subjects previously appropriated to traders and craftsmen,[2] the movement itself

---

[1] 'It is impossible that a society can long subsist and suffer many of its members to live in idleness and enjoy all the ease and pleasure they can invent, without having at the same time great multitudes of people that to make good this defect will condescend to be quite the reverse '—Mandeville, *Fable of the Bees* (6th ed.), 326. Contrast the saying of Edward VI.—' Wherefore as in the body no part hath too much or too little, so in a commonwealth ought every part to have *ad victum et non ad saturitatem* ' (Meredith, *op. cit.*, 86).

[2] Mandeville's main argument, which has a permanent interest, looks forward to the danger of recruiting a surplus army of ' clerks,' or, as he would have expressed it, of ' tradesmen and artificers '—*Fable of the Bees*, 328, 370. He reiterates a traditional view that the Church service and catechising should be sufficient to the needs of the labouring poor, ' without the assistance of reading and writing'—352 *sq.*

was not contrary to precedent ; it was neither so great a degradation as has been sometimes suggested, nor so great an advance as might appear from its advocacy of popular instruction. A system of teaching, essentially remedial in its objects and subordinated to the needs of industry and religion, followed, in fact, as a legitimate extension of Elizabethan principles. The status of the poor was still roughly predetermined ; education was as much a means of restraint as of improvement. The rescue-motive lay at the root of popular instruction, just as in later years the recovery of lost ground was the original object of the trade-union movement.

So far we have traced a connection between certain lines of educational policy and certain tendencies in economic organisation and political thought. In the period of reconstruction which follows the Reform Bill of 1832, there will be something like a reversal of these tendencies and corresponding changes in the aims of educational reform. The People's College at Sheffield and similar institutions which developed during the middle years of the nineteenth century, represent the intellectual side of a progressive movement whose aim was to raise the status of the masses, and which finds an illustration in the familiar antithesis between a training for livelihood and a training for life. The movement towards national education was already connecting itself with the vague conception of a 'common school.' The *carrière aux talents*, hitherto subordinate, was becoming a motive of primary importance in the direction of educational policy. The history of the intervening period of transition is concerned with changes in the economic structure of society which altered the character of social problems, and with the growth of new ideals and energies which led men to a higher level of social consciousness.

It has been suggested that the authoritative super-vision of national life in all its details, which was carried to a logical extreme in the system of ' thorough,' received a permanent blow from the constitutional struggles of the seventeenth century. During the hundred years which followed the Puritan Revolution, analogous abuses accumulated in the administrative systems of Church and State ;[1] a slackening of discipline and restraint being apparent no less in the sphere of religion and morals, than in different phases of economic regula-tion. The lax administration of the Poor Laws finds a counterpart in the gradual disuse of the practice of catechising and of the inquisitorial system, scrupulously carried out by many local authorities in the earlier half of the seventeenth century, which enforced attendance at divine worship and corrected indifferently contra-ventions of the law and forms of misbehaviour which lay beyond the scope of any legal enactment.[2] The rise of new industries, for which no provision had been made in the Statute of Artificers, was accompanied by the growth of population in urban areas beyond

----

[1] Pluralism in the Church, which was partly the result of insufficient endowment and one of the main causes of absenteeism, may be paralleled by inequalities in the distribution of magistrates between different parts of the country (Webb, *English Local Government*, i. 321) ; again, just as incompetent persons found their way into the magistracy (*ibid.*, 328 *sqq.*), so a faulty method of examination admitted unqualified candidates to Holy Orders (Sydney, *England and the English in the Eighteenth Century*, ii. 351). Negligence and irregularity in the conduct of the clergy are ascribed in a large measure to the decay of episcopal supervision (*ibid.*, ii. 338), just as the decline of diligence and efficiency in local government is ascribed to absence of the stimulus which was formerly brought to bear on magistrates and local authorities by the Privy Council through the Judges of Assize. Both in civil and religious matters the effects of misgovernment were most noticeable in the growing urban centres (*cf.* Webb, i. 85, 198 *sq.*, 328 *sqq.* ; Bosanquet, *London*, 126 *n.*).

[2] Roberts, *Social History of the Southern Counties*, 141 *sqq.*, 204 *sqq.* Overton and Relton, *English Church, 1714–1800*, 294.

the reach of Church discipline and magisterial control. But there is another side to the picture. If the decay of regulation is responsible for instances of physical and moral neglect, it produced also a comparative freedom of enterprise and gave a stimulus to new forms of thought. In the reaction from paternalism, opinion drifted by degrees towards a conception of 'natural liberty,' which found expression in the economic gospel of free competition and the opposition of early liberals to authoritative interference in the domain of thought and conduct. Further, if the actual decrease of State intervention prepared the way for a doctrine of *laissez-faire*, the materials for a conception of equality of opportunity were furnished by the rise of individuals at the commencement of the Industrial Revolution and by the influence of political and religious movements which, extending downwards in the social scale, had commenced a process of intellectual selection.

But the failure of paternal methods of government meant more than the growth of individualism and individual effort. The emancipation of the individual was a necessary step towards a wider policy of social reconstruction. If the removal of restrictions encouraged individual initiative, it gave rise also to new combinations and a new spirit of solidarity. The theory of 'natural liberty'—or rather the form which it assumed in the writings of Priestley and Adam Smith —is open to the same general criticism that applies, perhaps in a less degree, to Elizabethan statesmanship ; it was based on a study of conditions which were already passing away. Formulated at a crisis when new adjustments of regulation and discipline were becoming imperative, its influence on the condition of wage-earners is reflected in a widespread degradation of their habits and standards of living. It was a sense of weakness, quite as much as the instinct of monopoly, which led them to cling with impracticable conservatism to those forms of legal protection which belonged to a passing phase of economic development, and ultimately, as the old safeguards disappeared, to pursue their interests not as individuals, but as organised bodies working for a common end. In the new era of competition, as the unit of production was enlarged, the weakness of the individual labourer, standing alone, became increasingly apparent. Self-help and co-operation came to be almost interchangeable terms. Individual betterment was largely dependent on a general improvement in social conditions. Here, too, the tendencies which developed rapidly with the progress of the Industrial Revolution appear in an embryonic form in the years which preceded. From an early stage in the eighteenth century different forms of combination spread gradually among the labouring classes, which challenge comparison with a corresponding movement that occurred four centuries earlier. Friendly societies in town and country, trade combinations, debating clubs and reading circles, religious associations, musical and horticultural societies, were various manifestations of a new impulse, severally of little significance but important collectively as showing the current. The history of the Methodist Societies, which occupy a position in the group somewhat analogous to that of the religious gilds in the earlier movement, may be said to illustrate one aspect of the difference between two stages of civilisation. Not only was the social order less capable of assimilating without friction new forms of associated effort, but the conditions under which such activities developed, and the influences by which they were inspired, were in many respects fundamentally changed. An impulse which contains the germ of democracy may be seen advancing by slow degrees among new classes which had formed in the interval. The religious awakening which Puritanism had brought to the middle class extends with the progress of the Methodist Revival among a considerable part of the labouring population. Trade unionism and mutual assurance spread from the urban handicrafts to industries of an inferior grade. The transient combinations of journeymen in the mediaeval crafts are replaced by associations of different kinds which were destined, after more or less interruption, to acquire a permanent place in the industrial system.[1]

(1) *The Religious Revival*

The conclusion suggested by a recent inquiry into the religious state of the people—that the most vital forms of religion are found in areas which have developed since the Industrial Revolution, and represent rather a reawakening of spiritual consciousness than a survival from the past—has a peculiar interest in connection with certain phenomena disclosed in this period of transition. It was in districts which presented a model of paternal discipline, that religious observance seemed most liable to degenerate into a social custom. It was the new scenes of missionary labour that profited most from the growth of self-consciousness which underlay different phases of the Evangelical movement, originating among small groups of associates who met together for mutual edification and the promotion of good works.

The Religious societies of the eighteenth-century revival may be compared with associations which had arisen at different periods in the history of the Mediæval

[1] Webb, *History of Trade Unionism*, ch. i.

Church. As bodies of laymen supporting certain recognised forms of devotion, they bear a remote resemblance to the religious gilds. As a nucleus of the elect consecrated to a religious life and to works of charity and education, they performed to a limited extent and in relation to altered circumstances some of the functions which had devolved on the Monastic orders. In so far as they developed a mission to the oppressed and afflicted, their position is analogous, and sometimes closely akin, to that of the friars. There is, in fact, more than a superficial parallel between the Methodist Revival and the Franciscan movement which invaded England in the thirteenth century. The man who claimed the world for his parish, who developed an elaborate organisation and rules of procedure, and exercised a plenary jurisdiction in the choice and discipline of his subordinates, had the genius which would have given birth in the Middle Ages to a religious order or an heretical sect.[1] The Methodist body might be said to fall between these two categories. It consisted partly of an order of preachers loosely connected with the Established Church ; it was partly, also, a new sect. The doctrine of conversion involved a dubious attitude to the ecclesiastical system, and an organisation of converts whose position in the parish was an anomaly and a possible source of disturbance.

---

[1] The mingled approval, jealousy, and contempt which confronted the Methodist preachers in their dealings with ecclesiastical authorities and the religious world, find a parallel in the experiences of the early Franciscans ; incidentally, the same charges of illiteracy and ignorance were made in both cases. The religious conditions which gave birth to either movement were roughly similar ; in either case the clergy were losing touch with the vital needs of the people ; and as the Monastic orders had degenerated before the coming of St. Francis, so the dissenting bodies which preceded Wesley had lost in the eighteenth century much of their earlier zeal. But it is unnecessary to force the parallel ; the attitude of Wesley to the Establishment, after his conversion, differed materially from that of St. Francis to the system of the Catholic Church.

The unsectarian composition of the society, and the opposition which it encountered at the hands of the clergy, gave it the character of a distinct denomination. The atmosphere of the class-meeting and the practice of recruiting preachers from an uneducated class were at variance with the recognised system of Church discipline and the social traditions of the time.

' It has been a great fault all along,' wrote Walker of Truro, ' to have made the low people of your council '; and nothing in the Methodist organisation gave greater offence than the character and antecedents of many of its preachers and class-leaders. A circle of labourers or mechanics, led in worship or ' conference ' by one of their own rank,[1] stood on a footing essentially different from the middle-class gatherings of Churchmen and dissenters which appear at the commencement of the century, and from the type of parochial society which was a later product of the Evangelical movement. Much has been said both of the emotional side of the revival and of its effect on morals and parental responsibility. The part which it played in the political education of the masses has been as often misrepresented or ignored. Like every movement which makes a new demand on the poor, it formed in different neighbourhoods a bond of union between the most active and independent of their class. An exceptional degree of intelligence and attainment was not uncommon among Methodists of humble station and those who had been reared in Methodist homes ; and the same influence generally underlies the reading circles that are found occasionally among the labourers and artisans in rural areas. The class-meeting was a starting point for serious friendships, and often contained an inner circle of com-

[1] Wesley, *Journal*, June 13, 1757 ; June 18, 1777, etc. *Anti-Jacobin* (1801), 157.

panions more intelligent than the rest, who would meet
to converse on religion and matters of general interest
and occasionally entered on a course of reading.[1]

The effects of a spiritual awakening have been seldom
confined to the sphere of religious practice and beliefs.
Puritanism had given birth to movements and reactions
in politics, and was connected with underlying streams
of social and economic tendency. A similar interaction
of forces may be observed in the popular movements
of a later age. A group of Cornish Methodists became
interested in the American War of Independence.[2]
Paine's ' Age of Reason ' was accompanied by the
' Rights of Man,' and both were read by a circle of
Methodists in Lancashire who were moderate supporters
of political reform.[3] Politics and religion went together
in the debating societies formed among the artisans and
tradesmen of London and the provincial towns.[4] Though
it has been justly claimed that the religious movement
exercised a steadying influence on political agitation and
formed a defence against the cruder forms of infidelity
which were mingled with the spirit of sedition, there was
sufficient connection between disturbances in either
sphere to explain the attitude of alarmists who included
Methodism and radicalism under a common ban of
denunciation.[5] Both in religion and in politics new

---

[1] *Life of Samuel Drew*, by his son ; Bamford, *Early Days*, 52 *sq.* (ed.
1893). Drew, a Cornish shoemaker, was a man of exceptional talent
who owed his inspiration to the revival ; but it is clear from his biography
that smaller men might imbibe intellectual conceit.

[2] *Life of Drew*, 102 *sq.*

[3] Bamford, *Early Days*, 52 *sq.*

[4] *Cf.* Sydney, *England and the English in the Eighteenth Century*, ii. 165.
Brentano, *History and Development of Gilds*, remarks that, during the
Puritan Revolution, the London apprentices had been wont to pronounce
on the religious and political questions of the day.

[5] The attitude of the *Anti-Jacobin* to Methodism may be expressed
in the words of the Cardinal De Lorraine with reference to the Huguenots.
' If the secular arm fails in its duty, all the malcontents will throw them-

forces were astir beneath the surface, and within the framework, of traditional beliefs. In either case, examples of deep and earnest devotion, implying a new attitude to the problems of life, were disgraced by outbursts of unreason and emotional excess. In either case, those of the poor who became converts to a new teaching found their bitterest opponents in the multitude of their own class.

(2) *Political Unrest*

The familiar accessories of modern political agitation had their origin in the critical events which followed one another in rapid sequence from the accession of George the Third to the outbreak of the French Revolution. The public meeting—' a custom unknown to our earlier constitution '—acquired an increasing

selves into this detestable sect. They will first destroy the ecclesiastical power, after which it will be the turn of the royal power '—Smiles, *Huguenot Settlements*, 33.

A pamphlet entitled *The Rise and Dissolution of the Infidel Societies in this Metropolis*, by William Hamilton Reid (1800), describes the mutual provocation which arose between rationalist infidelity and the more extreme forms of religious enthusiasm. It appears that about 1795 a body of rationalists commenced a campaign among the working classes, organising open-air meetings and debating clubs, and invading benefit societies where they raised religious discussions and sang democratic songs. At the same time the Lady Anne's Preachers were holding meetings during the summer months in the Spa-fields and in Hackney, Islington, etc.—' a wandering tribe of fanatical teachers,' says Reid, ' mostly taken from the lowest and most illiterate classes of society; among whom are to be found raving enthusiasts, pretending to divine impulses, of various and extraordinary kinds, practising exorcisms and many other impostures and delusions and thereby obtaining an unlimited sway over the minds of the ignorant multitude.' They attacked the clergy, says the same authority, and visited the sick. A counter-movement was organised by their opponents. ' A very formidable party . . . assembled every Sunday morning at seven o'clock near the City Road; here, in consequence of the debates forced upon the preachers or their hearers, several groups of people would remain upon the ground till noon, giving an opportunity to the unwary passengers to become acquainted with the dogmas of Voltaire, Paine, etc.'

importance from the time of the Middlesex Petition.[1] Sunday newspapers came into existence during the American War of Independence;[2] and the influence of the cheap press may be traced at the same period in the growth of debating societies in the towns,[3] and in the appearance of the ' pot-house oracle ' as a new factor in rural life.[4] The intermixture of sporadic demands for constitutional reform with the general stream of radicalism during the opening phase of the French Revolution produced the form of propaganda which has covered the land with a network of political organisations, working through the medium of public meetings and private canvassing, through the distribution of literature or the more personal influence of lectures and debates.[5]

[1] ' These assemblies, in which the nation deliberated apart from its aristocratic chiefs, cannot be distinctly traced higher than the year 1769 ; they were now (1770) of daily occurence '—Cooke, *History of Party*, iii. 187. But we must not overlook the influence of the public meeting in open vestries ; and it is perhaps significant that an instance of political partisanship in vestry elections occurs in 1771—Webb, *English Local Government*, i. 113 *n.*

[2] Andrews, *History of Newspapers*, i. 273 ; *cf.* Buckle, *Civilisation in England*, i. ch. vii. 393 *n.*

[3] Sydney, *op. cit.*, ii. 165 ; Langford, *Century of Birmingham Life*, i. 243 *sq.* ; Cooke, *op. cit.*, iii. 412 ; Knight, *Pursuit of Knowledge under Difficulties*, iii. 76 *sq.*

[4] ' His features, though considerably relaxed by intoxication, bore the stamp of intelligence far above his situation. . . . It appeared that he read several newspapers, and in all probability is the oracle of every pothouse in the surrounding country '—' Pedestrian Tour through parts of England and Wales,' *Monthly Review*, viii. 619 (1797). Crabbe, *The Newspaper* (1785), ridicules and laments the appearance of this type.

[5] The London Corresponding Society (1792) was in touch with the Revolution Society, the Society for Constitutional Information, the Unitarian Society, etc. ; it formed centres in the large towns, and circulated pamphlets, newspaper cuttings, Paine's *Rights of Man*, etc. ; its emissaries are said to have canvassed in factories, ale-houses, barbers' shops, etc.—' individuals who, though deficient in education, had received talents from nature which frequently shone through coarse and vulgar language.' *Annual Register*, xxxiii. 115 ; xxxiv. 365 ; xxxviii. 8. *Cf.* Langford, *op. cit.*, ii. 285. ' Originally an obscure club, composed of a few mechanics and inferior tradesmen '—Cooke, *op. cit.*, iii. 413. *Cf. Annual Register*, xxxvi. 266.

Numerous reading rooms and lecture halls appear to have been closed as

How far this growth of agitation reflects a serious movement of public opinion, is a problem which is not simplified by the fact that a large number of the reformers found their inspiration in political developments which occurred abroad, their material in the distress of the people at home. There is certainly nothing in these earlier phases of radicalism to compare seriously with the massed forces of enthusiasm which concentrated in the next generation behind a definite demand for political reform. The positive incentives which arose from the new grouping of population in the manufacturing districts, and from the glaring contrast between ' changing social conditions and unchanging laws,' had not come to maturity before the close of the Napoleonic struggle. The political distractions of the intervening period were as much calculated to evoke the native conservatism of the masses as to incite them to revolt ; its economic incidents served rather to emphasise a divergence between the interests of the middle class and those of the rising proletariat, than to furnish a common platform on which both might unite. Sympathy with the cause of reform seems, in fact, to have been confined at the outset of the movement to a section of the aristocracy and a section of the artisan and trading classes ; and whatever influence it may have obtained during the period of distress which accompanied the war of the first Coalition, was more than counterbalanced by reaction against foreign ideas and by the patriotism which united all ranks, when opposition to the Revolution became associated with the cause of national defence.

The true explanation of the very different effects of

a result of the Seditious Meetings Act, 1795. On the distribution of radical literature, *cf.* Reid, *Rise and Dissolution of the Infidel Societies*, 86 *sqq.* ; *Remarks on the Poor Bill (1807), by one of H.M. Justices of the Peace*, 13 *sq.*

revolutionary teaching in England and in France, must be sought in an antecedent stream of circumstances which had been steadily emancipating English labour from those particular forms of oppression which in France prepared the materials for an explosion; [1] in historic conditions which led unerringly in the one case to an industrial, in the other to a political, revolution. The closest point of connection between English distress and the grievances of the French peasantry may be found in the injury to vested interests resulting from different forms of agrarian enclosure, and from the new phase of industrial competition which deprived the artisan of his customary wage. It is necessary merely to state the case in this form, to realise one fundamental point of difference which renders comparison between the two countries altogether illusory. France was passing through a phase of economic growth which finds its nearest English analogy in the decay of the manorial system and during the period of the Peasants' Revolt. Though there were parts of France where complaints were made of enclosure by landlords, yet on the whole the French cultivators represented a progressive force pressing against antiquated monopolies; whilst the English masses, already falling under the subtler oppressions of a triumphant capitalism, found that their interest lay, for the moment, in resisting change. In France the cause of the peasants was identified with that of all progressive sections of society in opposition to a privileged caste which had forfeited its power; in England the forces of civilisation were ranged on the side of a governing aristocracy, to whom the masses had not ceased to look for protection and redress. Meanwhile the

---

[1] Maine, *Early Law and Custom*, ch. ix.

condition of the French peasantry had been steadily improving, the position of the English masses in town and country was becoming on the whole more isolated and depressed. To the maxim which found in the ignorance of the multitude a safeguard of national stability, might have been added the more cynical assurance that a state of economic depression does not necessarily conduce to an effective confidence in sweeping reforms. The attitude of the skilled artisans in urban handicrafts, whose position was relatively secure and who formed for some time to come the backbone of democratic movements, stands in striking contrast to that of the newly organised masses who wavered between submissive appeals to the government and spasmodic insurrections equally devoid of purpose and effect.[1] How far the crowd-instinct has been leavened by rational motives and guided into the channels of a constructive policy, is one of the main problems to be considered at a later stage of political development. At any rate the unrest which followed at the close of the Napoleonic wars was very different from the discontents of the previous century. The failure of the government to redress their grievances had infused an element of solidarity and self-dependence into the scattered groups from which the labour movement arose. The whole course of repressive legislation, which for a time stifled every expression of discontent, worked ultimately in the same direction. When agitation revived, even the specific grievance of the Combination Laws was overshadowed by issues of a more fundamental and definitely political

---

[1] ' The prevailing tone of the superior workmen down to 1848 was, in fact, thoroughly Radical. . . . But their trade clubs were free from anything which could now be conceived as political sedition. . . . In the new machine industries (on the other hand) . . . both leaders and rank and file were largely implicated in political seditions, and were the victims of spies '—Webb, *Trade Unionism*, 76–9.

character.[1] And in the meantime the groundwork of society had been shaken by an economic upheaval, with which the modern phase of educational problems may be said to commence.

(3) *The Industrial Revolution*

The term Industrial Revolution has been applied to a series of changes in the technique and structure of industry, extending roughly over the interval between the accession of George the Third and the advent of the Reform Bill, of which economy in production may be described as the final cause, whose tendency was towards a general redistribution of economic functions and a more concentrated management of industrial resources, and which resulted socially in a ' new form of human settlement.' It is sufficient here to refer briefly to certain general features of the transformation which have a bearing, more or less direct, on educational problems. In the first place, a change in the technique of production was accompanied by an enlargement of the productive unit and by corresponding changes in the structure of social life. ' The small master-workman is superseded by the capitalist manufacturer, the small farmer disappears before the capitalist farmer '; the mass of the agricultural population tend to become grouped together on large farms under capitalist management, the mass of the manufacturing community in large establishments under the direction of the proprietor and his officials. Secondly, there was a widespread specialisation in the functions of the individual labourer,who became normally dependent on one source of subsistence, the wage of a particular line of employment. This was partly the result of a general growth of trade facilities, but it was also a

[1] Webb, *Trade Unionism*, 85.

corollary of enlargement in the unit of production. Industrial reorganisation tended to deprive the agricultural
population of the subsidiary means of support provided
by the domestic industries, and the manufacturing
classes of the element of subsistence-farming which they
had shared with other sections of the rural peasantry ;
while the enclosure movement gradually displaced the
type of labourer who had been engaged partly in farming
on his own account, or had supplemented his earnings
by the exercise of rights of commonage. Lastly the
movement of population and its numerical increase,
which were incidental to these changes, had social
effects of a revolutionary character. The centre of
gravity shifted from the south toward the north of
England, and from the country to the town. In due
course urban surroundings came to be regarded as the
normal environment of the labouring class, and exercised
an increasing influence on the general trend of social
thought. In more senses than one, ' commerce and
industrial enterprise ' had been ' grafted on the stock
of agriculture,' and the rural districts had ' become
the dependents of the manufacturing and trading
centres.'

It is important to realise the extent to which reformers
had been gradually prepared to welcome, on general
social grounds, changes which placed the resources
of the country in the hands of those who were most
likely to exploit them to the full, and to accept some form
of reorganisation on the lines which have been described
as a means of social discipline. The commercial policy
of the Whigs, which from the age of Walpole gave a
distinct advantage to the man of capital, was conceived,
at least incidentally, in the interests of the population
as a whole. As the Tudors were continually falling
back on personal government where ' democratic '

institutions had sunk into decay,[1] so a later generation
of statesmen came to rely on capitalism as a sovereign
remedy for social disorders. The widespread irregularity of employment, revealed in the records of the
period,[2] might serve to identify the cause of social reform
with some drastic measure of industrial development ;
and examples were not wanting, in which the civilisation of a backward district was a direct outcome of
commercial adventure.[3] Nor was the lightness of
organisation which offered the labourer a choice of
resources and gave him a certain detachment and
independence, so obvious or unmixed an advantage
as is sometimes suggested by writers at the present day,
who contrast it with the concentration and strain of
modern industrialism. ' Ease of living ' was associated
with a habit of ' lazy-diligence,' which Defoe remarked
as a leading characteristic of his age, and of which
examples might be found in times of prosperity alike
among the manufacturing and the agricultural classes.[4]
If the open-field system offered certain incentives
to thrift and a chance of rising in the social scale, it
gave no safeguard against idleness ; while the commons
afforded shelter to a parasitic population whose manner
of life was precarious and unprogressive. Behind the
economic wastage lay a moral waste, a lack of steady
enterprise and ambition without which advance in civilisation was impossible, an element of moral stagnancy
which flowed from a thriftless use of material resources.
Underlying the argument for enclosure is the conception
of a stricter discipline which should concentrate attention

---

[1] *Cf.* Meredith, *Economic History of England*, 139.

[2] *Ibid.*, 195.

[3] *Cf.* Smiles, *Brindley*, 272–4.

[4] Kalm, *Account of Visit to England, 1748* (tr. Lucas, 1892), 333. Young,
Northern Tour, iii. 248 *sq.*

continuously on a definite task, exacting more from the labourer and giving more in return.[1]

The origin of these ideas must be sought in a general view of economic necessities whose bearing on the welfare of the masses was at most indirect. A change of attitude on questions of social policy seems traceable to the growing importance of trade as a source of taxable wealth and a basis of national power, which suggested gradually a new conception of social progress. Government during the eighteenth century ceased to be concerned primarily with the ' breeding of men ' and the task of guaranteeing to each a reasonable and secure subsistence. It approached the problem, as it were, from the other end of the scale, by seeking to augment the general fund of wealth and plenty. The change, however, was not merely one of means and methods ; there was, also, a change of outlook and aim. There was at once a more definite conception of material progress resulting from an increased interchange of commodities, and a more exacting demand on the energies of the labourer. It was no longer sufficient that the worker should subsist ; he must contribute his full share to an economical system of production and exchange on which the common welfare depended ; and this involved a progressive division of labour, and its redistribution according to the needs of the market. Young's ' Political Arithmetic,' which expresses this train of thought, approaches the problem of reorganisation, for various reasons, from the side of agriculture and the land ; but his outlook extends over the whole field of commerce and industry, and the argument for large farms may be read also as a defence of the later factory system.

[1] Johnson, *Disappearance of the Small Landowner,* 96 *sq.,* 103 ; Eden. *State of the Poor,* i. p. xviii *sq.*

The reasoning proceeds from the general to the particular, from the good of the nation to that of the individual. The economic aim is to increase the net wealth of the community, the social aim is to increase the sum of employment, and these ends are ultimately the same. The argument, it is to be observed, is not assailed by a local decrease of employment and gross produce, such as followed the conversion of arable land into pasturage in certain cases of enclosure. Take the country as a whole and labour as a whole, and the aggregate of production includes the product of ' useless hands ' transferred from agriculture to the manufacturing industries. It is further argued that any incidental loss involved in the transition will be compensated by a general advance in comfort, owing to the growth of national wealth and its distribution in wages and to the discipline of higher standards of industrial efficiency.

From this standpoint, what may be described as an educational test may be applied to the economic tendencies of the period. It would appear that some form of reorganisation, imposing a severer discipline, was demanded as a complement to the increase of wealth. In industries which preserved the loose structure of the domestic system a rapid increase of earnings seems normally to have resulted in increased license and demoralisation.[1] On the other hand, it did not follow that a reorganisation of industry on a more economical basis would correspond in any strict sense to an educational process. Allowance must be made, in the first place, for a large element of friction in the readjustment of labour to altered conditions and new types of environment. Some of the arguments for enclosure betray an excessive confidence both in the fluidity of labour and in the possibility of converting

[1] *Cf.* Bosanquet, *The Strength of the People*, 79.

into effective workers those who had been used to a precarious existence on the land, by a simple change in agrarian conditions and the removal of commons. When the local demand for labour was diminished by enclosure, there was a tendency rather for the weaker elements among the peasantry to remain stranded on the land, with the result of depressing the rate of wages—a tendency afterwards repeated in the case of domestic industries, as the pressure of factory competition increased. The difficulty of adapting domestic workers to the discipline of the factory system was certainly a cause of one of its main abuses, an excessive employment of child labour. The argument, again, that labourers displaced from agriculture would find employment in the manufacturing centres, does not touch the question as to whether the new conditions were socially better or worse than the old. The growth of industrialism and town life introduced new forms of debasement, which enter into the educational problems of a coming age. Meanwhile, if specialisation was laying the groundwork of a new society, it involved also the unweaving of an earlier fabric of habits and ideas in which the good and the evil were closely intertwined. The phenomenon is noticed in an oft-quoted passage of Adam Smith, which describes the narrowing of personality that formed a moral counterpart to the division of labour in the manufacturing industries.[1] An equally striking example of the same tendency may be found in certain aspects of the enclosure movement. The reckless marriages, so often denounced at a later date as a sign of the demoralised state of the rural districts and ascribed directly to a pernicious system of outdoor-relief, have an earlier source in the social disintegration which

---

[1] *Wealth of Nations*, bk. v. ch. i. art. 2.

followed the upbreak of an old form of rural economy.[1] An increased wage, even if it had been realised, was no compensation for the loss of subsidiary resources, in so far as these stood for a sense of ownership and independence and were bound up with the traditions of a corporate life.

The impression that ' an increase in the quantity of human life ' has been attained ' at the expense of a degradation in its quality,' is most strongly suggested in the cases of agriculture and the textile industries, where the economic structure was most radically changed. The problems presented by the factory system have a special reference to the care and training of the young; and the main issues to which attention was drawn during its initial stages are among those which confront educational effort at the present day.[2] On the one hand, there was a decay, amounting in some cases to an extinction, of the influences of domestic training; on the other, a system of employment which consumed the energies of the child by excessive toil in an unhealthy environment, casting the young adrift at the close of their apprenticeship with faculties impaired and without the training requisite to a future career. Certain forms of child exploitation and a certain decay of home life among

---

[1] Slater, *English Peasantry and Enclosure of Common Fields*, 265. On the psychological and social effects of enclosure, see Denson, *Peasant's Voice to Landowners* (1819), also some remarks in a journal of Robert Burns—' The more elegance and luxury among the farmers, I always observe, in equal proportion the rudeness and stupidity of the peasantry. This remark I have made all over the Lothians, Merse, Roxburgh, etc. ; and for this, among other reasons, I think a man of romantic taste—a " man of feeling "—will be better pleased with the poverty, but intelligent minds, of the peasantry in Ayrshire (peasantry they are all below the justice of the peace) than the opulence of a club of Merse farmers, when he at the same time considers the vandalism of their ploughfolks, etc. I carry this idea so far, that an unenclosed, half-improved country is to me actually more agreeable . . . than a country cultivated like a garden.' —*Works of Robert Burns*, Cunningham, 64.

[2] *Cf.* Aikin, *Description of the Country round Manchester* (1795), 219.

the manufacturing classes are clearly prior in origin to the factory organisation; but the new system, with its extensive employment of women and children away from their homes, the social atmosphere of large establishments, and the physical strain imposed by machinery, had the effect of aggravating old disorders and producing others for which no precedent existed. It is not difficult to discover a superficial parallel to these evils in the condition of agricultural districts during the early part of the next century; in the decay of rural housing, in the organisation of labour under the 'gang' system, and in cases where the employment of women in field labour left them neither time nor energy to attend to the training of the young. The comparison, however, is instructive mainly as illustrating complementary, rather than parallel, effects of the same economic tendency in different spheres. In the manufacturing districts we have the chaos of a new society in process of formation; rural distress is connected with the dissolution of an old order of social life. In industry economic reorganisation is in the main a driving force; in agriculture it is largely a process of suppression. One of the tendencies of agrarian reform was to remove those intermediate positions between the labourer and the farmer which had opened to the small man a means of investment and a chance of advancing in the social scale; in the manufacturing industries the situation is so far reversed as to present a ladder of social opportunity which, if steep, ' is at least continuous,' while an apparently unlimited increase of production impressed ideals of material progress on the minds of the industrial class.[1] In agriculture, again, the destruction of the open-field system and the growth of new social divisions involved, in various

[1] Meredith *op. cit.*, 262, 301 ; Hammond, *Village Labourer*, 33.

ways, a loss of independence and mutual helpfulness and of the sense of membership in a corporate group ; in the industrial centres, there was the independence of large masses, and the opportunity for new forms of social co-operation. Lastly, while all these changes reacted on the traditional culture of the country-side, the advance of urban industry awakened new intellectual interests, partly through the effects of science and invention on certain kinds of employment, partly through the growth and conflict of political ideas. It was as if the school of social progress had been transferred to new and more adventurous scenes ; as if the economic process were destroying old opportunities in the country only to create new opportunities in the town. It is also, in some ways, a characteristic feature in the contrast, that, whereas in agriculture it was the man of capital who added field to field and the large landowner who initiated improvements, the lead in industrial movements fell in no slight measure to men of small means and humble extraction. A large proportion both of the great engineers and inventors and of the manufacturers who made fortunes in the textile industries were men who had risen direct from the ranks ; and in the varying types of character which they present, there is some suggestion of the effects of the Industrial Revolution on the mass beneath them. Just as the new directing class included, side by side with the rough diamonds of the cotton manufacture, others whose genius had been kindled by a constant struggle with large ideas and overwhelming difficulties ; so we shall find, among the new proletariat, men whose minds were forced into the groove of a hard struggle for existence, and others who had visions of an improved society and whose strivings after enlightenment are among the redeeming features of a commercial age. So too, if we isolate the factor of employment, there were tendencies which made the worker the slave of the machine, and there were occupations which induced him to understand it. If the Industrial Revolution was responsible for the ' factory hands,' it also called into existence a new race of mechanics.

In the attitude of Government to social problems during these critical years there are many symptoms of the political bankruptcy that marks the close of an era. A separation of class-interests, which rendered the political system incapable of comprehensive measures of social readjustment, was aggravated by a dearth of imagination in the ruling class. Popular discontent, in an age of unparalleled turmoil, was combated by methods of repression drawn from the armoury of Tudor tradition. A new literature was created to impress upon the poor the duties of religion, loyalty, and contentment. Magistrates combined to suppress amusements and assemblies of the common folk. Laws which sometimes confound independence with treason accompanied a general prohibition of collective bargaining, compromising every form of trade-union activity. Meanwhile there was no real counterpart to the constructive side of Tudor policies. Government drifted into a partial acceptance of new economic doctrines, without any effective attempt being made to protect the labourer's standard of living from rapid deterioration. Enclosure was carried on without adequate regard to the permanent interests of rural society. Poor Law reform ended in a courageous but abortive scheme of industrial training.[1] A single measure dealing with child-labour under the factory system was based on precedents already out of date.[2]

[1] Hammond, *op. cit.*, 149 *sqq.* (Pitt's Bill, 1796-7).
[2] Health and Morals of Apprentices (etc.) Act, 1802.

The neglect of remedies which might have preserved and educated the character of the masses found its nemesis in a form of poor-relief which added to their demoralisation. Yet it is fair to observe that the difficulties besetting the statesmanship of the period were, in a general sense, the legacy of problems left unsolved in the Tudor age and rendered formidable by a sudden change in economic conditions. Where it had been sufficient to restrain competition and enterprise, it was now necessary to define their relation to social ends. Where it had been possible to invoke the power and prestige of personal monarchy, it was necessary to reform the political system and to re-organise the machinery of administration on a new basis Elizabethan statesmanship was most successful when its action was guided by precedent and based on the strength of conservative traditions, while in the preceding period of transition there had been little change in the groundwork of economic thought. In the eighteenth century a rapid change in material conditions, producing problems unprecedented in kind, followed the dawn of a new theory of progress which for a time unduly restricted the sphere of State intervention.

It may be said of this, as of an earlier, period of social history that an ' illusion of increasing selfishness ' is produced by an ' increase in the opportunity for anti-social action,' and that in statements which testify to an extension of human suffering there is evidence, also, of growing sympathy and insight. The interests of the peasantry may be of little account in a question of enclosure, but there is no proof that an aristocratic Parliament would have acted differently, if possessed of the same uncontrolled authority and faced by a similar situation, at an earlier stage. It is important at any rate to recognise in certain proposals, which appeared when the movement was at its height, an attempt to remedy hardships which had long been endured. But for the revulsion caused by the French Revolution and the burden of a prolonged war, the last quarter of the eighteenth century might rank as one of the important phases in the awakening of a social conscience. Not only does the literature of the period supply the first examples of a detailed and systematic study of economic facts with reference to the condition of the labouring class, but the thought awakened by new forms of oppression goes to the root of problems which a weaker sense of responsibility had allowed to pass unobserved. The remarks of Dr. Percival on the factory apprentices are more than a criticism of the factory system ; they mark the beginning of a new attitude to the problems of childhood.[1] The new economic conditions illustrated and strengthened the plea for instruction advanced by Adam Smith ; whose aim, it may be observed, was not to increase the efficiency of the worker, but to develop the faculties of the man. Different streams of opinion were already converging in an educational movement which to this day bears the marks of an original conflict of social ideals. Repression was not the only result of the concentration of political forces towards the close of the century which gave birth to a conservative party. A more scrupulous discharge of magisterial duties, not wholly the outcome of reactionary panic,[2] was accompanied by an awakening among the parochial clergy, who busied them-

[1] The exploitation of physique drew attention to the exploitation of ' mind and spirit ' which had been a common accompaniment and result of child labour before the rise of the factories. Meredith, 267, cf. 268.

[2] Webb, *English Local Government*, i. 377 *sq.*

selves in visiting the poor, and in organising libraries [1] and other forms of instruction. Hannah More, who expounded 'Village Politics' and left the comforts of London society to teach the poor in a derelict country parish, was not an unworthy pioneer of that form of authority—assumed in turn by every fresh group of reformers—which sought to establish its influence by educating the masses. That it is difficult to draw any hard distinction between the principles of authority and self-control, is suggested by Bentham's aphorism which defined education as government acting through the 'domestic magistrate.' The attitude of the early liberals to educational questions displays, however, a distinctive bias proceeding from a fundamental re-

[1] Sunday Friendly Societies for the aged poor, 1798, at Bishops Auckland and Winston (Durham), in connection with which books and tracts were read and distributed. Parish Libraries at Steeple Morden (Cambridge) 1801, and Hunmanby (Yorks) 1805. Parochial Society for the purchase of Bibles at Melksham (Wilts) 1811. See *Reports of Society for Bettering the Condition of the Poor*, 1798, etc. There is no means of estimating the influence, for good or evil, of the incalculable mass of tracts flung broadcast in these years by supporters and opponents of Church and State. Sydney Smith, a privileged humorist, mentions a proposal that travellers, 'for every pound they spend upon the road, should fling one shilling's worth of these tracts out of the chaise window' (*Works*, i. 205). Wesley had published penny tracts for his converts, followed by an edition of his works in sixpenny numbers which brought him a considerable profit (Telford, *Life*, 321 *sq.*). From this we pass to Legh Richmond's *Annals of the Poor*; Rowland Hill's *Cottage Dialogues*; Hannah More's *Village Politics* and *Repository Tracts*, containing ballads, stories, Sunday reading, etc., published 1792–8 and circulated by local committees to the extent of some millions of copies. Thence to Mrs. Trimmer (1788–); *John and Dame or the Loyal Cottagers*, by a certain Pratt (1803); an *Address to the Mechanics, Artificers, Manufacturers and Labourers of England, on the Subject of the Threatened Invasion* (1803); *A Friendly Address to the Labouring Part of the Community, concerning the Present State of Public Affairs in Church and State* (1804); and *The Life and Adventures of Job Nott* of Birmingham (1793), which 'nobody can read without laughing, nor leave it off without being more loyal and more moral; . . . and to my Brother Artificers and the small fry my advice is, get a dab of overwork that you may be able to lay out threepence on a book wrote entirely for your use, information and amusement'—attributed, probably with some malice, to one of the local clergy (Langford, *Century of Birmingham Life*, ii. 117).

sistance to authoritarian tradition. Overrating the rational side of human personality, they tended to form an exaggerated conception of the speed with which results are achieved ; but they were also among the first to insist that a man's capacity for sharing in the life and culture of his time is not rigidly determined by his social status or the nature of his employment, and that his redemption from evil courses is to be sought by extending the range of his moral and mental interests. The theory of ' rational recreation ' was expressed by an enlightened writer of the conservative school at the close of the century, who pleaded that a decent observance of the Sabbath might be best ensured by tolerating amusements whose aim should be to ' raise the genius and mend the heart.' [1]

The educational movement in England during the eighteenth century is concentrated within two periods of about equal length, the one concluding with the death of Anne, the other commencing with the growth of Sunday schools in the eighties. The latter phase of the movement was in a broad sense a revival and continuation of the former, although its character and aims were strongly influenced by the intervening course of events. Popular education was still approached as a missionary enterprise for the uplifting of a neglected class, where earlier means of training had failed. But the class which could be so described had become so large, especially in the towns and manufacturing districts, that organised instruction could no longer be regarded as the exceptional need of recipients of charity. In the meantime the maxim that every child should learn to read the Bible had appeared as one of the first-fruits of religious revival. Thus

[1] Eden, *State of the Poor,* i. 446.

there was a definite advance towards the idea of national
education, involving incidentally a change of method
and a stricter differentiation of social aims. Industrial
training retained a place in the programme of educational reform;[1] but there was no longer the same
attempt, as in the earlier years of the century, to include it as an integral factor in the school curriculum.
The school of industry developed as a distinct institution dealing with exceptional cases of affliction and
neglect; the main stream of philanthropy passed it
by, in an attempt to extend the elements of religious
and literary instruction to the majority who were
already in the way of earning a livelihood. The special
incentive in this later movement was the hope of securing
a decent observance of Sunday. Partly for this reason,
partly also because it was natural to select a time when
the industrial population was most accessible and
assistance in teaching could be most readily obtained,
effort was concentrated on the promotion of Sunday
schools, which remained for an indefinite period the
most widely organised medium of instruction for young
and old and the starting point for further experiments.[2] The Sunday school led back to the day school,
and was often connected with a system of night classes
during the week. Even at this early period there were
developments which recognised the principle of the
continuation school, leading forward to higher grades

---

[1] Schools of industry, 1791 onwards, at Lewisham, Kendal, Banburgh
Castle and elsewhere, see *Reports of Society for Bettering the Condition of
the Poor ; Monthly Review*, iii. 431 ; Lyson, *Magna Britannia*, i. 482.
Day industrial schools were sometimes formed in connection with Sunday
schools, and we find the wish expressed that ' some institution could be
established for the idle children ' ; Jenkins, *Charles of Bala*, ii. 15, 10 *sqq.*

[2] For a view of Sunday schools as agencies intended to make up for
the absence of home training, ' compensatory institutions highly creditable
to the teachers but very discreditable indeed to the parents,' see Miller,
My Schools and Schoolmasters, 39.

of instruction. Thus in 1789 the Sunday school teachers of Birmingham formed a society, with the object of continuing the education of their former scholars, which was subsequently amalgamated with a local scientific association and developed on the lines of a Mechanics' Institute.

Another distinctive feature of the period, and one perhaps of still greater importance, was the remarkable growth of educational activity among adults of the working class, both as teachers and learners, which characterised the closing years of the century. It is in the wider outlook, and in the demand for knowledge produced by the religious movements of the period and the economic and political consequences of the Industrial Revolution, that we must seek the origin of those ideas of democratic government which have entered so largely into adult education in recent times. The intellectual awakening showed itself in various ways : in the growth of adult Sunday schools and the rapid spread of night classes in the north of England, in the formation of book clubs,[1] reading societies and discussion circles, and in the beginnings of scientific and technical studies. The examples which fall within the last category illustrate different types of organisation which are continually recurring. Thus at Birmingham in 1794 a small group of artisans, known as the ' cast-iron philosophers,' were attending lectures at the house of Thomas Clarke, a local patron of science.[2] Two years later, they were merged in the Brotherly Society, an association which advertised instruction in elementary and more advanced subjects, provided a newsroom, lectures and classes free of charge to

[1] *Monthly Review*, iv. 275 *sqq.*, mentions a book club formed by a few mechanics in Lincolnshire.
[2] *Mechanics' Magazine*, i. 307 *n*,

working-class members, and in the following year started the first Artisans' Library.[1] About the same time, Professor Anderson invited workpeople to attend his course on Experimental Physics at Glasgow University. His successor, Dr. Birkbeck, delivered lectures to a crowded audience of mechanics, who for a short time, after his departure in 1804, continued to hold meetings of their own accord, the class being revived subsequently as the nucleus of a Mechanics' Institute. But it is to the religious rather than to the scientific renaissance that we must look for the manifestation of that corporate spirit which is the most abiding characteristic of the new democracy. The modern Adult School movement is lineally descended from a small group of students who met at Nottingham in 1798 to learn Bible-reading and the elements of secular knowledge; and, if its distinctive feature at the present day is an effort to discuss the problems of life on terms of mutual forbearance and Christian fellowship, it may trace back its pedigree a stage further—to some of the more fruitful examples of the Methodist class-meeting.

[1] *Mechanics' Magazine, l.c.; cf.* Hudson, *Adult Education,* 29.

PART II
THE FIRST HALF OF THE NINETEENTH CENTURY

CHAPTER IV

In the comparison between English and German educational systems—once a familiar topic, now distasteful by common consent—it was customary to refer back to the course of political events in the seventeenth and eighteenth centuries, which in the one country increased the authority of the State over social institutions and in the other weakened its power of constructive intervention, leaving behind a legacy of social discord which opposed a lasting obstacle to any broad measure of educational reform. But though this circumstance may account for wide differences of opportunity, it does not fully explain the different ways in which ideas were developed and opportunity employed. School attendance was already being enforced in at least one of the German states during the earlier decades of the seventeenth century, at a time when the power of the central government in England was still vigorously exercised in many branches of social discipline without extending in the same degree into the sphere of education.

It was due to something more than political accident that the basis of a national system appeared earliest in countries which had carried out the religious changes of the sixteenth century with drastic effect, and that

145

in England, where it had been the ideal of the best Churchmen to steer a middle course between rival extremes, national education was indefinitely delayed. In England, though there was an eminent group whose hopes centred in education,[1] there was no counterpart to the organised zeal which accompanied the most vigorous phase of the Lutheran Reformation, or to the democratic force of the Scottish movement. The reforming party, led by the government, showed a characteristic reluctance to admit the consequences of a new departure. Their watchword was renewal rather than revolt, and they held generally to the principle of reconstructing on safe lines which threatened the least disturbance to the political system and the inherited fabric of social ideas. Henry the Eighth ordered a copy of the English Bible to be placed in all churches, and gave instructions that the laity should be encouraged to read it, that they might better understand their duties ; [2] but the privilege was afterwards curtailed and held in abeyance for fear of dissension.[3] The young of all classes were to be instructed in the Paternoster, the Articles of Belief, and the Ten Commandments, which were to be delivered in writing to 'them that can read and will desire the same. '[4] Parents were exhorted to 'bestow their children . . . either to learning, or to some honest exercise, occupation or husbandry,' to prevent idleness and to preserve the State.[5] On the broader question of providing schools for the masses there was no authoritative pronouncement, though individuals realised that the need existed and Cranmer

---

[1] Craik, *The State in its Relation to Education* (*English Citizen Series*), 4.

[2] Burnet, *History of the Reformation*, iv. 91, 138 (Instructions to the Clergy).

[3] *Ibid.*, i. 517.   [4] *Ibid.*, iv. 91.   [5] *Ibid.*

developed a 'scheme of new schools for every class.'[1]
On the other hand he rebuked those who would have
diverted educational endowments to the exclusive
benefit of the higher ranks, reasserting in the name of
religion the traditional claims of the poor with talent.[2]
The canons of 1604 show the same tendency. The
educational system, as it existed, was placed under the
sanction and control of the Church, the aim being to
ensure efficiency and soundness of doctrine; and it
was ordained, further, that the 'youth and ignorant
persons' should receive catechetical instruction in the
parish church.[3]

A more democratic impulse came from the Puritan
side, and emerged under the Commonwealth. At one
time it seemed possible that education would be reorganised and a general system of schools established
on a statutory basis. Outside Wales, however, the
design, if it existed, never matured. Public instruction
in the turmoil of the age was little more than a side
issue, and after the Restoration the provision of schools
was left again to voluntary effort.

New factors made their appearance in the eighteenth
century—on the one hand, the growth of organised
philanthropy developing a network of schools for the
poor; on the other, a fundamental antagonism to the
idea of universal instruction. Class-feeling went far
towards establishing monopolies in higher education,
and opposition to the Charity Schools derived support

---

[1] Craik, *op. cit.*, 4.   [2] Strype, *Cranmer*, i. 127.
[3] Canons 59, 77–79; Cardwell, *Synodalia*, i. 280, 291. The fifty-
ninth canon, dealing with catechetical instruction in churches, repeats
—with the addition of the Catechism—Henry VIII's Instructions to the
Clergy, issued in the year 1536, which particularise a method of oral
teaching, adding that books containing the subject-matter are to be
pointed out to those who were able and desirous to read them (Burnet,
iv: 91).

from an economic conception of class-gradations which
had survived from an earlier age. The mediaeval view
of learning as an alternative to labour was interpreted
to mean that labour is incompatible with rudimentary
knowledge. The oral teaching which the Church had
authorised as the minimum required for all classes was
taken as the standard of popular enlightenment. ' There
is a prodigious difference,' wrote Mandeville, ' between
debarring the children of the poor from ever rising higher
in the world, and refusing to force education upon
thousands of them when they should be usefully employed ' ; and his opinion gained adherents in later
years, at a time of conservative reaction and amid
revolutions which heralded the advent of democracy.
The criticisms which appeared at the commencement
of the nineteenth century are governed by the same
traditional preconception, that education is normally
a means of rising in the social scale and that any widely
organised instruction of the people would incapacitate
them for necessary labour and diffuse an atmosphere
of social unrest.[1]

If the defects of school-training have been most

---

[1] ' A vast number of those who had been brought up at Sunday
schools were wandering from their proper callings, had become fanatical
teachers, had deemed themselves qualified to hold disputations on religious
topics, had turned sceptics, infidels and anarchists, and were spreading
a malignant influence throughout the mass of the community '—*Anti-
Jacobin*, Oct. 1800 ; *cf.* the royal injunction, 1541, that laymen reading
the Bible should not take upon themselves public disputation (Burnet,
op. cit., iv. 138). Even Hannah More had been charged with promoting
fanaticism and sedition (Overton and Relton, *History of English Church,
1714–1800*, 248) ; and twenty years later Brougham had to protest in
the House of Commons against this form of attack on popular education.
' It is doubtless desirable that the poor should be generally instructed
in *reading*, if it were only for the best of purposes—that they may read
the Scriptures. As to *writing* and *arithmetic*, it may be apprehended that
such a degree of knowledge would produce in them a disrelish for the
laborious occupations of life '—*Remarks on the Poor Bill ; . . by one of
H.M.'s Justices of the Peace in the County of Lincoln*, 1807 ; a fair
representation of moderate conservative opinion.

commonly remarked precisely among those sections of the poor which supplied the chief materials of controversy, it does not exculpate those who in opposing education closed their eyes to the problems arising from economic changes and the competing demands of urban and rural life, and to the new facts which made it necessary to remodel social discipline and give a healthy outlet to growing aspirations. Nor has the criticism which education encountered merely that degree of significance which belongs to a negative and transitory phase. It opposed a continual obstacle to deliberate measures which might have saved the situation, and it favoured compromises which prevented efficiency and helped to create the evils against which it prophesied. Yet the English habit of compromise is not without its advantages. It has secured a wide liberty for voluntary experiment and for the clash of rival ideals, which may prove in the long run the surest way to a higher synthesis reconciling freedom with order, and comprehending all that is of permanent value in a variety of social traditions. It has, also, given to the history of English education its peculiar attraction as a record of the national character in every phase of its growth. Just as philanthropic enterprise in the early years of the eighteenth century had reflected the business methods of the period, so the movements which commenced a hundred years later are impressed with the spirit of the Industrial Revolution. There can be little doubt that the forms of child-labour and labour-saving machinery which appear in Lancaster's ' plan ' and the monitorial system played an important part in recommending education to public patronage. The imagination is haunted by the prospect of a ' clear easy practical system,' carried out with a maximum reduction of labour and expense and bringing speedy and calculable returns.

The language of philanthropy combines with disinterested benevolence the hardened optimism of a
commercial prospectus.[1] The movement commenced
with the strife of rival leaders, Joseph Lancaster and
Dr. Andrew Bell ; and it accorded well with the spirit
of the age that the matter should be left in the hands of
two great competing associations, summing up in themselves the history of former conflicts of creed and tradition—the National Society formed in allegiance to the

---

[1] ' We meet to erect a perpetual standard against ignorance and vice,
to confirm and render permanent an establishment intended to train up
the children of this town in knowledge and virtue. We expect thousands
of children will here be taught not only the grounds of human science,
but the first principles of Christian religion, that religion which,' etc.—
Speech of the Treasurer at the opening of a gigantic Sunday school built
by the mill-owners of Stockport, 1805 (Ure, *Philosophy of Manufactures*
(3rd ed.), 408).   One is tempted to mention Robert Pemberton's *Address
to the people on the necessity of popular education in conjunction with emigra-
tion, as a remedy for all our social evils* (1859), announcing the formation
of a ' People's Shilling Company for Popular Education ' on the author's
system, which was to ' give general knowledge and produce excellent
mechanics and good scholars at fourteen and the finest orators at twenty-
one ; wonder not, for this is the scientific age of discovery.'   In a *Report
of Proceedings at the Inauguration of Mr. Pemberton's new Philosophical
Model Infant School, for teaching languages native and foreign on the natural
or euphonic system* (1857), it is stated that he had devised a ' Nursery
Chromatic Barrel Organ, for the express purpose of developing the
musical attribute of the infant and naturalising on its mind from birth
the perfect language and harmony of music.'
     Incidentally it may be remarked that Lancaster himself seems to have
derived inspiration from other than industrial and religious sources.
The son of an old soldier, he retained to the close of his life the spirit
of a recruiting sergeant.   His system was essentially one of drill, everything being reduced to rule and regulation ' with the object of saving the
teacher's time and thought.'   The children were to be kept in ' constant
activity,' each having ' at every moment . . . something to do and a
motive for doing it ' ; and it seems that badges or other small marks of
distinction were distributed as a reward for good conduct (Binns, *Century
of Education*, 1908, 8–20).   Mrs. Trimmer, according to Sydney Smith,
accused him of preparing the materials for a rebel army.   ' On half-
holidays,' we are told, ' he would marshall his scholars in order, the monitors
acting as captains over their class, and sally forth to some outlying village,
with sports and games in the fields.'   The system which modern writers
have described as mechanical and barren of result, was probably associated in his mind with those ideas of discipline and *esprit de corps* which
have found expression in Lads' Brigades, etc.

Established Church (1811), and the British and Foreign School Society (1814), an outgrowth of Lancaster's Committee and the Royal Lancasterian Institution (1808) which had succeeded it in the interval.

(1) *General Lines of Development*

The resolution of Lancaster's Committee, ' to constitute themselves a society for the purpose of affording education, procuring employment, and as far as possible to furnish clothing to the children ' of the poorer classes,[1] is evidence of an underlying continuity in educational thought, and carries us back to the aims with which philanthropy had started a hundred years earlier. Lancaster had already spoken of adapting his system to the teaching of agriculture and handicrafts.[2] To connect education with manual employment was the policy of his rival, Dr. Andrew Bell.[3] During the century and a half following the birth of the Charity School movement the idea was continually reasserting itself, without any permanent effect.[4] Apart from the

---

[1] Binns, *op. cit.*, 32.   [2] *Ibid.*, 22.
[3] Adams, *Elementary Schools Contest*, 59.
[4] Montague Burgoyne in an *Address to the Governors and Directors of Public Charity Schools* (1829) refers to the alleged tendency of the ' present system of popular education to unfit the poor for those laborious situations in life in which they would have to move, making them aspire to preferment which they cannot reach.' He proposed to establish an industrial agricultural school at Potton, Bedfordshire, where in addition to ordinary elementary subjects the boys might learn tailoring, shoe-mending, gardening and agriculture, and the girls needle and laundry work, dairying and housewifery. *Cf.* a minute drawn up for the guidance of the Committee of Council (1839)—to ' include instruction in industry as a special department of the moral training of children,' and to give ' such a character to the matter of instruction in the school as to keep it in close relation with the conditions of workmen and servants.' There was a ' Colony-at-Home ' established by William Allen at Lindfield, Sussex, where he purchased a property in 1826 and proceeded to erect labourers' cottages and a schoolhouse, with an infant department and an industrial day-school for boys and girls—Allen, *Plan for Diminishing*

question of expense, there was a growing opposition, on economic and educational grounds, to any scheme which bore the appearance of converting the school into a substitute for the workshop.   There was also a tendency for elementary schools to become monopolised by a comparatively select class of children, for whom manual training was not always an immediate or apparent necessity.

It is probable that the main stimulus to philanthropy, all along, had been the hope of dealing with the sources of crime and destitution and civilising a class whose ignorance was a menace to society.   The difficulty of reconciling this aim with any general scheme of education based on voluntary enterprise was soon realised, especially in the urban districts.   The tone of a school and its standard of discipline would improve in proportion to its success.   It would attract by degrees a superior class of children, and appeal to a more respectable and fastidious class of parents.   The managers, finding it difficult to accommodate all under the same system of discipline and instruction, would drift from their original aim into safer paths of financial security.[1]   It followed that successive groups of philanthropists were continually rediscovering a submerged class for whom nothing was done, and whose condition grew more ominous and lamentable in proportion to the general progress of manners and intelligence.   Just as

the Poor Rates (1833), 3 ; Stephen Grellet, *Memoirs*, ii. 183.   Industrial Schools for waifs and strays—*Select Committee on Education*, 1834, QQ. 2697–2749 ; Langford, *Century of Birmingham Life*, ii. 363.

[1] Thus Matthew Arnold reports that in British and Wesleyan schools in his district the children of the poorest were not found ; small farmers, skilled artisans, etc., paying a considerable fee, ' often object as much as the classes above them to the contact, with their children, of the children . . . of the class found in Ragged Schools ' (1853) ; again, ' Ragged Schools, rather than National Schools, take the really poor of London who are not Roman Catholics '—*Reports on Elementary Education*, 19, 151.

in the eighteenth century the establishment of Charity Schools had been followed by a special provision for waifs and orphans, so a hundred years later, a generation after the founding of the great national societies, we find a supplementary group of rescue movements working strictly on a poverty test. One line of experiment, which aimed at isolating children of the destitute and criminal classes in permanent institutions, is represented by the Children's Friend Society, whose origin coincides very nearly with the centenary of the Foundling Hospital.[1] Another is seen in the more flexible organisation of the Ragged School Union. A ragged school might start as a Sunday school, a day school, or an evening class. It might include industrial classes, a library, and a provident club, and become a centre for

[1] The Children's Friend Society for the Prevention of Juvenile Vagrancy was founded through the exertions of Captain Brenton, R.N., who in 1830 opened a small house of reception in West Ham. By 1837, when he wrote an account of the work, there were (1) the Brenton Asylum, 150 boys, (2) the Victoria Asylum at Chiswick for girls, supported by the society, with branch committees in the Colonies. Upwards of a thousand children had been rescued from workhouse, street, and prisoner's dock. They stayed about six months, receiving an industrial and general education, being kindly treated and constantly employed. The Brenton Asylum stood in ten acres of ground cultivated by the inmates. At the end of their time the boys went to the Colonies to be apprenticed—Brenton, *The Bible and the Spade* (1837); *Fanny Forster, a Sequel* (1837); *Select Committee on Education* (1834), Q. 2576 *sqq.* Kay-Shuttleworth, *Social Condition and Education of the People*, i. 394 (1850), reckons that there were 30,000 destitute, filthy, lawless children in London alone, the source of nineteen-twentieths of the crime committed. The Royal Asylum of St. Ann's Society (1702), the Foundling Hospital (1739), and the Marine Society (1757, which collected street arabs and trained them for sea service) may be mentioned as corresponding types of rescue work in the eighteenth century. We may refer, also, to the work of City Missions in London and elsewhere, which commenced about the year 1825 and seem to have been inspired by the ideal of a ' Ministry for the Poor,' emanating from America—Kay-Shuttleworth, *Four Periods of English Education*, 46–115 ; *Social Condition and Education of the People*, i. 414 *sq.* ; Langford, *op. cit.*, ii. 581. Knight, *Passages in a Working Life*, iii. 86 *sq.*, relates how a stockinger, named Brooks, came to Birmingham in the forties and instituted a ' Ministry for the Poor,' which led to a Ragged School, a People's Instruction Society, a Provident Institution, Sunday schools, evening classes, etc.

social and religious meetings and different forms of amusement. It might develop into a boarding institution, a reformatory or home for destitute children.[1]

The work of Bell and Lancaster had helped to reassert the principle of full-time attendance at a day school, for a varying period between the ages of six and eleven, as the basis of an educational system; but for some time the greater part of the industrial classes, both young and old, found their only means of instruction on Sunday. The rapid growth of Sunday schools in the manufacturing districts is one of the most important signs of social advance during the early years of the nineteenth century ; and in two respects the movement possesses a special interest in the history of education. The Sunday school seems to have afforded the teacher a more general opportunity for exercising a personal influence than was possible in the large classes of a day school under the monitorial system [2] It supplies also the first traces of a course of instruction pursued consecutively for a number of years and covering the critical period of adolescence.

In 1816 the number of adults attending Sunday schools in East London was estimated at about six hundred ; at Manchester, a few years later, the ages ranged from six to twenty-five, and some scholars were known to have attended for twenty years in

---

[1] C. J. Montague, *Sixty Years in Waifdom.* The clientele of the early Ragged Schools was not entirely composed of illiterates. Thus about 100 of all ages, 16–35, attended a reading room at the Marylebone Ragged School, being attracted by the warmth and sociability of the place and gradually getting interested in the books ; many had previously read a good deal in the way of penny dreadfuls—*Committee on Public Libraries,* 1849, Q. 3194 *sqq.*

[2] At the Stockport Sunday School, mentioned above, the monitorial system was discarded and small classes insisted on. Ure, *Philosophy of Manufactures* (3rd ed.), 408 *sqq.*

succession.[1] Where attendance was thus commenced in childhood and carried on for a considerable period, there might be some chance of arranging a continuous course of instruction. Such, indeed, was the object of the Sunday Society established at Birmingham towards the close of the eighteenth century, and of the senior classes which became a common addition to Sunday schools at a later date.[2] But in these early years, when scholars of all ages were beginning to learn, the distinction between a juvenile and an adult class would not necessarily imply much difference of curriculum.[3] Putting aside differences of age, the schools admit of a twofold classification ; according as the religious teaching was conducted on denominational or on unsectarian lines, and according as instruction was or was not extended to include secular subjects. Not uncommonly a sharp distinction was drawn between reading (which implied reading the Bible) and writing and arithmetic, which were considered secular, besides being difficult to teach effectively in the time available.[4] It appears that in 1834 the average length of attendance in London might be estimated at three years, in the manufacturing districts at four, and in the country at five ; [5] that there was little time

---

[1] *Select Committee on Education*, 1816, 76 ; 1834, Q. 2312, 2323.

[2] Watson, *First Fifty Years of the Sunday School [Union]*, (1853).

[3] The Adult Sunday School, as a distinct institution, first appears in the form of classes for men and women started by Fox and Singleton at Nottingham in 1798, which have continued to the present day. The *Bristol Institution for Instructing Adult Persons to read the Holy Scriptures* (1812) was the means of spreading Adult Schools over the country and enlisting the support of the Society of Friends. After an interval of decay (the attention of the Churches being concentrated on the needs of children), the movement was revived by Sturge of Birmingham between 1845 and 1852.

[4] *Cf.* Rowntree and Binns, *History of the Adult School Movement*, 13. Bamford, in his *Early Days*, speaks of a Methodist Sunday School where the ordinary subjects of an elementary education appear to have been taught.

[5] *Select Committee on Education*, 1834, Q. 1224 *sqq.*, 1498.

for secular instruction; and that the majority were fortunate, if they left with a fair knowledge of reading. A number of schools, however, had subsidiary evening classes during the week, where the more promising scholars might learn to write legibly in the course of three years.[1]

Night schools grew up in rapid succession in the North during the last years of the eighteenth century, and afterwards extended over all parts of the country.[2] They became scenes of considerable energy, and helped to satisfy the desire for self-improvement inspired by certain aspects of the Industrial Revolution. At a candle factory in Vauxhall, in the year 1847, some dozen boys set an example by starting a night class on their own initiative, 'hiding . . . behind a bench two or three times a week, after they had done their work and had their tea, to practise writing on scraps of paper with worn-out pens begged from the counting house.' Their efforts received judicious encouragement from the managing director, and made the beginnings of a well-planned scheme of social betterment.[3] From the early years of the century, there are instances of day schools remaining open at night for the benefit of lads in employment,[4] so that the evening class may have gradually come to be regarded as a continuation of

---

[1] *Select Committee on Education*, 1834, Q. 310, 1233 *sqq.*, 2310.

[2] Sometimes under the auspices of local associations, e.g. the Benevolent Evening Schools Society of Bristol (1806)—Hudson, *Adult Education*, 15–17. The Adult Institution for Berks and Bucks (1814) provided for all ages from 10 upwards: the villagers might be seen in cottages of a night seated round a table, learning to read the Bible—Knight, *Passages in a Working Life*, i. 189.

[3] *Quarterly Review*, Dec. 1852, No. 183, art. 1.

[4] The Royal Lancasterian Free School at Birmingham had an elementary class for factory lads three evenings a week, 1816—Langford, *op. cit.*, ii. 372. The Roby Day and Sunday Schools at Manchester had evening classes in writing, arithmetic, grammar, geography, and drawing for mill-hands over 13—Hudson, *op. cit.*, 19 *sq.*

the day school no less than as a supplement to the teaching received on Sunday. But the familiar hindrances appear from the outset. Juvenile employment, which interfered with the day school, handicapped every attempt to provide a substitute. Children were often too exhausted after the labour of the week to make a regular attendance on Sundays; and night schools were liable to fail for similar reasons. It was often as hard to find scholars, as to secure competent persons to volunteer the service of teaching.[1] When a class had been successfully enrolled, the difficulties were not at an end. 'The evening school,' wrote a Government inspector in 1840, 'which only affords instruction for four hours in the week, and that when the scholars are jaded with twelve or thirteen hours of toil, cannot educate those who attend it.'

(2) Success and Failure

During the second quarter of the century, much attention was directed to the state of elementary schools and the condition of the rising generation. The results include a series of estimates, possessing at the time no doubt considerable value as a means of stirring public opinion, but comparatively useless for historical purposes. There is evidence not only of an increase in the number of schools and of the children receiving some form of instruction, but also of some general improvement in manners and intelligence. Otherwise the conclusions formulated at intervals during these years are a set of vain repetitions, leaving the history of the period, so far as the quality of education is concerned, to all appearance a complete blank. Allowing for irregularity of attendance, the average

[1] *Select Committee on Education*, 1834, Q. 311; 1835, Q. 389.

length of school life rises on a favourable estimate
from about one year in 1835 to about two years in
1851 ; [1] but in either case an overwhelming majority
leave school before, or shortly after, the age of eleven,
and there is little, if any, sign of improvement in the
results achieved. In 1834 the curriculum in the better
class of national schools was limited in the main to
religious instruction, reading, writing, and arithmetic ;
in some country schools writing was excluded for
fear of evil consequences ; at the central schools of
the British Society, ' children remaining one year '—
the normal period—might ' read well, write fairly, and
have a tolerable knowledge of the first four rules of
arithmetic : this is, however, above the average of
the whole.' [2] In 1850, we find that ' even of the children
of the poor who have received some instruction, very
few know anything ' beyond the rudiments. [3] Seventy-
five per cent., writes the inspector of the Midland
division, leave school unable to read the Bible. [4] ' Many
children,' again, ' say they can read when they only know
the letters of the alphabet, or can at most pronounce
monosyllables . . . and in like manner, comparatively
few who state that they have learnt to write are capable

---

[1] 1834–5, average attendance (day schools) : London, just over a
year ; manufacturing towns, a few months longer ; agricultural districts,
two years continually interrupted by jobs ; few stay after eleven—*Select
Committee on Education*, 1834, Q. 64, 258 *sqq.*, 715, 2246 ; 1835, Q. 12.

1845–50, average attendance (day schools) just over a year, ending
at eleven in manufacturing, at nine in agricultural, districts—Kay-Shuttleworth, *Public Education*, 267, 281 (1845), *Social Condition, etc., of the People*,
i. 587 ; ii. 475 (1850). *Census Report* (1851) puts the number of children in
England between 3 and 15 years at 5,000,000, of whom 2,046,848 were at
school, 49 per cent. staying till 11, 28 per cent. till 13. Dr. Sadler estimates
average attendance of working-class children (5 to 15) at about 4 years,
brought down in practice by irregularity to about 2 years—*Special
Reports (Education Department)*, ii., No. 20, 449.

[2] *Cf. Select Committee on Education, 1834*, Q. 60, 252–267, 274, 2071 *sq.*

[3] Kay-Shuttleworth, *Social Condition, etc.*, ii. 462.

[4] Kay-Shuttleworth, *Public Education*, 291, 309.

of writing a sentence legibly.'[1] School inspectors were continually commenting on the absence of globes, maps, blackboards and other apparatus, especially in village schools, and on the habitual use of the Bible as a textbook of general instruction, problems in arithmetic being extracted from the pages of Exodus and Joshua.[2] Complaints as to the scandalous state of accommodation certainly showed no tendency to decrease as the years went by.[3] The teaching profession in 1850 was still thronged with uneducated and 'worse than incompetent' men and women, who traded on their physical infirmities or had failed in other walks of life.[4] In 1848, as in 1834, three months was the average period of training at the establishment in the Borough Road. It might be said that, from whatever aspect the situation was approached, the further the inquiry was carried, the more terrible the nakedness of the land appeared.[5]

The explanation is simple. At the stage of development through which education was passing under the voluntary system, calculation by averages is essentially misleading. Take the industrial population as a whole, and it is found that a majority have received no instruction. Take the school children throughout the country or in a particular district; the notorious defects of

---

[1] *Children's Employment Commission (1843), Digest,* 171, 206 *sq.*

[2] Kay-Shuttleworth, *Public Education,* 238, 257, 303 *sq.* ; Horace Mann, *Report of an Educational Tour* (ed. Hodgson, 1846), 268 *n.*

[3] 'Thousands of such schools in all parts of England and Wales . . . many which are held in cellars, garrets, chapels and kitchens, badly warmed, wretchedly ventilated, dirty, unfurnished, dark, damp, unhealthy '—Kay-Shuttleworth, *Social Condition, etc.,* ii. 474.

[4] Kay-Shuttleworth, *Public Education,* 215–19, 228, 270 ; *Children's Employment Commission (1843), Digest,* 171–4, 205 *sq.*

[5] Statistical societies, formed at Manchester and elsewhere to repudiate charges of insufficiency of education, revealed uniformly a state of ignorance and neglect which had been only dimly suspected to exist. Adams, *Elementary Schools Contest,* 94 *sq.*

private schools will probably account for the greater part of the results. Take the schools under some responsible management over a considerable area; small and ill-supported rural schools or over-crowded schools in the larger towns will tend to predominate. Whatever mode of classification is adopted, there is always an excess of scandalous instances which bring down the average. It must be remembered, too, that in the course of the inquiry the standard of values was continually rising. Methods and results which had been received with uncritical enthusiasm at the outset of a new movement passed to the wrong side of the account as the movement progressed. Lastly, the difficulty of organising a populous district increased directly with the growth of its population.

To the historical student it is precisely those isolated cases of improvement which are lost in the flood of averages and generalisations, that possess at such times of slow transition the highest importance. Dr. Sadler has justly repudiated the excessive attention which has been paid, ' in estimating the quality ' of education, ' to the facts disclosed in regard to the large towns and the poor results obtained at the dame schools.' ' If we could take the ordinary school in a moderate-sized village, or in a small town, where the population had not increased too rapidly for the school accommodation to keep pace with it, we should find a more satisfactory state of affairs than is generally imagined.' [1] It is equally true that in every kind of neighbourhood, in large manufacturing towns, among mines and collieries, and in agricultural districts, a better class of school was making its appearance. [2] Even the adventure

[1] Sadler, *Special Reports (Education Department)*, ii. 450.
[2] E.g., a superior school in St. Mark's parish, Sheffield, offering geography, history, vocal music, algebra and elementary mechanics, attended (1845) by nearly 700 children, whose parents paid £180 annually—

schools, which played so large and ominous a part in English education, were not without a redeeming remnant. ' My school,' writes Thomas Cooper, ' was a perfect passion with me for a time. I was in the schoolroom often at five in the morning until nine at night, taking my meals in a hasty, imperfect way while the boys were gone home to theirs. I had quill pens to make in great number, the first work in the morning, and for a time I had early classes each morning. Then, again, in the evenings, although other day-schools broke up at five, I drew the older scholars around the globe, and described the countries upon it until a late hour, or talked to them on some part of history, or described the structure of animals or, to keep their attention, even related a story from the Arabian Nights. I spent at least fifty pounds on the walls of the large club-room, by covering them with pictures of every imaginable kind, and filling the corners with plaster figures and busts. The sill under every window of the schoolroom was fitted up with small divisions so that the boys might have a miniature museum of pebbles, coins, etc. I was intent on making their schoolroom their delight.' [1]

(3) Sources of Improvement

The work of public authorities may be left to a later survey. It was too early, at the close of this period, to expect much from the influence of inspectors and

---

Kay-Shuttleworth, *Public Education*, 298 *sq.* At the Killingworth Colliery, three large schools (one an infant school) were opened by the owners in 1840 ; attendance 528, paying threepence a week—*Our Coal and Coal Pits, etc.*, by a Traveller Underground (1853), 211. Similar schools at the lead-mines of Alston Moor—*Children's Employment Commission, Digest,* 193 *sqq.*

[1] Cooper, *Life*, 74. School opened at Gainsborough 1828 ; average attendance 80, mostly working class.

the new scheme of supervision and encouragement
fore-shadowed in the government minutes of 1846.
Until recently, the State had practically confined
itself to distributing money between the two largest
voluntary organisations which together exercised
some of the more delicate functions of a central
authority.

The annual reports of the British Society, from
1832 onwards, deal with important questions of school
organisation—the necessity, for instance, of broadening the curriculum and introducing better methods of
instruction ; the training of teachers ; and the compila-
tion of suitable textbooks. From an early period the
Model Schools had set an example. In 1823 it was
reported that a ' select and small number of boys '
had been ' instructed in the elements of grammar,
geography and geometry " as a reward for good
conduct." ' [1]   Later on, subjects such as singing, linear
drawing, and mathematics were added, and the methods
of Pestalozzi adopted to some extent. Between 1837
and 1858 a number of improvements gradually spread
from London to the provinces. The ' barn-like buildings ' of the monitorial system were broken up into
classrooms. Science and music appeared in the curricula.
The Scripture lesson was supplemented by the reading
of primers and the institution of school libraries, from
which the children were encouraged to borrow books,
taking them home to read and to show to their parents.
The training of teachers was to form, for many years,
one of the gravest and most difficult problems. Early
in the forties, the establishment in the Borough Road

[1] ' Those remaining three or four years (at the Borough Road School)
will both read and write well and perform any sum in the usual books of
arithmetic ; they will acquire also a considerable knowledge of geography,
can draw maps and are made acquainted with the elements of geometry '—
only a small minority. *Select Committee on Education, 1834*, Q: 262_sq.

was enlarged and became the scene of interesting experiments. Soon afterwards we hear of special classes and lectures in history and mathematics for the London teachers, and a summer school at which their fellows from the country assembled during the harvest vacation.[1] But if it was premature to expect much from State interference, either for good or evil, it is easy to award a disproportionate share of credit to the great societies. The best schools, as well as the worst, were beyond the sphere of their influence; and in any case such were the conditions of organisation that improvement in the quality of teaching depended principally on local initiative. The comparative failure of British schools outside the large urban areas has been attributed in no small degree to the absence of persons qualified to assist and encourage the teacher, such as might be found in the case of schools attached to the Church.[2] On the other hand, the two standard examples of excellence in rural education were due to the personal efforts of Professor Henslowe and Richard Dawes, Dean of Hereford.[3] At this, even more than at a later period, the secret of improvement must be read in the lives of individuals in different ranks of society: some of them, as clergymen or employers, occupying a

[1] Binns, *Century of Education*, 113–17, 157–62. I take the British and Foreign School Society as an example, because the information concerning its work comes nearest to hand.

[2] *Ibid.*, 221.

[3] The dean's school at King's Somborne is mentioned as exceptionally good by Matthew Arnold (1853, *Reports on Elementary Education*, 21), its influence on the agricultural labouring class being due to the 'union of instruction in a few simple principles of natural science, applicable to things familiar to the children's daily observation—with everything else usually taught in a national school.' See Lubbock, *Addresses, Political and Educational (1876)*, 84. Prof. Henslowe, ex-Professor of Botany at Cambridge, taught a botany class (42, ages 8–15) in a Suffolk village school; an early and successful example of nature study, well received—*Public Schools Commission, 1864*, Dr. Hooker, Q. 21–27.

position of trust and influence, others standing in no official relation to the masses but impelled by genius or the force of circumstances to venture beyond the beaten track.

Concerning the attitude of employers much the same might be said in general terms as at the present day. The Manchester men were held to be generally favourable to the education of their people. Some of them were munificent and enthusiastic, others in practice apathetic and even hostile; well-regulated schools affording a strange contrast to the notorious coal-hole seminaries improvised in contempt of the Factory Acts. In isolated cases, from the earliest years of the eighteenth century, iron-masters and owners of collieries and mines are found building chapels, opening pleasure grounds, and supporting schools of the accepted type.[1] The new directing class which rose a hundred years later, as a result of the Industrial Revolution, commenced afresh on a larger scale. To this period may be traced the origin of those organised settlements which have contributed in various ways to raise the standard of social enterprise throughout the country. A new factory erected in rural surroundings, where ties of loyalty might grow up between master and man, became the centre of an organised community, decently housed, with facilities for physical exercise and various aids to health and cleanliness, and a large school-house established in a prominent position which served the purposes of instruction, worship, entertainment and social inter-

---

[1] Sir Ambrose Crowley builds a chapel at the iron-works, Winlaton, near Newcastle—Richardson's *Reprints of Historical Tracts, Travels of Defoe, etc.*, 17 *n.* (1705). Charity schools maintained by Welsh mine-owners and a Yorkshire iron-master—*List of Several Charity Schools* (1707). Later, Richard Reynolds at Madeley, near Coalbrookdale, lays out extensive walks through the woods on Lincoln Hill, for his iron-workers—Smiles, *Industrial Biography*, 95. *Cf.* Young, *Northern Tour*, ii, 288 *sqq.*

course.[1] Later on, in the second half of the century, as the population increased and the town extended its dominion, came a series of movements back to the country: Saltaire, Bourneville, and other more recent experiments. Meanwhile the schools provided by the more responsible class of employers appear to have been considerably above the average, possessing in the matter of equipment the advantages which might be expected of business capacity and a ready command of capital. The buildings were large, well lighted and ventilated, and furnished with appliances which stood the test of expert criticism for many years to come. The teaching was plain and thorough ; the curriculum was decidedly advanced according to the standards of the time ; and importance was attached to punctuality, neatness, accuracy, and the various qualities which made up the virtue of the middle class. The care exercised in selecting competent teachers was no small advantage at a time when broken adventurers, male and female, monopolised a large share in the training of the young.[2]

[1] Messrs. Greg, new cotton mill near Manchester, 1832 ; cottages, Sunday schools, baths, evening parties, outdoor exercise—Knight, *Passages in a Working Life*, ii. 85. *Cf.* account of Thomas Ashton's mills in township of Hyde—Ure, *Philosophy of Manufactures* (3rd ed.), 349 *sq.*, *cf.* 353. Clay Cross Company (collieries and ironworks) founded by George Stephenson, 1838 ; a system was gradually evolved, by which in return for a fortnightly subscription, levied on all employés, the following privileges were guaranteed—(1) day schools for all children ; (2) night schools for lads—optional ; (3) access to Workmen's Institute with lectures, reading room and library ; (4) medical attendance ; (5) sick and disablement funds ; (6) fortnightly dance ; (7) bands and Choral Society ; (8) cricket club ; (9) prizes for cottage gardens, and flower show. Smiles, *Life of Stephenson*, 479–81 ; *Machinery Market*, Aug. 1, 1891, 5–7, 17.

[2] The following examples appear to be typical of the best schools founded by employers at this period. (1) Robert Owen, New Lanark Mills, 1816 (see p. 166 *sq.*). (2) Messrs. Bright, Rochdale. For some time before a school was built, Mrs. Bright, mother of John Bright, gave elementary instruction to employés in their homes ; and an office was set apart in the mill, where the younger employés received lessons

The system established by Robert Owen in 1816 in connection with his cotton mills at New Lanark stands in a class by itself, deserving the reputation which brought innumerable visitors every year from all parts of Europe. The full curriculum, commencing in an infants' department and extending over three grades of elementary instruction for children up to the age of twelve, concluded with evening classes which covered

in reading under Joshua Haigh, each one coming separately and then returning to his place in the mill and sending the next. 1840, Fieldhouse School was built, large and well equipped, Mr. John Greenwood, of Heptonstall, being engaged as schoolmaster, 'a man of cultured tastes' (says his grandson, to whom I am indebted for these notes), 'who strove to give his students an interest in many subjects beyond the 3 r's.' To a newsroom attached to the schoolroom was removed a library which had been kept in the mill ; books were let out at 1d. a week, the money being spent on additions. The schoolroom formed a convenient centre for week-night lectures, public meetings, etc. Subsequently a music master was engaged to give singing lessons in the winter. 1846–7, when nearly all the cotton mills had stopped work, Messrs. Bright fitted up a room in the new mill as a night school, engaged a master and six assistants, and provided books and slates, offering instruction free to all comers. From the first there appears to have been a night school for adult employés, in which Jacob Bright displayed an interest, 'purchasing school-books which were lent free to the students and at one time himself teaching special classes' in geography, history, and English grammar. Long afterwards men and women who had attended the night school, treasured memories of the benefits derived, 'the wider outlook upon life' and the 'interest in literary and scientific subjects which would' otherwise 'never have been brought within their reach.' It was remembered of the Brights among the manufacturers of the neighbourhood that 'no other family did so much personal work.' (3) Messrs. Chance, Smethwick. Spon Lane Schools, 1845 (Girls and Infants, 1846), the first complete set of schools with teachers' residences built by a Midland firm : a 'set of buildings which even now (1887), in the presence of the magnificent schoolrooms erected by Boards, still vie with them in general adaptation to their purpose, and especially in respect of spaciousness, light and ventilation.' Between 1845 and 1887 (after which the schools were transferred to a School Board), about 10,000 were educated ; the schools were open to all in the neighbourhood and attended from distant parishes. From the first, free-hand drawing was a special feature in the curriculum. 'Half the school learn to draw, and some have arrived at great proficiency in drawing scrolls and other forms used in ornamental art' (H.M. Inspector, 1851). A small fee was charged after much deliberation. The firm established a reading room and library for adults, with the usual forms of entertainment, and took a prominent part in the promotion of evening classes.

a five years' course in history, geography, music, and scientific and technical subjects. But it was on the earlier stages that its fame rested. The great aim, which represents all that is best in Owen's philosophy, was to instil habits of good-breeding and mutual consideration from earliest childhood and to develop every perfect gift. The dawning intelligence was stimulated by music, pictures, and object-lessons ; and it was a maxim of the founder (which he abandoned with reluctance) that formal instruction should not commence before the age of ten. A constant change of employment banished monotony and kept the faculties alert. Manual training and bodily exercise were allowed their share in the building up of mind and character. Among the older children, a certain time was set apart for gardening and recreative employments. The boys danced in the Highland costume, and both sexes sang and drilled together, performing military evolutions to the amazement of all comers and the confusion of some. ' We heard no quarrel,' was the report of a Yorkshire deputation, ' and so strongly impressed are they with the conviction that their interest and duty are the same . . . that they have no strife but in the offices of kindness.'

The new Lanark experiment has a twofold interest. It drew attention to the problems of the infant school, and it represents the first important attempt made in this country to base a practical scheme of education on an original study of the child. The work of Owen was continued by Wilderspin and others, whose efforts gave rise to the Infant School Society of 1836. Experience had shown the inexpediency of attempting to instruct infants by methods commonly applied to older children, and attention was drawn periodically to the systems of Pestalozzi, Froebel, and other continental teachers. The fact that the problem is still one of primary importance, although its urgency was recognised and treatment successfully applied in isolated cases from an early period, affords an example of the slow movement of new ideas and a warning against generalisations based on favourable instances.[1] Nevertheless these experiments have probably done more than anything else to raise the question of educational aims and methods.

Before the middle of the century an appeal arose from a different quarter. The early secular schools are remembered chiefly as an item in the long catalogue of abortive attempts to override the religious difficulty. Their real significance is found in the idea of recasting the curriculum of elementary schools on scientific principles, and in a conception of equality of opportunity which sums up the liberalism of the period.[2] The philosophy of the movement was supplied by George Combe, a disciple of Spurzheim, whose ideas he developed and promulgated until his death in 1858. Education, whose object was a healthy development of the individual in preparation for the manifold duties of life, consisted, first, in the training of mind and body by appropriate exercises, secondly, in instruction in various sciences relating to the constitution of man and his place in nature and human society. The two sides of the process, though logically distinct, were actually inseparable ; for the mental faculties could not be trained

---

[1] Wilderspin ' discovered much of the true nature of the child, and employed such materials and methods in his work as are too seldom found in some of the very best infant schools at the present day '—Holman, *English National Education* (1898), 41 *sq.*

[2] The Lancastrian (afterwards National) Public School Association (1847), advocated a national system of secular schools, maintained by ' equal taxation,' free and open to all classes (the ' Common School ' ideal) : the scheme included infant schools, evening classes, and industrial training—George Combe, *Education*, ed. William Jolly (1879), 224, 237 *sqq.*

except through the act of acquiring knowledge, and instruction could succeed only on the basis of a healthy constitution. Combe, in short, complained that in existing schools the element of training was too often disregarded, while the course of instruction was an inadequate preparation for practical life.[1] His attempt to discover the laws of mental growth with the aid of phrenology was in some sense a foretaste of psychological experiments, relating to a science of teaching, which have been undertaken in more recent times.

In 1848 he founded the Edinburgh Secular School. A few months earlier, similar efforts had been set on foot in London by William Ellis and Lovett the Chartist, working at first independently of Combe and of one another but stimulated by the same general idea of enabling children ' intelligently to know themselves and their surroundings in nature and social life.' Ellis opened a day school at the London Mechanics' Institute, the first of a series of schools subsequently established in different parts of the Metropolis and named in memory of Dr. Birkbeck. Lovett followed suit at his National Hall in Holborn. Each attempted to bring some branch of science within the comprehension of school children. Ellis took up social science.[2] Lovett turned to anatomy and physiology, the elements of which he taught by means of diagrams to separate classes of girls and boys, endeavouring to impress upon their minds in a simple manner some of the fundamental laws of health.

[1] Combe, op. cit., pp. xvii–xliii.
[2] In 1846 he had given simple lessons in social science at a British School in Camberwell, and was surprised at the ease with which the children grasped his meaning. For the growth of secular schools, see Combe, op. cit., 201–59.

CHAPTER V

IF elementary education is connected with the religious movements of the eighteenth century, higher popular education may be said to spring from the Industrial Revolution and the stirrings of political discontent. Its familiar methods—the lecture, the class, and the discussion circle, culminating in some form of corporate institution—had made their appearance at one or two centres before the close of the eighteenth century. In the course of the next fifty years they were widely established; and it becomes possible to discuss their merits, and to enter on the study of certain problems of organisation which have reappeared in all subsequent movements.

The network of industrial settlements which sprang up over the Midlands and the North of England during this period, opened the way for a new class of teacher following in the wake of the itinerant schoolmaster. By the middle of the nineteenth century, lecturing before popular audiences was developing into a profession which specialists did not disdain to pursue.[1] Men of science and letters volunteered their services in East London;[2] while some of the most successful lecturers, especially in the manufacturing and mining

---

[1] *Committee on Public Libraries, 1849*, Q. 2432 *sqq.* ; *cf. Mechanics' Magazine*, Nov. 1823 (opening of London Mechanics' Institute).
[2] *Ibid.*, Q. 2713.

districts, were self-taught amateurs, often of the same class as their hearers.[1] Commencing with science, the subject-matter extended gradually so as to include literature, politics, and religion ; and its treatment showed a corresponding variety of aims and methods. There were courses of lectures for a circle of students, propagandist addresses, and single lectures whose object might be described as entertainment rather than instruction.

Class-teaching with an element of discussion, which forms a recognised complement to the lecture in modern schemes of higher education, finds its origin in one of the most characteristic aspects of voluntary enterprise. The intermediary stage between private study, of which the eighteenth century affords so many examples, and organised instruction under an expert teacher, was supplied by the formation of societies for 'mutual improvement.' The plan was exceedingly simple, and might be easily adapted to varying needs. The members arranged to meet at each other's houses, or hired a room for the purpose, accumulating meanwhile a small supply of books and stationery. They would proceed to lay down a few simple rules, to appoint teachers, and to arrange a programme of classes, essay-readings, and discussions. · Such societies were constantly

[1] Hudson, *Adult Education*, 200 (1851), mentions ' Mr. Richardson, a self-educated man,' who had been busy for the past fifteen years lecturing ' on electricity, pneumatics, etc ' in the villages of Northumberland and Durham, travelling about day by day with his apparatus valued at £500 ; ' somewhat provincial in his dialect, perfect as a manipulator, and correct in his statements.'

One of the best lecturers was Detroisier, at one time a factory operative, who acquired a knowledge of French, Latin, and various branches of science and mathematics (*Select Committee on Education*, 1835, Q. 855). His practice of performing chemical experiments in the pulpits of dissenting chapels, to the scandal of the congregation, may recall James Mill's egregious scheme for the conversion of the Church of England into a National Mechanics' Institute (Dicey, *Law and Opinion*, 321).

springing up in the large towns during a depression of trade, and dissolving as rapidly when the novelty wore off or employment increased;[1] but in certain cases, notably in the West Riding of Yorkshire, their history extends over a period of years, and it is possible to trace the stages of their development into organised institutions. A society founded at Leeds by a small body of operatives in the summer of 1844 is a typical instance. The members commenced by assembling every evening for elementary instruction at a 'Garden-house' on Richmond Hill; one of them presiding in the 'house' as teacher, and the rest hanging about the door among broken flower-pots and rakes. As winter drew on and their numbers increased, they hired a room in the town and proceeded to organise a discussion-circle and classes in French and chemistry. Six years later they had migrated to more commodious premises, and were in possession of a museum and a library of three hundred volumes; there were eighty members, subscribing threepence a week.[2]

It is in the 'mutual improvement' circle that we find the connecting link between the science lectures which Dr. Birkbeck addressed to the Glasgow artisans at the close of the eighteenth century, and the organisation of Mechanics' Institutes in which he took a leading part some thirty years afterwards.[3] The

---

[1] *Committee on Public Libraries, 1849*, Q. 1990 *sq.*

[2] Hudson, *op. cit.*, 95 *sq.* Such institutions were common in the West Riding, where there were a number of Oddfellows' Literary Institutes, each with its library, reading-room, and evening classes, generally handicapped by want of money—*Committee on Public Libraries, 1849*, Q. 1984 *sqq.* Lovett mentions a literary society of workmen and others, called the 'Liberals'; when he opened his coffee-house (London), in 1834, he provided newspapers, periodicals, and a library, and set apart a Conversation Room for classes, recitations, and debates—*Autobiography*, 34, 88 *sq.*

[3] Dr. Birkbeck's class for mechanics at Glasgow was continued after his departure in 1804 by the enterprise of the members, and subsequently

Mechanics' Institutes, and the Schools of Design which commenced a decade later under the auspices of the Board of Trade, supply the first traces of an organised system of technical instruction. 'This Society,' ran the prospectus of the Manchester Mechanics' Institute, ' has been formed for the purpose of enabling mechanics and artisans, of whatever trade they may be, to become acquainted with such branches of science as are of practical application in the exercise of that trade, that they may possess a more thorough knowledge of their business, acquire a greater degree of skill in the practice of it, and be qualified to make improvements and even new inventions in the arts which they respectively profess. It is not intended to teach the trade of the machine-maker, the dyer, the carpenter, the mason or any other practical business ; but there is no art which does not depend more or less on scientific principles, and to search out what these are, and to point out their practical application, will form the chief objects of this Institution.' Birkbeck, in his inaugural lecture at the London Institute, spoke in a similar strain of the 'projected union of science and art,' and of the advantage to be derived from a study of the scientific principles underlying industry and invention ; but his standpoint was different. What gave the movement its initial stimulus, was not so much the thought of commercial expediency as a desire to cultivate the minds of the artisan class, by appealing to objects within the sphere of their daily experience which seemed to present the widest range of intellectual interests. The Institutes, in fact, were continually varying their

revived in the form of a Mechanics' Institute. *Cf.* the Mechanical Institution founded by Claxton and a few kindred spirits of the artisan class, who met weekly in different parts of London between 1817 and 1820 to discuss arts and sciences.

programmes and accumulating the apparatus of general culture. Science-teaching alternated with lectures on drama and the fine arts, and with classes in literature, languages, vocal music, and elementary subjects; natural history museums were ranged side by side with workshops for practical training; and instruction was supplemented by entertainments and social gatherings, which under happier circumstances might have formed the centre of a vigorous corporate life.

Every phase in the history of the movement—its high promise, its universality, its imposing statistics, its blighted hopes, and its long decline—has a special message for later times. It was the beginning of battles yet undecided. On November 11, 1823, a mass meeting, two thousand strong—journeymen, masters, politicians, and philanthropists—assembled at the *Crown and Anchor* to consider the advisability of founding a Mechanics' Institute in the Metropolis; and some hundreds of members were enrolled on the spot. Within a few months the institution was at work at the Southampton Buildings, in Chancery Lane. Two years later it moved into new premises, containing a spacious lecture hall—opened by Royalty—a lending library of two thousand volumes, a reading-room, newsroom, chemical laboratory, machines, maps, and diagrams, as well as suitable accommodation for classes, and an elementary school. In the first year Francis Place had seen 800 artisans attending a lecture on chemistry, and there were 1300 of their class already on the books. Institutes sprang up rapidly throughout London and the provinces, in large manufacturing centres, watering-places, villages, and hamlets. Manchester and Liverpool erected huge fabrics replete with every requirement of luxury and learning. The Wellingborough Institute was established in a workhouse. The villagers of Ripley, in the West Riding, met in a hayloft. Everywhere, under all circumstances, the same enthusiasm prevailed. In 1850 there were 610 Institutes in England, and 12 in Wales, with a total membership of over 600,000.[1] Meanwhile the cry had arisen that the Mechanics' Institutes were losing their mechanics. In the early forties it was ' universally acknowledged, that the members . . . are, nineteen-twentieths of them, not of the class of mechanics, but are connected with the higher branches of handicraft, or are clerks in offices, and in many cases young men connected with liberal professions.' [2] The membership of the London Institute, after various fluctuations, fell in 1845 to 600; and James Robertson, a somewhat uncertain authority, asserted that for some years the number of artisans in attendance had not averaged 200 annually.[3] The Institutes at Manchester, Liverpool, and Huddersfield, and in the smaller towns and villages of the West Riding, are cited as exceptions; but when Brougham went to Manchester in 1835, he noticed the small number of mechanics on the register, and apparently the same thing was remarked at Liverpool. The large enrolment of artisans at Huddersfield and the West Riding centres was, indeed, exceptional; of which the reason will appear.

The London Institute had not been in existence a year when the mechanics drew up a bill of grievances.

---

[1] Hudson, *op. cit.*, p. vi *sq.*

[2] James Hole, *History and Management of Literary, Scientific and Mechanics' Institutes*, 21 ; *cf. Comm. Pub. Lib., 1849,* Q. 1956.

[3] The Hackney Mechanics' Institute, soon after its foundation, changed its title to ' Literary and Scientific,' because the expression ' Mechanics' ' was no longer applicable—*Mechanics' Magazine,* Jan. 1828.

They complained that the rules were crude and unintelligible, the lectures desultory and unpractical, and the library deficient in technical works of reference. The criticisms which came periodically from this source refer in general to the teaching, the question of management, the rate of subscription, the influx of well-to-do tradesmen who put the poorer members out of countenance, and the exclusion of political controversy.[1] ' Nothing can persuade us but that all systems of education are false which do not teach a man his political duties and rights.' [2] It was precisely in the extent to which it offered larger opportunities than the mutual improvement circle, that the Mechanics' Institute encountered problems of a new and formidable character. The work of a permanent institution, with a numerous roll of members, involved administrative difficulties of a kind which did not arise among a small group of friends and equals controlling their arrangements from day to day. Skilled instruction was an advance on the co-operation of unskilled students, but a teacher did not necessarily understand the needs and mind of his class in the same way that a band of fellow students realised one another's perplexities. It was difficult, moreover, in a large institution, with no traditions to build upon, to secure the same motive power and binding force that developed naturally among a circle of intimates meeting on equal terms. The manifold sources of friction which arise in the mingling of different social strata and in uniting groups of teachers and students occupying different ranks of life, were a side

---

[1] *Mechanics' Magazine, passim.* *Social Science* (Prize Essays, Cassell, 1859). *Cf.* Ludlow and Jones, *Progress of the Working Class*, 174.

[2] *Mechanics' Magazine*, Sept. 11, 1824, etc. The Blaydon-on-Tyne Mechanics' Institute, at which there were political, social, and ' theological' lectures (Holyoake, *History of Co-operation*, i. 504), was exceptional.

of the problem which the founders of the enterprise ignored.

The complaint of the London mechanics raises a more immediate issue. The subjects introduced during the first year of the parent Institute range from ' jurisprudence ' to the ' structure of chimneys,' from ' hydrostatics ' to ' Greek and Roman antiquities,' and from ' mummies ' to ' savings banks.' It was no wonder that Dr. Playfair, a generation later, should describe the lectures as unsystematic and the teaching as cumbrous and inefficient. One of the most promising features of the movement was the importance attached to class instruction, which might be expected to afford greater opportunity than the lectures for close and connected study. Here, too, the same kind of criticism was continually repeated. ' Each class is to a great extent isolated. . . . There is no regular course of study through which a student is expected to pass. To working men these classes often present few, if any, advantages, except the acquirement of elementary knowledge ; and those really desirous of obtaining in the Mechanics' Institutes a knowledge of the principles of their trades, seldom find that knowledge there.' [1] The serious students were the first to leave, making way for a heterogeneous company which had little in common with the original members. The programme was then diversified by the inclusion of lighter subjects and various forms of entertainment, with the result of increasing the disorder and further alienating the student element.

But if the supply was ill-organised, the reason was to be found to a large extent in the inadequacy of the demand. Where, in the early days, ' as many as ninety lectures were delivered on one branch of natural philo-

[1] *Cf.* Hole, *op. cit.*, 60.

sophy,' the number had fallen to two or three a year by
the middle of the century.[1] Excellent scientific apparatus was left to rust, and museums of natural history
failed to secure attention. At Manchester lectures on
chemistry were discontinued after a three years' trial;
and the number of science lectures delivered annually
decreased by sixty per cent. between 1835 and 1850.
At the Liverpool School of Arts, where there was a
connected scheme of evening classes in eighteen departments under twenty-six masters, chemistry and natural
philosophy had been dropped owing to the egress of
working mechanics. One writer complains that even
those who came to study desired only as much instruction as had a direct bearing on their trades.[2] Another
found, 'from a comparison of a large number of
institutes,' that the attendance at evening classes com-
prised 'less than one-sixth of the total number of
members,' and that even the classes for elementary
instruction had not increased 'in proportion to the
number of members,' and 'those for more advanced
studies still less so.'[3] Nor is this remarkable, when we
remember that the majority had received no previous
schooling or had lost the habit of application.

James Hole, who wrote a history of Mechanics'
Institutes, observes that 'small means and small
advantages mutually alternate as cause and effect.'
The artisan 'does not subscribe to the Institute, for he
can gain little by so doing; and the Institute can give
him nothing because he furnishes no means.'[4] The

---

[1] Cf. Report of Society of Arts on Industrial Instruction (1853), 37.

[2] A secretary of the Leeds Institute—Traice, Handbook of Mechanics'
Institutes (2nd ed., 1863), 11.

[3] Hole, op. cit., 34 (1852).

[4] Ibid., 88. The Secretary of the Warrington Institute writes: ' Our
subscription is so low that we cannot afford to pay teachers and are
dependent on gratuitous aid '—Report of Society of Arts on Industrial
Instruction (1853), 193.

annual subscription varied from six to twenty-four shillings, the latter sum being often prohibitive, especially where the payment was quarterly. Hole asserted that the tendency to reduce subscriptions had gone too far ; and that, if efficient teaching were provided to meet their needs, working men might be trusted to contribute their share, which could be supplemented from other sources. Assuming that their demand was for elementary instruction, there was one eminent example which seemed to bear out the argument. The Huddersfield Institute was maintained on a weekly subscription somewhat above the average, supplemented by generous contributions from the local manufacturers. It offered an elementary course, conducted by an efficient staff of paid and unpaid teachers, which was largely recruited from the neighbouring college. In 1852 there were 800 students in attendance, the great majority of them working men.[1] In so far, however, as the Institutes held to their original design of providing ' higher ' education, the argument is little to the point. The evidence seems to show that, if there had been any considerable demand for teaching of an advanced standard, the financial problem would have been comparatively small. The difficulty was to allocate funds to the support of a science class which only a small, perhaps an infinitesimal, minority could be induced to attend.

Two methods of reconstruction were suggested, the one directly, the other incidentally, by the early experiences of the movement. The first aimed at reestablishing the Institutes, or broadening their resources, by a process of federation. The second introduced

---

[1] Hole, *op. cit.*, 34, 39, 93.

the principle of differential grading—or, in other words, of adapting different institutions to different demands.

The Yorkshire Union of Mechanics' Institutes [1] was the most conspicuous of a series of county federations commencing in the year 1837. Its original aim was to engage a permanent staff of lecturers, who should visit the affiliated Institutes in rotation and give concurrent courses on chemistry, mechanics, political economy, and general subjects; but, though the principle of effecting economies by wholesale purchase was in itself a pregnant discovery, the scheme seems to have met with little success. The real work of the Union commenced a few years later, when the sum of £200 was raised among the Yorkshire gentry and a salaried lecturer, or organiser, was appointed to go the round of the Institutes, any of which might obtain his services at a reduced fee. By means of its annual report, the Union was able to advertise plans and suggest improvements. It published a list of available lecturers, offered manuscript lectures on loan, gave the names of gentlemen willing to render gratuitous service, and issued a catalogue of second-hand books. The organiser spent his time travelling about the district, giving instruction, advising local committees, and promoting new Institutes. Lastly there was an annual meeting of delegates, to discuss the business of the Union and to compare the experiences of the past year.[2] In 1859 it was asserted that the Yorkshire Institutes 'not only supply the educational wants of working men, but are mainly supported and in many cases actually managed by them'; forty years later, there were 274 affiliated societies, many of them in a vigorous condition, with

[1] It developed out of the West Riding Union, founded in 1837.
[2] Hole, *op. cit.*, 123–6.

a total membership of 58,000.[1] Notwithstanding the
failure of ' higher ' education,[2] the Union succeeded in
securing for its constituents a career of even prosperity
and preserved them from the chequered fortunes which
elsewhere characterised the history of the movement.
A number of societies throughout the country perished
as soon as the original following withdrew. Some
lingered on as billiard saloons in the hands of a clique.
Others, in the latter half of the century, transferred their
premises and appointments to the local authorities
under the Public Library Acts. A certain number survived as the home of Government Evening Schools.
The Mechanics' Institute at Manchester developed after
a long period of stagnation into a School of Technology.
The parent Institute in London became a branch of
the City Polytechnic.

The Institutes represent one side of a general movement for the Diffusion of Useful Knowledge, necessarily
experimental in its methods and from the outset handicapped by assumptions the falsity of which became
the text of a later generation of workers who built on its
ruins. Birkbeck's first efforts were full of promise.
His enlightenment was free from the taint of patronage.
He wished to share with others the fruits of his learning,
and he made a silent appeal to the comradeship of his
hearers. The decision of his artisan students at Glasgow
to continue their class, when he left the city in 1804,
showed that he had been working on right lines. But

---

[1] Barnett Blake, paper on Mechanics' Institutes of Yorkshire (Ludlow
and Jones, op. cit., 170). Greenwood, Public Libraries, 476.

[2] A statement in 1860 shows that very little provision was made for
teaching other than elementary, and adds that not more than one-third
of the members attended classes and that many of those attending were
children—see Mansbridge, Survey of Working-Class Educational Movements, 31. Cf. ' In most places where they (the Institutes) have succeeded,
there are only boys and girls attending ' (Manchester)—Report of Society
of Arts on Industrial Instruction (1853), 187.

it may well have been too soon for him to draw the moral of his own success; and when later on he was called to assist in an organised movement, he became associated with lesser men who had neither his humility nor his perception of the difference between education and instruction. It is probably less true to say that they overrated the intelligence of artisans than that they failed to discover it. The effort of which this class is capable revealed itself gradually at a later stage to those who approached them as individuals, and whose primary aim was not to enlighten the masses, but to get in touch with their minds. It is clear that the Mechanics' Institutes failed to utilise the corporate sentiment which had begun to permeate industrial movements, while it is doubtful whether the best means of arousing enthusiasm lay in an appeal to intellectual interests directly related to material pursuits. The importance of the second method of reconstruction, to which we have referred, is that it not merely involves an attempt to analyse the popular demand, but introduces also new preconceptions and forms of appeal which distinguish the movements commencing in the latter half of the century under the influence of Maurice and the Christian Socialists.

The first experiment was on behalf of the masses, for which the Mechanics' Institutes were manifestly too advanced. The Lyceums which were opened in 1838 at Manchester and other centres were Institutes of a lower grade, combining recreation with miscellaneous instruction of an elementary type. They promised well so long as the novelty lasted, but they appear to have developed little corporate vitality and failed to maintain their hold.[1] A People's Instruction Society,

[1] For a time ' eminently successful, the people eagerly availing themselves of the novelty . . . of cheap newspapers, recreation and mutual improvement'—Goddard, *Life of Birkbeck*, 142. *Cf.* Hole, 26 ; Hudson, 140.

founded a few years later at Birmingham by a working man named Brooks, seemed to foreshadow a new order of things. The equipment—consisting of a reading-room, chess-room, and library, with a debating society, lectures, elementary classes, and music, not to mention the provision of refreshments, tea-parties, and excursions, all for a nominal subscription—may have differed little from that of a Lyceum; but there was evidently a higher tone among the members, assisted no doubt by the personality of the founder, and a sense of pride in an institution which they could call their own. Charles Knight, who visited the society two years after its foundation, described it in prophetic language as an ideal working men's club.[1]

Meanwhile, as regards the approach to higher education, a counterpart to the club appears in the conception of a Working Men's College—a term chosen, in preference to 'Institute,' to convey an ideal of humane culture reared on a basis of democratic comradeship. While the Mechanics' Institutes were falling into decay, social unrest provided a stimulus and motive to educational effort that had been previously lacking. To those who interpreted public events from the standpoint of Christian socialism, the most impressive feature in the Chartist agitation, side by side with its evidence of social disunion, was the absence of ideals and guiding principles in any way commensurate with the passion it evoked. The moral purport of the movement was a claim on the part of the industrial classes to political manhood; but its source lay in an unhealthy state of society. The new forces which had been called into play seemed likely to waste them-

---

[1] Knight, *Passages in a Working Life*, iii. 84 *sq.* Brooks was a stockinger and Methodist, one of the many examples of poor men who understood the needs and spirit of their class.

selves in ineffectual, because ignorant, revolt, and to degenerate on the return of prosperity, for want of higher ideals, in the pursuit of selfish and commonplace ambitions. It was necessary that education should start with the problem of social reconstruction, and should be grounded on a deeper and more spiritual analysis than had underlain earlier movements. The new ideal was not information, but the enrichment of personality; a conception which at the outset tended to draw a hard distinction between liberal and technical studies. The development of individuality was approached through an appeal to corporate feeling. Lastly, following out the conception of social reunion and admitting the postulate of human brotherhood, it was claimed that education is a reciprocal process, involving an interchange of thought between teachers and learners and a persistent reaction of mind on mind. It is perhaps more than a coincidence that the fiasco of the last Chartist petition in 1848 was followed within six months by the reorganisation of the People's College at Sheffield on a democratic basis. It is certain that the founders of the Working Men's College in Red Lion Square claimed the twofold inspiration of Chartism and the Sheffield experiment.

CHAPTER VI

LIBRARIES AND LITERATURE

In the early days of the British Society School in the Borough Road the children were taught to read from the Bible, no other textbook being admitted; but those who made sufficient progress at this stage were enabled to study further on their own account with the help of the school library. The authorities did their best to encourage an inquisitive spirit, and let it work its way.[1] In so far as the business of a teacher is to induce his pupils to educate themselves, the method was commendable; and it was one which reflected the general course of mental development among the working classes of the period. In the schools few children were taught, and few adults aimed at acquiring, much more than the elements; but, given the power to read with tolerable fluency, knowledge of some sort would follow in its train. The Library formed the most valuable feature in a Mechanics' Institute, and remained a centre of attraction when classrooms and lectures had been generally abandoned. The mass of the people, for whom no organised instruction was provided in after life, depended for information almost

In the notes to this chapter *C.P.L.* is an abbreviation for *Select Committee on Public Libraries, 1849*.

[1] 'We find that, if once an inquisitive spirit is excited in their minds, knowledge they will have and will not rest till they obtain it'—*Select Committee on Education, 1834*, Q. 275.

entirely on the standard or ephemeral literature which was accumulated in newsrooms and popular libraries, or which they were able to purchase.

In a valuable monograph by Edward Edwards on the 'Paucity of Libraries open to the Public in the British Empire,' dated April 1848, the writer reckons the number of ' Public ' Libraries in the United Kingdom at thirty, two-thirds of which were University and other collections not really accessible to the general public. In Great Britain, he added on a later occasion, ' there are no free lending libraries . . . of any kind.' [1] The nearest approach to a public library, in the modern sense, was to be found in the Chetham Library at Manchester and the Williams Ecclesiastical Library in the City of London. Neither of these could be described as popular or modern in its equipment and resources ; and, though the former was frequented by artisans and factory operatives, the reason appears to have been that it served the purpose of a newsroom and contained a supply of quarterly periodicals.[2] The first instance of a library supported out of the rates occurs at Warrington, where in June 1848 a reference library was formed in conjunction with a museum under the Museums Act of 1845 ; a similar course being pursued at Salford in the following year.[3]

It is misleading to compare England with other countries where State action was more fully organised,

---

[1] *C.P.L.*, Q. 281.

[2] *Ibid.*, Q. 1167 *sq.* The Williams Library, like the Chetham Library, required applicants to write their names and addresses in an entry book (Q. 980 *sqq.*) ; the British Museum Library required a voucher of respectability (Q. 154). Both appear to have been used to a slight extent by artisans (Q. 1006, 1038, 2829).

[3] *Ibid.*, p. xiv, Q. 1685 *sqq.* *Libraries and Museums Returns, 1852–3,* P.P. 312. The Warrington Library was used by the working classes (*C.P.L.*, Q. 1711).

without taking into account the growth of voluntary enterprise, which afforded some compensation and gave play to a large amount of public-spirited enthusiasm. The Artists' Repository established at Birmingham in 1797, and the village libraries and book societies of which there is some record towards the close of the eighteenth century,[1] set an example which was widely followed during the next fifty years. Libraries were formed in connection with elementary schools, ragged schools and schools of design, churches and chapels, factories and Poor Law Institutions, and coffee-houses frequented by the working class. Parochial and village libraries sprang up in towns and rural districts, from Buckinghamshire to the West of England, and from the collieries of Staffordshire and South Wales to the mining centres of the North. In some cases the village library would form the centre for a mutual improvement circle; while Friendly and Co-operative Societies and other adult organisations had often a museum and library at their places of meeting. There were also special libraries, on a larger scale, for artisans and apprentices at Liverpool, Sheffield, and Nottingham.

Most of the literature in school and parochial libraries appears to have been derived from the Society for Promoting Christian Knowledge, the Religious Tract Society, and the Kildare Place Society in Dublin, and consisted of moral and religious pieces, history books, biography, poetry, stories of travel and adventure, magazines for the young, and elementary treatises on industry and science. In other cases the nature of the supply varied enormously. The principal Mechanics' Institutes in the manufacturing districts possessed a varied collection of standard works on mathematical

[1] See Chap. III. A circulating library was opened at Birmingham by William Hutton, bookseller, in 1751—Hutton, *Life of himself*, 279.

and scientific subjects.[1] Smaller societies were inundated with gift books, Annual Registers, and religious magazines.[2] The supply in some institutions was subjected to a rigid censorship which excluded light literature, politics, and controversial theology;[3] and others purchased nothing but fiction.[4] This exclusiveness was partly responsible for a noteworthy and characteristic development. If fiction and periodical literature were all that the majority of men could be expected to relish after the day's work, a library composed mainly of fiction, and one that put a veto on controversial topics, were alike distasteful to the politician and to the more serious readers. It was not unusual, therefore, for the latter to collect libraries of their own;[5] while others combined to form library societies, commonly lodging their books in the public-house where the group met for reading and discussion.[6] A difficulty common to all these forms of voluntary effort, with the exception of a few opulent institutions, was to maintain a continuous supply of fresh material. It was comparatively easy to start a library; but it often happened that, when

---

[1] Hudson, *Adult Education*, 197 ; *Handbook of Mechanics' Institutes, 1839* (Society for the Diffusion of Useful Knowledge), 55.

[2] *C.P.L.*, Q. 1212.

[3] *Ibid.*, Q. 1220, 2494.   [4] *Ibid.*, Q. 1194, 1200.

[5] ' I know a great number who have very respectable libraries '—*C.P.L.*, Q. 2796 (Lovett).

[6] Thus a group of readers, objecting to the exclusion of controversial works from the Operatives' and Artisans' Library at Nottingham, withdrew and ' formed a new library, and the books are kept in public-houses, and there they go and pay a small subscription, and perhaps take a glass of ale and read . . . the books are mostly novels . . . still there are a great many political works '—*Ibid.*, Q. 1216 *sq.* Library of 800 formed by Spitalfields workmen—*ibid.*, Q. 2709 ; *cf.*, Q. 1244, 1327 *sq.*, 2490. Ludlow and Jones, *Progress of the Working Class* (1867), refer to a mutual improvement society of wood-carvers, founded 1833, which acquired a valuable collection of books, casts and engravings (p. 179 *n.*) ; also to a book-buying and lending society formed by six workmen of Sunderland, who collected old English ballads (p. 180).

the original stock was exhausted, interest waned and the books were ultimately sold for what they would fetch.[1] The simplest remedy, which was adopted in some cases, was to create a maintenance fund by levying a small weekly subscription or a charge on the loan of books, the proceeds of which might be devoted to fresh purchases.[2] An extension of this method is seen in the circulating libraries which were established by Mechanics' Institutes and developed with permanent results by means of federations covering a wide area.[3]

From the problem of library organisation we pass back to more general questions concerning the supply of literature available for purchasers of small means. The situation at the commencement of the century, when many of the poor had acquired some taste for reading and were compelled to rely for materials on the local market, was singularly discouraging. The scenes which Charles Knight witnessed as a youth near his home at Windsor are a fair indication of what occurred on market days in every provincial town. There was the artisan who spent ' his sixpence upon an antiquated manual of history or geography, to which he would devote his brief and hard-earned hours of leisure ' ; the ' careful matron tempted to buy the first number of the " Pilgrim's Progress " or the " Book of Martyrs "—

[1] *C.P.L.*, Q. 303, 1951 *sqq.*

[2] *Ibid.*, Q. 2053 *sqq.* ; the practice appears to have been general in parochial libraries.

[3] The Chichester Mechanics' Institute circulated books among the villages of the county, placing them under the charge of some farmer or responsible person—*Handbook of Mechanics' Institutes (1839)*, 61. Circulating libraries were organised by the Northern Union of Mechanics' Institutes (founded 1848), the Lancashire and Cheshire Union (1848), and the Yorkshire Union. The Yorkshire Village Library, formed in 1858 by amalgamating with the Library of the Yorkshire Union two other local itinerating libraries, has had a prosperous career; in 1913–14 its circulation exceeded 240,000.

perhaps one less discreet bestowing her attention upon the " History of Witchcraft " or the " Lives of Highwaymen "—each arranging with the canvasser for their monthly delivery till the works should be complete, when they would find themselves in possession of the dearest books that came from the press, even in the palmy days of expensive luxuries ' ; and for the young there were ' sixpenny novels with a coloured frontispiece, whose very titles would invite to a familiarity with the details of crime—something much more dreadful than the old-world stories, the dreams and divinations of the ancient chap-books.' [1]

Commercial enterprise and the effort of philanthropic or propagandist groups were already contributing to improve the situation ; both phases of the movement during the first half of the nineteenth century having this in common, that they aimed not so much at circulating standard works in a cheap edition as at producing a special literature for popular use.[2] The first important advance is ascribed to religious associations, of which the Society for Promoting Christian Knowledge is a characteristic example. The nature of its aims is shown by the development, between 1812 and 1832, of anti-infidel and general literature committees, which by

[1] Knight, *Passages in a Working Life*, i. 226 *sq.* ' Are you able to state how the lower classes in London are supplied with literature ?—By accident altogether. It is a scramble in London ; whoever can get a penny, buys a book. There is no provision in London in that respect for any poor person '—*C.P.L.*, Q. 1242.

[2] Moritz, *Travels in England in 1782* (English ed., 1886), 36, mentions ' The Entertaining Museum and Complete Circulating Library,' a series issued in weekly numbers (sixpence to ninepence each) and consisting of English classics and translations from the best foreign literature. *Cf.* the following item in Lacey's *Library for the People* (1827)—' The Chimney Corner Companion . . . an exhaustless and everlasting magazine of the curiosities and good things in the entire circle of literature, books and knowledge, adapted to all tastes, fancies, ages and conditions, and containing the quintessence of many thousand volumes, and everything worthy of being read that ever was printed, in history, biography, politics, medicine, law,' etc. (prospectus, see *Mechanics' Magazine*, March 31, 1827).

means of a network of district organisations promoted libraries and distributed a multitude of tracts, narratives, and educational treatises on most branches of knowledge. It is to some such operation that Cobbett refers in 1821, when, in the course of a tour in the Forest of Dean, he came upon ' two lazy-looking fellows, in great coats and bundles in their hands, going into a cottage.' ' Vagabonds of this description,' he exclaims, ' are seen all over the country . . . they vend tea, drugs and religious tracts.' [1]   In the same year appeared a publication of a very different kind—the *Labourer's Friend and Handicrafts Chronicle*, a monthly periodical sold at sixpence, the first of a long series of magazines dealing in technical and general information, which anticipated the trade journals of a later date.   The most successful of the earlier group was the *Mechanics' Magazine*, which was started by Hodgskin and Joseph Robertson in 1823 and issued monthly at threepence. Professing chiefly to instruct artisans in the history and principles of their respective trades and to keep them informed of the latest improvements, it commanded a large sale from the outset and seems to have maintained its popularity for several years. Working men contributed articles, and their correspondence gives the modern reader an insight into their point of view on education and self-improvement and into the numerous embarrassments to which their efforts were exposed.[2]

---

[1] *Rural Rides*, Nov. 14, 1821.

[2] Similar magazines, started at the same time, became rapidly extinct. The earliest trade-union journal was the *Trades' Newspaper and Mechanics' Weekly Journal*, founded 1825 by the Committee of the London Trades' Delegates. After the revival of trade unionism in 1843, we have the *Potters' Magazine*, the *Mechanics' Magazine* (Steam Engine and Machine Makers' Friendly Society, 1841–7), and the *Flint Glass Makers' Magazine* (monthly, octavo, pp. 96, founded 1850 ; it advocated the 'education of every man in our trade' ; 'we say to you . . . get intelligence instead of alcohol . . . it is sweeter and more lasting ')—Webb, *Trade Unionism*, 178–80.

In the meantime the idea of a special series for the
people had commended itself to a few well-known
publishing firms. Constable commenced his weekly
Miscellany in 1827, to 'extend useful knowledge and
elegant literature . . . within the reach of every class
of reader.' Lacey followed with his *Library for the
People*; and Chambers, with the *Edinburgh Journal,
Information for the People, Papers for the People*, and
Educational Course.

The most attractive figure in the cheap literature
movement is Charles Knight, to whose writings every
student of literary enterprise owes a debt of gratitude.
The son of an enlightened bookseller at Windsor, he
inherited a taste for letters and developed a keen
interest in social affairs. With ample opportunity
for observing the disadvantages under which poor
men struggled in quest of books, he convinced himself
that a large amount of crime and disorder in the country
might be traced to unclean reading or to provocative
literature which was circulated among the people in
an age of unrest. The notion of counterbalancing
what was cheap and obnoxious with a supply of wholesome material, which should come as far as possible
within reach of the poorest, runs through his correspondence from an early period. In 1814 he spoke
of publishing in weekly parts a series of treatises on
law, religion, history, art, science, and matters of
general interest, but with no immediate result. His
first venture was the *Plain Englishman*, a newspaper
intended for the working man, which commenced in
1820, but failed to attract attention. His opportunity
came some years later, when he was formally engaged
as publisher to the Society for the Diffusion of Useful
Knowledge—an organisation founded by Brougham
and others in 1826 with the object of imparting ' useful

knowledge to all classes of the community, particularly to such as are unable to avail themselves of experienced teachers or may prefer learning by themselves.' Its publications, including the *Penny Encyclopaedia*, the *Libraries of Entertaining and Useful Knowledge*, and the *Penny Magazine*, were advertised and dispensed by local committees in the principal towns, and enjoyed a period of apparent success.   Ultimately the circulation fell and the Society suspended its work in 1846, having incurred a heavy deficit.   Two years before, Knight had made a new venture on his own account, which was in some ways a fulfilment of his original scheme.   He published, first weekly and then monthly, shilling octavo volumes, of 300 pages each, which he suggested might form the basis of ' Book Clubs for all readers.' He shared the fate of his patrons, and gave up the under-taking on financial grounds after a four years' trial.

There is no kind of association better able to cover its retreat with a cloud of statistics and testimonies, than one engaged in disseminating literature with a philanthropic object. Instances were produced from the poorer parts of London, in which casual labourers had thrown aside their periodical horrors and invested in the *Penny Magazine*; while an artisan, in his autobio-graphy, takes occasion to inform us that, having borrowed the first volume, he found means to purchase the re-mainder of the series by abandoning the use of sugar in his tea.   The Tract Societies could point to similar achievements, and might justly claim to have commenced a revolution in the supply of textbooks and stories for the young.   But neither the Useful Knowledge Society nor the religious associations met generally with the success for which they hoped.   The common criticism that the former aimed too high, the latter too low, affords at least a partial explanation.   Knight somewhere complains that the Society for Promoting Christian Knowledge addressed 'working people as if they were as innocent of all knowledge, both of good and evil, as in the days when their mothers committed them to the edifying instruction of the village schoolmistress.' Its apologist would be justified in retorting that Brougham and his friends went to the opposite extreme. Their treatises were 'valuable,' but 'by no means adapted to the wants of the classes for which they were ostensibly intended.'[1] The *Penny Magazine* laboured under the same disadvantage—'perhaps too good, because too scientific,' as its friends explained. The firm of Chambers were wiser in their generation. Their journal combined amusement with instruction, and outlived its rival.

Knight himself suggested a more fundamental cause of failure. In the year that his society suspended operations, he refers to the revival of a taste for inferior literature. There were fourteen penny and halfpenny magazines on the market, twelve social and economic journals, and close on forty weekly sheets and booklets of a sensational character. Foremost among the popular magazines stood the *London Journal,* the *Family Herald,* and *Reynolds' Miscellany*—sold by thousands every week and patronised by factory girls, clerks and apprentices in the back streets—which he describes with some contempt as harmless productions, devoid of originality and matter. The language is significant. There is reason to suppose that many of the worst prints had disappeared from the market, and that the societies had played their part in raising the standard.[2]

[1] *Journal of Society of Arts,* ii. 438. *Cf. Handbook of Mechanics' Institutes* (Knight, 1839); *Mechanics' Magazine,* Jan. 3, 1829, Feb. 23, 1833; *Quarterly Review,* No. 168, 1849.

[2] Martineau, *History of the Peace,* i. 580. Knight, *Passages, etc.,* ii. 328; *The Old Printer and the Modern Press,* 300. Ludlow and Jones, *Progress of the Working Class,* 182 *sq.*

It is equally probable that, in so doing, they had stimulated competition from another quarter and to some
extent prepared the way for an ephemeral literature
whose aim was to satisfy, rather than to educate,
a popular demand. It was left for a future generation to realise more fully the comparative uselessness
of creating an artificial supply, and the necessity of
so developing a taste for letters in early life that
the laws of supply and demand may operate with
beneficial effect.

When we turn from the mass to the individual,
the signs of progress are more easily discerned. From
the earlier generation whose achievements are written
in the ‘Pursuit of Knowledge under Difficulties’ to
that of Francis Place and Thomas Cooper,[1] the succession

---

[1] It is characteristic of Francis Place that, when out of work and half
starved, he waded through ‘ many volumes in history, voyages, politics,
law and philosophy, Adam Smith and Locke, and especially Hume’s
Essays and Treatises.’ This was in 1793, when he was a journeyman
tailor, aged 22. Previously he had mastered ‘ histories of Greece and
Rome and some translated works of Greek and Roman writers ; Smollett,
Fielding’s novels, and Robertson’s works ; some of Hume’s Essays, some
translations from French writers, and much on geography ; some books
on anatomy and surgery ; some relating to science and the arts. . . .
Blackstone, Hale’s Common Law, several other law books and much
biography.’ Most of these books were borrowed for him by his land-
lady, who had the care of chambers in the Temple—Wallas, *Life of Place.*
Cooper’s time-table, during the period when he worked as a shoemaker at
Gainsborough, will explain a serious breakdown in health from which he
recovered with some difficulty. ‘ Historical reading, or the grammar
of some language, or translation was my first employment on week-day
mornings, whether I rose at three or four, until seven o’clock when I sat
down to the stall. A book or a periodical in my hand while I breakfasted,
gave me another half-hour’s reading. I had another half-hour, and sometimes an hour’s reading, or study of language, from one to two o’clock,
at the time of dinner. . . . I sat at work till eight, sometimes nine at
night ; and then either read or walked about our little room and committed Hamlet to memory, or the rhymes of some other poet, until
compelled to go to bed from sheer exhaustion. . . . I was seldom later
in bed than three or four in the morning ; and when, in the coldness of
winter, we could not afford to have a fire till my mother rose, I used to
put a lamp on a stool which I placed on a little round table ; and standing
before it, wrapped up in my mother’s old red cloak, I read on till seven.
. . . In the finer seasons of the year I was invariably on the hills, or in

of students among the poorer classes had never failed.
It was natural that their number should increase
during the first half of the nineteenth century.
Educational facilities were improving; competition
and steam-power had lowered the price of good literature and extended the supply; and the stir of life,
accompanying economic change and political movement, created a thirst for knowledge in many directions.
It is unsafe to generalise from the case of popular
libraries reporting an increased circulation of works
on Mechanics, Philosophy, History, and Science ; [1] but it
was a common observation that, as a man settled down
to a course of reading, his taste in selection gradually
improved.[2] This is suggested by typical examples
which enable us to form some conception of the progress
made under varying circumstances and among different
groups. Thus in rural Buckinghamshire, where there
was great ignorance and little time for reading, the
'Pilgrim's Progress,' 'Robinson Crusoe,' and 'Cook's
Voyages' are mentioned among the most popular
works in a village library.[3] In an institution attached
to the parish of St. Martin-in-the-Fields, Scott's novels
attracted some of the younger subscribers, who belonged
to the labouring class, and were said to interfere with
their attendance at church.[4] Elsewhere, especially in
the manufacturing and mining districts, a serious use
of literature was becoming every year more common.
A reading pitman in the Tyne Valley would have on

the lanes or woods, or by the Trent by sunrise or before ; and thus often
strolled several miles with my book in my hand, before I sat down in the
corner to work at seven o'clock '—Cooper, *Autobiography*, 59 *sqq.* He
afterwards came in touch with Charles Kingsley, and his career clearly
suggested certain passages in *Alton Locke* ; in one place he is mentioned
by name.

[1] *C.P.L.*, Q. 1960 *sq.* [2] *Ibid.*, Q. 2426.
[3] *Ibid.*, Q. 1381 ; the S.P.C.K. etc. did good work in this sphere.
[4] *Ibid.*, Q. 2053 *sqq.*

his shelf one or two of Scott's novels, a vol ume of mathematics or English History, and perhaps a few Methodist classics.[1] There were artisans who knew something of the works of Milton, Byron, or Shelley; and some, it was said, had considerable portions of Shakespeare by heart.[2] Astronomy was often popular ; and studies in natural history were pursued with great keenness by small groups in Lancashire and even in the crowded parts of London, who collected literature on the subject and made periodical excursions into the neighbouring country in search of specimens.[3] Political reading was encouraged by the events of the period ; and, where the opportunity existed, there was some attempt to discover both sides of an argument.[4] There was occasionally a turn for more abstract speculations in philosophy and religion.

A branch of literature which exercised perhaps the widest influence remains to be considered.   Newspapers and partisan or sectarian tracts were said to drive the educational magazines from the market.[5]   Newsrooms formed the most popular feature in the Lyceums and in a number of the Mechanics' Institutes.   To exclude from a working-class library writings which had a bear-

---

[1] *Our Coals and Coalpits*, by a Traveller Underground (1853), 218, 225.

[2] *C.P.L.*, Q. 1372 *sqq.* ; Engels, *State of the Working Class*, 240.

[3] ' I have often heard working men, whose fustian jackets scarcely held together, speak upon geological, astronomical and other subjects, with more knowledge than the most cultivated bourgeois in Germany possess '—Engels, *op. cit.*, 239.   Mrs. Gaskell, *Mary Barton*, ch. v, refers to the botanists of Kersal Moor.

[4] ' I find that when their means admit of it, they never allow themselves to be confined to their own side ; . . . they take Blackwood, Tait and so on '—*C.P.L.*, Q. 1327.   It is said that the early Socialist movement developed an interest in continental theories of society, and that a few had got so far as to read foreign literature in the original—see Engels, 229 ; *C.P.L.*, Q. 1199, 1240 ; *A Working Man's Way in the World*, by a Journeyman Printer, 65 *sq.*, 92 *sq.*

[5] Gaskell, *Manufacturing Population*, 280 *sq.* ; *Select Committee on Education, 1835*, Q. 83–6.

ing on politics and current events was the best way of
ensuring its decline.

Controversial literature has made part of the stock-
in-trade of every popular movement since the people
became responsive to a written appeal. It was employed
by radicals at the close of the eighteenth century,
and revived in the critical times which followed the
Peace of 1815. From the rise of the Hampden Clubs
to the last phase of Chartism, every agitation—political,
social, or religious—had its paraphernalia of tracts and
handbills, printed at headquarters and industriously
dispersed. In the course of time, pamphlets of a more
elaborate and impartial character, together with the
leading quarterly Reviews, might be found at coffee-
houses and at various libraries and institutions accessible
to the working class. The coffee-houses played also
an important part in popularising the daily and weekly
press. At the commencement of the century few
artisans had the energy to look at a newspaper.[1] At
times of excitement, during a General Election or at a
critical stage in the war, the journeymen in a workshop
might club together to take in the *Courier* or the
Independent Whig, employing one of their number
to read its contents ;[2] but interest was apparently
not maintained. The cheap coffee-houses, which multiplied rapidly in London and the provinces in later years,
provided a meeting-place at which they could assemble
for meals and obtain the papers *gratis.*[3]

Few developments in the eighteenth century are

---

[1] *Westminster Review,* x. 476.

[2] Knight, *Memoirs of a Working Man, by a Tailor,* 90, 170.

[3] *Westminster Review, l.c.; Select Committee on Education, 1835,*
Q. 810. Coffee-houses, etc., containing newspapers, periodicals and
libraries up to 2000 vols.—*C.P.L.,* Q. 2773 ; *cf. Porter, Progress of the
Nation* (1850), 686 *sq.* Even in the early years of the previous century,
a foreign observer speaks of ' workmen ' beginning the day ' by going to
coffee-rooms in order to read the latest news '—De Saussure, *op. cit.,* 162.

more significant than the process by which journalism
passed from a bare narrating of events to the discussion
of policy, ending in a direct appeal to the man with a
grievance, which was renewed on the recrudescence of
agitation after the Peace of 1815.[1]   From the beginning
it had been viewed by conservatives with consistent
suspicion, and the profession of 'news-writing' was
held in contempt; but when to the discussion of policy
was added the criticism of established institutions, a
sharper contrast came to be drawn between expensive
newspapers which professed respectability and circulated among the wealthier classes, and the products of
the cheap press which came within reach of the poor.
That violence was confined to no party, and that the
cheap press on the whole had probably the merit, claimed
for Cobbett's *Political Register*, of winning the people
from purposeless riots to more deliberate forms of agitation pursued by relatively peaceful methods, were
arguments which involved subtle distinctions and were
not calculated to allay suspicion.   The discourse which
came home to an uneducated populace was of the kind
for which no excuse is offered by friends or accepted by
opponents; and it attacked with undisguised ferocity
most of the institutions and beliefs to which the governing classes attached social importance.   It was remarked
that in 1816 every manufacturing town of any size had
its 'seditious' journal, and that a Manchester weekly
reserved a special column to advertise anti-Christian
literature at a price accessible to the artisan.[2]   The

---

[1] A considerable impulse was given to this type of journalism by
Cobbett, who in 1816 reduced the price of his *Political Register* to 2*d.*,
devoting the first number to an ' address to the journeymen and labourers '
of the United Kingdom; it immediately attained an immense popularity—Knight, *Passages, etc.*, i. 188 ; Bamford, *Passages in the Life of
a Radical*, 7 (2nd ed., 1848).

[2] Knight, *Passages*, i. 234 ; *cf.* Walpole, *History of England*, i. 457.

very names of such publications as the *Gorgon*, the
Black Dwarf, and *Medusa's Head*, betokened no desire
for safe paths and easy compromise. In the legislation
which followed, neither of the great parties appears to
advantage ; but the Tories had at least the courage of
their convictions. Southey's advice to Lord Liverpool :
' You must crush the press or it will destroy the Constitution,' is more generous than the companion utterance of
Brougham : ' The Radicals have made themselves so
odious that a number even of our way of thinking
would be well enough pleased to see them and their
vile press put down at all hazards.' The sequel is
instructive. The stamp duty on whole-sheet newspapers which had been raised to fourpence in 1815
was extended in 1819 to all daily and weekly periodicals
costing less than sixpence.[1] That the measure was
intended as a weapon of defence appears from the fact
that certain publications, which were considered harmless, were permitted to pass unstamped. None the less
it was open to the objections which may be urged against
prohibitionist legislation in general, besides incurring
special odium as a ' tax on knowledge.' No form of
espionage could prevent the weekly circulation of a
multitude of illicit prints, which were often the des-
perate effusions of souls embittered by the struggle for
liberty. At the same time the cost of papers which
might have presented a different view of the situation
was maintained at a prohibitive rate. All duties connected with the publishing trade were sooner or later
condemned as a ' premium on rubbish,' and were
gradually repealed.[2]

[1] In 1820 a Constitutional Association was formed ' for supporting
the laws for suppressing seditious publications,' etc. It was known
popularly as the Bridge Street gang.

[2] Stamp duty reduced to 1*d.* 1836, repealed 1855 ; advertisement
duty repealed 1853 ; paper duty repealed 1861. Hetherington, Cleave,

The Owenite and Chartist movements produced a series of journals which sprang suddenly into existence and often disappeared within a few months of their birth, or became incorporated with others of a similar tendency. The early co-operative papers, which were beyond the means of the working class, were succeeded by penny monthlies and weeklies which had a considerable sale in Lancashire and Cheshire. The claim that they were the only popular periodicals ' which dealt with religion and politics and recognised science as one of the features of general progress ' is exaggerated ; [1] but that they stimulated thought and dispensed a good deal of useful information, need not be questioned. The Chartist papers were generally of a different description. ' A ribald sincerity and a frantic courage ' is Kingsley's comment. Some of them, however, edited by men of ability, flourished for a time.

The decline of the Chartist movement was followed by a period of comparative quiet and unbounded confidence in the future. The optimism inspired by free trade, which applied to the press as to other phases of national activity, is echoed in the last words of Charles Knight, as he looked back on the struggles of a lifetime, on the whole well content with an improvement which fell short of his earlier hopes. ' Let the cheap press purify itself. We have got beyond the scurrilous stage—the indecent stage—the profane stage —the seditious stage. Let us hope that the frivolous stage, in which we are now to some extent abiding,

and James Watson are remembered as the trio who defied imprisonment for the free press ; and it is said that 500 of Hetherington's sellers suffered in this way (Holyoake, *History of Co-operation*, i. 102). Hammond (*Farm Servant and Agricultural Labourer*, 34) estimates, about the year 1850, that 29,000,000 unstamped periodicals were circulated annually in defiance of the law.

[1] Holyoake, *op. cit.*, i. 143.

will in time pass on to a higher taste and sounder mental discipline.'

The newspapers and magazines served not only to exercise the power of reading acquired in the elementary schools, but gave also some scope to composition; articles, verse, and correspondence being not infrequently contributed by working-class readers.[1] The modern plan of essay-writing in connection with adult education was foreshadowed in a series of prize compositions, which were encouraged by Mechanics' Institutes and publishing firms. The Prize Essays on Social Science published by Cassell in 1859 represent a good deal of serious effort; but that the practice was open to abuse, is shown by the case in which a prize was offered for the best novel by a working man. The examiner on this occasion complained of 'wading for days together through hopeless trash.'[2]

Spontaneous composition appeared mainly in the form of pamphlets on social and economic questions, verse, and autobiographical sketches. The north country, and in particular the Craven district of Yorkshire, was at this time full of rhymers and versifiers—Frank King, the Skipton minstrel, 'no scholard' but a man of parts, accustomed to improvise songs and ballads, vulgar and heroic, to suit all companies from the manor to the village tavern; John Broughton, and Will Cliffe, Lang Tom fra' Winskill, and Robert Story, the author of many pieces, lyrical, narrative, dramatic and political—men who made up for technical defects by a fund of native humour, a grasp of

---

[1] *C.P.L.*, Q. 1368 *sqq.*

[2] Knight, *Shadows of Old Booksellers*, 177. Mention may be made of a curious and lengthy religious epic, entitled *Musings of a Working Man on the Pains and Praise of Man's Great Substitute*, by Thomas Brown of Cellardyke, 1861; the author explains that it was an essay in mental recreation, and urges others of his class to follow his example.

local tradition, and a knowledge of their kind. The pamphlets[1] and reminiscences come, as a rule, from writers of some attainment ; they display considerable force and clearness of expression, and afford in some cases valuable material to the student of social history.

It is fitting to conclude with a reference to two remarkable men, whose writings possess some interest, and whose names are intimately associated with the fortunes of the class from which they sprang—Samuel Bamford, the Radical, and Thomas Cooper, the Chartist. Bamford was the son of an intelligent weaver, from whom he inherited his passion for literature. His early manhood was taken up with the political agitation which followed the close of the Napoleonic wars, and the course of which he has described in his ' Passages in the Life of a Radical' and in various pieces of occasional verse composed at the time. In later years, after a brief tenure of a government clerkship, he devoted himself to letters, the handloom, and the society of a few chosen friends. The circumstance that he was brought up in a Lancashire village towards the close of the eighteenth century gives the memoir of his ' Early Days' a peculiar fascination. It may be doubted whether there is any single work which brings the reader into such close personal contact with the inner history of the great economic revolution which was transforming the social life of the industrial classes. ' Passages in the Life of a Radical' takes up certain phases of the same development at a later stage, being an account of the political unrest which was temporarily suppressed by the passing of the Six Acts in 1819. The narrative is graphic, full of naïve criticism, singularly

---

[1] Pamphlets by trade unionists ; Webb, *Trade Unionism*, 76 *n.*, 104 *n. A Peasant's Voice to Landowners, etc.*, by John Denson, labourer, of Waterbeach, 1829. *Letters to Working People on the New Poor Law* (a defence of it), by a working man (John Latey), 1841.

impartial and lit up by quiet sallies of humour—such as his description of the indomitable herb-doctor marching up a contingent of villagers to 'Peterloo,' with skull and cross-bones floating in the breeze before them, as if he were ' heading a funeral procession of his own patients.' These two autobiographical pieces have been reprinted in a decent edition, prefaced with a very readable introduction. The volume of collected verse has no intrinsic merit. Keen intelligence and a kind of hardy culture are displayed in every page of his writings ; but the ' Early Days ' abounds in passages analysing his emotions which reveal unmistakably his lack of training and the sense of proportion.

Thomas Cooper also has left reminiscences which describe the vicissitudes of his career from childhood to old age in correct and straightforward English. Like Bamford, he attended a variety of schools, receiving what would then be considered a very fair elementary education, and in after life suffered imprisonment, though in a cause which the former was never disposed to appreciate. Both men developed altogether out of proportion to their early training, and displayed in their public life a sensitiveness of manner and an independence of judgment which set them above their fellows. Both, too, possessed a strong conservative instinct which came out with more than usual force as life advanced. Here the resemblance ceases. Cooper was a man of unique capacity and, in a peculiar sense of the term, a born student ; and his character was enriched by the softening influence of a deep religious experience, an inspiration which his predecessor apparently lacked. A strenuous self-discipline, which might have destroyed a man of less robust constitution, enabled him to pursue a wide range of studies in the intervals of manual labour. He became in due course a schoolmaster, a publicist and political agitator, a man of letters and a minister of religion, and formed the acquaintance of Kingsley and Carlyle. His works, which include an autobiography and sundry reminiscences, a volume of poetry, miscellaneous sketches and addresses on religious subjects, never attained any wide celebrity; but the student of men will not look in vain for evidence of an extraordinary character and a versatile intellect, and for the sage impressions born of the life-long experience of one who laboured for the common people and paid them the compliment of serious criticism.[1]

[1] *Life of Thomas Cooper*, by himself, 4th ed., 1873 ; *Wise Saws and Modern Instances*, 2 vols., 1845 ; a volume of poetry, including two epics noticeable mainly for their erudition (*The Purgatory of Suicides, a Prison Rhyme*, composed in Stafford Gaol, 1842, afterwards republished in a cheap edition by request of his admirers ; and the *Paradise of Martyrs*), and various shorter poems, ballads, and political songs ; several volumes of a Christian Evidence Series, based on lectures delivered throughout the kingdom in the latter half of his life ; *Thoughts at Fourscore*, 1885.

CHAPTER VII

EDUCATION BY COLLISION [1]

'Whatever might be the case in some other constitutions of society, the spirit of a commercial people will be, we are persuaded, essentially mean and slavish, wherever public spirit is not cultivated by an extensive participation of the people in the business of government in detail; nor will the desideratum of a general diffusion of intelligence among either the middle or lower classes be realised, but by a corresponding dissemination of public functions and a voice in public affairs'—J. S. Mill, *Dissertations and Discussions*, ii. 25 *sq.*

'Universal teaching must precede universal enfranchisement'—*Id., Representative Government* (1861), 160.

MILL'S Essay on 'Representative Government' concludes a series of dissertations which connect the philosophical radicalism of an earlier generation with more recent attempts to formulate a defence of democracy. The basis of his argument is a definition of the twofold aim of political institutions. The test of a political system is, partly the efficiency displayed in the management of public affairs, partly its success in promoting the 'general mental advancement of the

[1] 'In a large town the influences which educate a man against his will are almost incessant; there are so many public meetings. . . . That forms the most valuable part of the education which an Englishman receives?—Yes. It has put us beyond some of the nations of the Continent who have more school instruction. . . . Do you hold that this *Education by Collision*, as it may be called, is the best of all?—It makes them citizens' (*Committee on Public Libraries* (1849), Q. 1359–62). *Cf.* Harriet Martineau's estimate of the Anti-Corn-Law campaign in the agricultural districts. 'By means of exercising the minds of the labouring classes on affairs interesting to them and within their comprehension, the League Leaders did more for popular education than has yet been achieved by any other means'—Martineau, *History of England during the Thirty Years' Peace*, iv. 296.

community.' Democracy is not simply a device for balancing rival interests; it is, at a certain stage of social development, an indispensable means of education. 'It is from political discussion and collective political action, that one whose daily occupations concentrate his interests in a small circle around himself, learns to feel for and with his fellow citizens and becomes consciously a member of a great community; but political discussions fly over the heads of those who have no votes or are not endeavouring to acquire them.'

This recognition of an educational purpose or ideal in the growth of public institutions forms a cardinal distinction between the political theories of the eighteenth, and those of the later nineteenth, century; but, as may be seen from Mill's treatment of the question, it does not necessarily involve an unlimited acceptance of popular government. His argument suggests, in fact, a reaction from the creed of Bentham and his immediate successors, proceeding from a closer analysis of the forces which determine political action and the formation of opinions. Retaining a firm belief in the power of reason and the efficacy of public discussion, he is aware also of counteracting tendencies, whose strength may increase as democracy advances in its career. 'The position which gives the strongest stimulus to the growth of intelligence is that of rising into power, not that of having achieved it'; for a body of men strong enough to prevail against reason will no longer listen to its warnings, or invoke its aid. In other words, the value of popular movements as educational agencies will diminish as they succeed in achieving their immediate ends, unless some higher stimulus is brought into operation. It may be truer to say that political argument gravitates towards the mental level of those to whom it is addressed. The obstacle to political education, under any form of government, is not any conscious unwillingness to listen to reason, but the ease with which men are led to adopt conclusions and even trains of argument without going through the process of reasoning on their own account. Where power extends in advance of education, the art of organising delusion threatens to keep pace with the agencies which aim at diffusing enlightenment.

If the progress of the democratic movement has been attended by an increase of mental activity, the result may be ascribed, in part at least, to two safeguards which are not always taken into account. In a modern state no victory in politics is final or complete. Whatever form the constitution may assume, power will ultimately depend on knowledge ; and the force of this principle is realised only when the preliminary triumphs have been won. The intelligence required by a class to render its power effective in action is much greater than that which was needed to assert a right to it. In so far as intellectual effort can be shown to have been directly influenced by politics, there is no evidence that it has diminished permanently as a result of enfranchisement. The forms of instruction which are connected with the political awakening of the masses in the early part of the last century cannot be compared seriously with the systematic studies undertaken by artisans in recent years and stimulated by a desire to assist in the solution of social and economic problems. In the second place, it is necessary to examine the assumption, more often implied than expressed, that the mass of the people have no history and no accumulating experience. Writers on democracy have paid insufficient regard to those changes in the character and outlook of a people, produced by widening opportunities and their own efforts for self-improvement, whose tendency is to raise an increasing number to the level of responsible citizenship and to place them in a position to think for themselves. The nature and the effect of these changes, and the extent to which a process of education may be traced in the sequence of social events, are questions which must be considered in estimating the prospects of popular government.

The point at issue may be illustrated by analysing the connection between the growth of political consciousness and recurring periods of prosperity and economic depression. The natural outcome of depression, in an age of progress, is social unrest, awakening visions of a new social order from which misery and injustice have been for ever expelled. The natural outcome of prosperity is contentment and a certain degree of complacency. The former, if continued indefinitely, might end in despotism or anarchy; the latter in the extinction of large ideals. Mutually related as alternate phases of social experience, they provide complementary forms of discipline and encouragement. A period of distress reveals the mass of human suffering, calls into play new forces of enthusiasm and revolt, and brings new groups into action.[1] The return of prosperity opens the way to a calmer and more detailed study of social facts and the development of practical policies. In so far as these vicissitudes enable us to interpret the history of last century, it may be said that a period of awakening consciousness, in which

[1] It is true that a class may be brought too low by economic depression to feel confidence in large ideals and drastic remedies, and that, as a class advances in prosperity, it becomes conscious of its strength and the more likely to chafe at obstacles to its further advancement; but it is incontestable that, taking the nineteenth century as a whole, periods of distress are the great periods of revolt, or those, at any rate, in which the feeling of revolt takes its rise.

enthusiasm was stirred by vague ideas of social reconstruction, was followed by an interval of detailed thought and practical experiment, succeeded in its turn by the challenge of new disorders and a new widening of the mental horizon. In a broad sense the course of events has an educational influence, whose results may be tested by the growth of political aims. The difference between modern labour policies, since the revival of socialism in the eighties, and the vague idealism of the Chartist period shows the influence of administrative experience, of which the foundations were laid during an interval of relative quiet. It is more difficult to decide how far these influences extend beyond the leaders and penetrate the mass of organised labour; and, again, how far the lesson learned during one phase of experience is actually continued in that which follows.

Martineau's history of the 'Thirty Years' Peace,' from 1816-46, covers a well-marked epoch in the political life of the unfranchised classes. It was a period of chronic distress and of social change, which revived the forces of unrest and enlarged their sphere. New industrial conditions hardened the opposition between labour and capital. The decay of paternalism removed influences which had kept labour in a state of disunion and held it in play.[1] Class consciousness was strengthened by the conservative reaction which followed the close of the Napoleonic wars, by fiscal injustice and organised repression.[2] These circumstances, which hastened the

[1] The wages and apprenticeship clauses of the Statute of Artificers were repealed 1813-14; *cf.* the drastic reform of the Poor Law in 1834, intended to sweep aside the demoralising tendencies which were a legacy of paternal government, and to reassert the principle of self-dependence.

[2] Webb, *Trade Unionism*, 85. *Cf.* Effects of Corn Law, 1815—Prentice, *Historical Sketches, etc. of Manchester*, 90 *et passim.* Dicey, *Law and Opinion in England*, 123. Benn, *Modern England*, i. 97 *sqq.*

birth of an industrial democracy, turned the current of its energies into idealistic and revolutionary channels. Within a few years of the repeal of the Combination Laws, the labour movement became involved in struggles to effect a universal remedy for social ills. With the conception of political equality, which found expression in Chartism, went the Owenite gospel of social regeneration and the vision of a 'new moral world.' The character of the period is no less clearly defined by comparison with the thirty years which followed. In the prosperous times ushered in by the repeal of the Corn Laws, the pursuit of panaceas gave place with unusual abruptness to detailed schemes of reform and the business of securing advantages under existing conditions. Both the co-operative and the trade-union movements showed a reaction from the universalism and heroic assurance of the Owenite propaganda, and, at the same time, a much steadier grasp of administrative details and of possibilities within their immediate reach.[1] The same practical attitude, combined with a wider outlook, is seen in the beginnings of parliamentary action which became effective during the early seventies.[2]

No two periods of activity appear, at first sight, less related to one another in aim and achievement. In the first, a succession of enthusiasms seem to vanish without result, as if to illustrate by repeated trial the helplessness of the masses, the incompetence of their leaders, and the impracticability of their ideals. In the second, more limited and less generous aims gave rise to permanent and effective organisations whose history shows at every stage an advance in business capacity, discipline, and intelligence. From the outset a mutual antipathy, developing in some cases into active antagon-

---

[1] Webb, *op. cit.*, 199 (*cf.* 168 *sq.*), 206 *sq.*   [2] *Ibid.*, 223 *sq.*

ism, appears to separate the movements which are characteristic of either period. Owen had little sympathy with free trade, and disowned the 'commercial co-operation' which was to prove a lasting success.[1] Official Chartism was equally hostile to developments which fell short of its demands. On the other hand, what was left of the trade-union movement after the crisis of 1834, parted company with the Owenite agitation; and the unions were never connected with Chartism as they had been with earlier political movements, and occasionally came into conflict with it.[2] Indeed the New Unionism, which made its appearance in the forties, derived its characteristics in no small degree from groups which had passed unscathed through the turmoil of the heroic age, from a new generation which had no part in the experience of former years, and from the influence of ideas of middle-class origin.[3] The nucleus of a new form of organisation was found in unions which had held aloof from earlier movements, and which had a superior record.[4] Where individual societies moved in support of the old ideals, the protest came not from 'cautious elders' who had outlived past failures, but from the younger men who had never shared their beliefs.[5] It was especially among the younger genera-

[1] Podmore, *Robert Owen*, 453.
[2] Webb, *op. cit.*, 158–61.   [3] *Ibid.*
[4] *Cf.* the engineering and printing trades—*ibid.*, 152. For growth of the 'new model' led by the Amalgamated Society of Engineers (development of orderly business methods and appointment of salaried officials), see *ibid.*, 185 *sqq.* Webb notices an increased desire to get at facts and an exact knowledge of the points at issue, which he attributes largely to the entrance of the printing trades into the trade-union movement; their proceedings had been characterised throughout by moderation, formality, and a desire to deal with concrete facts—*ibid.*, 178. *Cf.* the proceedings at the Miners' Conference 1863, where the meeting was organised on the model of the National Association for the Promotion of Social Science, being divided 'into three sections, on law, on grievances, and on social organisation, each of which reported to the whole Conference'—*ibid.*, 287.
[5] *Ibid.*, 161.

tion that an improvement was observed in the tone of
political discussion.[1]

It is true, none the less, that the first half of the
century was the parent of the age which followed. The
Rochdale co-operators of 1844 recognised Owen as their
prophet and laboured in a soil already prepared. The
trade-union movement in the forties emerged from the
storm of revolutionary unrest which had diffused ideas
of solidarity and was the necessary prelude to a saner
mood. It was in the course of a hopeless struggle to
combine all labour in a general union that the wage-
earning class had passed finally from an ideal of conservatism to an ideal of progress. The shortcomings of
the earlier period lie on the surface. There was more
rhetoric than knowledge, and more conviction than
clearness of thought. ' A few, but they are very few,
are well educated and know something of physical and
political science . . . and of those truths of political
economy which all educated persons admit and understand.' [2] Of a group who were tried in connection with
a Chartist outbreak in the manufacturing districts, a
large proportion could scarcely read or write.[3] But the
human material was different from what it had been
half a century earlier. Intelligence, ' in a degree which
was formerly thought impossible,' had spread to ' the
lower and down even to the lowest rank ' ; and with
intelligence went the faculty of disciplined action and
an adherence to principle. Place remarked on the
agitation led by the orator Hunt at the commencement
of the period (1816)—' There was no want of energy,
but it was not the mischievous energy of uncultivated
madmen, but the energy of much more cultivated men

[1] Re Debating Societies, see Committee on Public Libraries (1849),
Q. 1319 sqq.
[2] Kay-Shuttleworth, Social Condition and Education of the People, i. 584.
[3] Ibid., i. 379.

than these classes in former times contained ' ; [1] and his testimony is supported by later events. The spirit of insurrection persisted ; but it was modified by new influences which survived the moments of passion and excess. Chartism bequeathed to the Lancashire operatives that power of principled endurance which possessed them at a later crisis occasioned by the American Civil War. Yorkshire had supported Wilberforce in his crusade against slavery ; but there was no earlier example of a starving population suffering quietly in defence of principles which were to the advantage of an alien and distant race and detrimental to their own immediate interests.[2] It was a typical product of the ' heroic ' age.

Not less significant was the growth of an intelligent minority which was to supply the elements of constructive leadership. In each movement there were a minority of thinkers and a minority of extremists, between whom the battle was waged [3] ; and the former were quietly winning recruits. Lovett, writing to Francis Place in 1834 during the lull which preceded the Chartist agitation, analyses the mental experience through which many must have passed in these troubled times : starting with the dawn of political consciousness, passing through the stage in which loyalty to principle is distinguished from partisanship, and ending in the disillusionment which is the beginning of wisdom. ' I have known,' he says, ' many persons under thirty who a few years since were dissipated, ignorant and besotted, and are now sober, intelligent and excellent members of society. . . . If I now enter a mixed assembly of working men, I find twenty where I formerly met with one who knew any-

---

[1] Place, *Add. MSS.* (B.M.) 27827, p. 220.
[2] *Cf.* Howell, *Labour Legislation, etc.,* 140–2.   Dicey, *op. cit.,* 250 *sq.*
[3] Lovett, *Autobiography,* 68 *sqq.*

thing of society, politics or government. . . . I have been in the habit of corresponding with societies and individuals in different parts of the country, and I have perceived a great change in their opinions, social and political. Formerly they worshipped political leaders —now they seek the establishment of principles. Formerly they thought that Universal Suffrage, annual Parliaments, and the vote by ballot would bring the means of comfort home to every man's door—now they see that something even more than Republicanism, as hitherto understood, is necessary to effect it.'[1]

How much of this progress is to be ascribed directly to the influence of organised movements, how much to a wider range of experience and incentive less easily defined ? It is necessary to start with some conception of the materials which presented themselves. The agitation of the period had not to deal with an un-differentiated mass of weakness and ignorance. It formed part of a process extending back into the past, and acted on social groups at different levels of political development. It was itself the product of energies which it guided into a new channel.

The skilled handicraftsmen of the Metropolis during the early years of the century occupied a position far removed from the mass of workers in the textile trades.[2] Their economic status was relatively secure ; they had had long experience of the forms of ' corporate government ' ; and they were closely in touch with the class above them.[3] They supply the chief examples of a

---

[1] Lovett to Place, Nov. 17, 1834. *Place MSS.*, 30.

[2] Webb, *op. cit.*, 75–7.

[3] Cobden notices the success of middle-class liberal movements (e.g. Free Trade) with the London artisans, who ' are all intermingled by their occupations with the class above them more completely than in any other large town '—Morley, *Life of Cobden*, ch. xii.

type which was not uncommon ; men possessed of much general knowledge and of organising ability. Their influence gave an element of stability to the trade-union movement ; and they furnished recruits to the mutual improvement societies which knew no master and acknowledged no limitations.[1] Their defects were those naturally produced by contact with many streams of thought at the centre of affairs. The ' *élite* of the London democracy' included a proportion of certified enthusiasts who displayed an undiscerning appetite for new ideas.

The manufacturing districts of the North presented a different picture. There, the industrial population started at a lower level of political experience ; and coming unprepared to a struggle with economic forces

---

[1] Lovett mentions a ' Literary Society ' composed mainly of working men, who met in Gerrard Street, Newport Market (about the year 1821), to discuss literary, political and metaphysical subjects ; they formed a select library—*op. cit.*, 34. In 1814, on the failure of his co-operative store in Greville Street, he reopened the premises as a coffee-house, setting apart a room for debates, classes, readings and recitations ; there he established a small society, the ' Social Reformers.' ' I look back,' he says, ' upon those two years of my life with great pleasure and satisfaction, for during this period I gained a considerable amount of information and was, I believe, the means of causing much useful knowledge to be diffused among the young men who frequented the place ' ; he mentions a chronometer-maker end a cabinet-carver as intelligent and accomplished members—*ibid.*, 88 *sq.* For similar instances, see *A Working Man's Way in the World*, by a Journeyman Printer, 14 *sq.*, 65 ; also Thomas Cooper, *Autobiography*. Webb notices that the skilled workmen of London were radicals and generally free from ' sedition,' and ' from their ranks came such organisers as Place, Lovett, and Gast '—*op cit.*, 76. *A Working Man's Way in the World*, 8–10, refers to a journeyman printer who had come from London to Bristol—' He possessed a fund of information upon all popular topics, and knew much of the personal history of the public characters of the day. He had travelled all over England, and wrought in most of the principal towns, and had received a substantial testimonial, at a period when testimonials were not hourly occurrences, for his successful advocacy of the rights of working men upon occasion of a strike in the north. Upon every topic, except Christianity, he reasoned gently and modestly, and was the means and medium of much pleasant and useful information to his companions. He was a great admirer of Franklin, whom he was continually quoting and whom he confessedly made his model.'

which cut at the roots of their independence, they were easily misled. In Lancashire ill-organised insurrection followed the rioting of loyal mobs.[1] By degrees a new order was evolved out of the chaos, as a constructive faculty began to assert itself. Before the close of the Chartist period there were already signs of that genius for association which is in a peculiar sense characteristic of these industrial areas. Some of the northern stores survived the collapse of the co-operative movement in the thirties; and it was at Rochdale that a new phase of the movement commenced. In the course of the Owenite agitation initiative passes gradually from London to Lancashire.[2]

It is too readily assumed, however, that democracy in the North was a specific product of the Industrial Revolution. Among the northern weavers were a class corresponding to the more intelligent of the London artisans; and the first signs of democratic advance appeared—side by side, as it were, with the new industrial system—among the survivors of an earlier social condition. The transitional stage is less clearly represented in the beginnings of trade unionism than in

---

[1] Prentice, *op. cit.*, *passim.*

[2] Lloyd Jones, *Life of Owen*, 293 *sqq.*—' We had among us in Manchester more life and energy, united to an active system of teaching. We possessed a number of men who had proved their fitness to teach, and we were therefore determined to throw ourselves into the movement' (1836). There follows a sketch of the propaganda round Manchester. His reference to an ' active system of teaching ' is illustrated by an account of a school opened by the supporters of a co-operative store in Salford. The store wound up its business in 1831, and ' we set to work in a different fashion. We had counters and shelves and a few tables and chairs, so we took a couple of large rooms and opened a school for the instruction of boys and girls and such adults as might think it worth while to learn what we had to teach. We had among us two carpenters who were found useful in turning the shelves and counters into desks and forms.' A house-to-house canvass drew pupils of all ages (12 to 40); subjects— drawing, music, singing, dancing, and the three R's. No fees. The school continued for six years. Sunday meetings, with essays and lectures on social questions.

an agitation for parliamentary reform which followed
the Peace of 1815 and was terminated by the Peterloo
massacre four years later. Bamford has left a vivid
picture of the formation of Hampden clubs in the
neighbourhood of Manchester. The people thronged to
village assemblies, to listen to readings and speeches
on the subject of Reform; local poets contributed
their effusions; and the cottagers left their looms
at the close of day to drill upon the heath. The
episode is purified by a breath of romance and country
air, which contrast with the noise and stifling atmosphere of the London trade clubs. It is the last
appearance of an organised peasantry, which was to
transmit much of its spirit to the new proletariat;
and the movement is significant on many grounds.
Sunday schools, which appear to have been exceptionally
democratic in the manufacturing districts, prepared
the way for the Hampden clubs; [1] and they were closely
connected with the effects of the Methodist Revival.
The legacy of these religious influences played an
immense part in determining later events.

Two streams of agitation converged in the trade-
union movement in the early thirties—one inspired
by the ideal of political democracy, the other by that
of social democracy as presented in the teaching of
Robert Owen.[2] The two aims were never completely

[1] 'The Sunday schools of the preceding thirty years had produced
many working men of sufficient talent to become readers, writers, and
speakers in the village meetings for parliamentary reform' (Hampden
Clubs, 1816)—Bamford, *Passages in the Life of a Radical*, 7 *sq.* (ed. 1848).
For a sketch of the London trade clubs, which plainly offended his æsthetic
temperament, see 23 *sq.* 'Amongst the quiet but effective labourers . . .
had been the Sunday school teachers. . . . With the single undeviating
purpose of promoting the eternal welfare of their pupils, they were
preparing them for the fit discharge of their social and public duties.
They were creating *thought* amongst the hitherto unthinking masses'—
Prentice, *op. cit.*, 116.

[2] Webb, *op. cit.*, 139.

dissociated, however vaguely they may have been linked together in the minds of the working class. But the agitations which they provoked developed, in the main, on different lines ; and their mode of appeal and the ways in which they affected thought and character in typical cases may be broadly distinguished.

The Hampden clubs mark the beginnings of a political movement which issued in Chartism. With it may be connected, for purposes of analysis, the earlier and later stages of the Anti-Corn-Law propaganda and the agitation for sundry specific reforms. Their common characteristic is that they drew attention to particular laws, or the state of the constitution, as immediate or ulterior sources of evil. In so far as they set men thinking of remote causes and general effects, thereby substituting deliberate action for spasmodic outbursts of vengeance, they accomplished an elementary stage of political education. In so far as reliance was placed on the force of numbers and what was a means to an end tended to become confused with the end itself, the original impulse was counteracted and repressed. Both tendencies are foreshadowed in the personality and career of William Cobbett. His writings were an effective means of restraining violence, and sowed the seeds of constitutional agitation.[1] An untiring propagandist, touring the country and lecturing in town and village, he was the precursor of Cobden and the League. He had also less favourable characteristics.

---

[1] 'At this time (1816) the writings of William Cobbett suddenly became of great authority ; they were read on nearly every cottage hearth in the manufacturing districts of South Lancashire ; in those of Leicester, Derby, and Nottingham ; also in many of the Scottish manufacturing towns. Their influence was speedily visible ; he directed his readers to the true cause of their sufferings—misgovernment ; and to its proper corrective—parliamentary reform. Riots soon became scarce, and from that time they have never obtained their ancient vogue with the labourers of this country '—Bamford, op. cit., 7

The idea of a change in the political system, which was to remedy every grievance, became a narcotic no less stupefying than the breaking of machinery. Ruthless invective degenerated easily into the grosser forms of flattery and abuse which rendered Chartism the least effective of popular movements.

The agitation led by Robert Owen had much wider and less practicable aims; but it was saved, as an educational force, by elements which made it a direct antithesis to the political movement. The object of Chartism was a political deliverance. The object of Owen was social regeneration and the creation of a 'new moral world.' The one might be achieved by Act of Parliament; the other demanded a 'revolution of the human mind.' Whereas Chartist leaders were continually appealing to class-antagonism and to the power of numbers, the new social order was to evolve through the effort and example of voluntary groups, creating for themselves an independent livelihood and joining in the work of mutual improvement. It is as futile to judge Owen by his communistic utterances, as to judge a religion by its formal theology. The ideas which he suggested were of more value than the system in which they were embodied. A vision had been granted, and character was being formed. When all his schemes had ended in bankruptcy, there were men prepared to continue his work.

The ideal set before the Owenite Societies was that of acquiring land and 'living in community.' The Brighton Co-operative Society, founded in 1827, went so far as to purchase twenty-eight acres which were cultivated in connection with their grocery store. Members were admitted on a test of moral respectability; mental improvement was to be a means and complement to material progress; and one of their first objects was to provide for the education of their children. They spent their leisure in reading and mutual instruction, and appointed one of their number librarian and schoolmaster.[1] None of the early societies seem to have advanced much further. They became small trading and producing groups, performing to some extent, in the supply of their immediate needs and in relief of unemployment, functions which were afterwards divided between the trade union and the distributive store. But the ideal with which they started is not insignificant; it is mentioned in the original programme of the Rochdale pioneers; and it must be considered in valuing the experiments of this earlier period, which were not simply exercises in economic co-operation and the conduct of business. The idea of a self-contained, self-developing community carried with it the vision of social harmony and of a life well ordered, symmetrical and complete. It was the nucleus of aims whose realisation on a larger scale is part of the general progress of society. The higher ideals were never wholly obscured. Some provision for education and social intercourse was a characteristic, and often the most persistent, feature of these early experiments.[2] At the central institutions where Owen expounded his system there were weekly festivals, with dance and song, which he refused to abandon in a season of general distress.

---

[1] Holyoake, *History of Co-operation*, 592 *sqq.*; Podmore, *Robert Owen*, 389 *sqq.*

[2] A group of stocking-frame weavers in Sutton-in-Ashfield (Notts), to protect themselves from the middlemen, after the trade-union crisis in 1834, determined to start co-operative production. Their leader informs Owen that they have devoted the remains of their 'late union fund' to renting a building for the purpose, and 'believing that knowledge is power, we shall appropriate the upper room . . . to the purpose of a school, lecture room, etc,'—Podmore, *op. cit.*, 449 *sq.* *Cf. n.* 2, p. 217.

In 1835, after the simultaneous collapse of the
'Trades-Union' and the early co-operative movement,
the followers of Owen devoted themselves to a propagandist crusade which extended roughly over a period
of ten years. The 'Association of All Classes of All
Nations' was the measure of their enthusiasm; its
later name, the society of 'Rational Religionists,' defines
the quality of their aims. An organisation was rapidly
called into existence, which borrowed from the example
of orthodox religious bodies. The kingdom having
been divided into districts, social missionaries were
appointed to go their rounds, lecturing and holding
discussions. In some of the towns 'halls of science'
were erected, where a form of service was held; and
many of the branches opened schools for young and old.
The distribution of tracts alone was sufficient to alarm
the Churches. In 1841 there were eighteen missionaries and paid lecturers at work, in addition to many
who rendered voluntary service, travelling long dis-
tances in their scanty leisure. The avowed object was
to hasten the social millennium, by preaching the
principles of Owen, denouncing the evils of the present
order and stirring men to a practical effort. Many of
those who took part in the movement were emotional
and ill-informed; but their sincerity was undoubted.
Their rhetoric was that of missionaries of a new faith
who were prepared to face contumely and misrepre-
sentation and who drove home, amid much crude
dogmatism, certain simple and necessary truths. If
they attacked apathy in high places, there were also
unsparing critics of ignorance and vice among their
own class. They were among the foremost advocates
of temperance and self-discipline, which they aided
by their example; and they preached education as
the basis of all reform. There was some organised,

and much casual, opposition ; and they were occasionally the victims of loyal mobs.[1]

All this bears a superficial resemblance to an earlier movement, which had been connected in many ways with the growth of democratic consciousness. The socialist crusade was in certain respects a secular rendering of the Methodist Revival, and affords a striking illustration of the change of circumstances which has brought to bear on social problems something akin to religious enthusiasm. Both Wesley and Owen asserted the universality of their mission. One claimed the world for his parish, the other founded an association which was to embrace mankind. The gospel of Owen was narrower than Methodism, in that it was essentially of this world ; it was broader in so far as it unfolded a vision of social progress ; where its influence was limited, it appealed to the *élite* rather than to the elect. The distinction is not simply verbal. The colony at Greenwood consisted of picked men ; the halls of science, at any rate in London, were frequented by a prosperous class ; and Owen was criticised on one occasion for neglecting the poor.[2] But the difference may be exaggerated. The early co-operators and their successors at Rochdale belonged to that class among the poor to whom Wesley had appealed with greatest effect ; and the co-operative movement loses its virtue and recuperative power where its traditions and benefits are not held in trust for the weaker brethren.

The main point at issue between the social and the

---

[1] Lloyd Jones, *op. cit.*, 294–388 ; Holyoake, *op. cit.*, 244 *sqq.* The moral influence of the Harmony Hall Community (Hants) was remarked in the neighbourhood—Somerville, *Whistler at the Plough*, 109, 115.

[2] The subscription at the Gray's Inn Road Institution seems to have been prohibitive—Podmore, *op. cit.*, 426.

political movements was one of precedence. Socialists, wrote a disciple, are Chartists ' in the abstract'; but they would first have the people educated and placed in a position of social independence. Then, too, the case for political reform would be better worth advancing and more likely to succeed. Above all, ' exhibitions of brute force ' were to be avoided on principle.[1] Lovett, who represented the moderate section of Chartist opinion, seems to start from a contradictory premise. The franchise, he maintained, was the ' best of schoolmasters '; and history showed that prosperity and enlightenment followed the attainment of political rights.[2] This did not prevent him endeavouring to develop thought among the masses, and advocating national education that they might be empowered to assert their rights and prepared to use them. Although the franchise was needed to effect any considerable improvement in their material condition, much benefit might be derived from ' moral culture ' and self-control; and it was important that the change should come ' without violence ' and through the pressure of organised moral force. The course of events matured his conviction that education was the only way, if the movement was to succeed and if success was to be a permanent benefit. ' True liberty,' he concludes, ' cannot be conferred by Act of Parliament . . . but must spring from the knowledge, morality, and public virtue ' of the people.[3]

The Working Men's Association, for which Lovett wrote, had formulated the Charter, but exercised very little control over the course of the movement. It had been organised in 1836 to promote radical causes,

---

[1] Podmore, *op. cit.*, 455.

[2] *Address to the Working Classes of Europe ; Address to the People of England* (1838). Lovett, *Autobiography*, 158, 175.

[3] *Address to the Working Classes on the Subject of Education*, 1837; *Address to the Political and Social Reformers, etc.*, 1841. *Ibid.*, 135, 245.

to collect and sift information on labour questions, to unite the intelligent sections of the working class, and to educate public opinion. It provided a meeting-place for a mixed group of reformers ; and though its influence was not widely extended, a number of branches were formed in the provinces. In 1841 the London members undertook the promotion of an educational scheme which Lovett had outlined during his imprisonment in the previous year. A national hall was opened in Holborn, containing a library and coffee-room for the use of members, and providing lectures, concerts, and classes, which were open to the public on reasonable terms. The premises were used as a Sunday school ; and subsequently a day school was added, affording a superior elementary education to the children of a superior class. The movement seems never to have extended beyond the Metropolis ; and the dearth of ' book knowledge ' among the general body of the Chartists is lamented by their most favourable critic.[1] A hopeful experiment started by Thomas Cooper at Leicester [2] went to pieces owing to a depression of

[1] Gammage, *History of the Chartist Movement*, 111.

[2] The Shakespearean Association of Leicester Chartists, so-called from the ' Shakespeare Room' in which they met (1841). ' I formed,' writes Cooper, ' an adult Sunday school for men and boys, who were at work on week-days. All the more intelligent in our ranks gladly assisted as teachers ; and we soon had the room filled on Sunday mornings and afternoons. The Old and New Testaments, Channing's *Self-Culture* and other tracts, of which I do not remember the names, formed our class-books. And we fancifully named our classes, not first, second, third, etc., but the " Algernon Sydney Class," " Andrew Marvell Class," " John Hampden Class," etc.' Among the members were two minor poets, a stocking-weaver and a ' glove-hand,' whom Cooper induced to write hymns for the Sunday meetings. ' We now usually held two or three meetings in the Shakespearean Room on week-nights, as well as on Sunday night. Unless there was some stirring local or political topic, I lectured on Milton and repeated portions of *Paradise Lost*, or on Shakespeare and repeated portions of *Hamlet*, or on Burns and repeated *Tam o' Shanter* ; or I recited the History of England, and set the portraits of great Englishmen before the young Chartists, who listened with intense interest ; or I took up geology, or even phrenology, and made the young

trade. 'What care we about reading, if we can get naught to eat ? '

Lovett had served his political apprenticeship in the co-operative movement; and the addresses which he issued to the public between 1836 and 1845 were strongly imbued with the spirit of Owen. He contrasted the policy of physical force with that of uniting the working classes ' upon principles of knowledge and temperance, and the management of their own affairs.' He would have the political leaders proclaim ' unpalatable truths ' ; and he protested against the atmosphere of beer-shops in which meetings were held. The democracy was to be eminently ' respectable.' Working men were to meet for mutual instruction and to blend study with rational amusement. They were to exclude drunkards and immoral persons from their ranks. They were to ' quicken the intellects ' of their wives and children. The scheme of voluntary association which he published in 1841 is almost certainly borrowed, in outline, from the socialists. He proposed that halls should be erected, to be used as schools in the day time ; that paid missionaries should be appointed ; that there should be circulating libraries, and a distribution of tracts ; and that the instruction of adults in physical, moral, and political science should be combined with the lighter influences of dance and song. How far the underlying conception of a change of mind and character is due to the influence of Owen, it is useless to inquire. Lovett belonged to a superior class of artisans who had no recognised leader and were preparing to exercise an authority of their own. They drew inspiration from many movements, and were too much in advance of

men acquainted elementally with the knowledge of the time.' Incidentally, he preached temperance and administered the pledge to several hundreds— Cooper, *Autobiography*, 164–9.

their generation to be complete disciples. The Working Men's Association had aims sufficiently elastic to comprehend every phase of radical opinion. It offered a common platform to men so widely sundered as Owen and Francis Place; and its programme betrays the influence of the middle-class group who were interested in the diffusion of useful knowledge. It marks the climax in a series of efforts to organise a 'peaceful expression of public opinion,' and it goes a step beyond. Its object was essentially educational; and it is the first example of a democratic organisation whose programme was not wholly or primarily sectarian. It proposed to collect information on economic conditions, and to found its propaganda on a basis of exact knowledge.[1]

[1] Programme of the *Working Men's Association for benefiting politically, morally, and socially the useful classes* (1836): (1) 'To draw into one bond of unity the intelligent and influential portion of the working classes in town and country'; (2) political and social equality; (3) a free press; (4) national education; (5) to collect information on labour questions, e.g. wages, habits and condition of labourers; (6) to meet and digest this information, and plan accordingly; (7) 'To publish their views and sentiments in such form and manner as shall best serve to create a moral, reflecting yet energetic public opinion, so as eventually to lead to a gradual improvement in the condition of the working classes, without violence or commotion'; (8) 'To form a library of reference and useful information,' and to maintain a place of meeting—Lovett, *Autobiography*, 92 *sq.* Lovett had been induced to found the Association by Dr. James Black of Kentucky, who came to London in 1834 with the idea of promoting Working Men's Educational Associations; but the movement had English antecedents. The National Union of the Working Classes and Others (1831), in which Lovett took a leading part, started with the same general social and political aims, including that of collecting and organising a 'peaceful expression of public opinion,' which does not seem to have met with much success. Another possible influence is suggested by a circular, among the *Place MSS.*, proposing a 'Society for the Diffusion of Political and Moral Knowledge,' with the following programme: (1) to publish works at a suitable cost; (2) to sanction works published elsewhere; (3) to promote educational measures in Parliament. A meeting was called in Roebuck's rooms for Jan. 14, 1833—Place, *Add. MSS.* (B.M.), 27827, 39.

CHAPTER VIII

THE SOCIAL OUTLOOK

THE repeal of the Corn Laws in 1846 was suggestive of a profound change which had passed over English society since the eve of the Industrial Revolution. Agriculture, still the largest industry, had ceased to govern the policy of the nation; rural life no longer supplied a recognised model. The agricultural labourer, at any rate in the South, had scarcely emerged from a long experience of physical depression and social displacement. In material condition he was slightly in advance of the domestic manufacturer, a companion in misery;[1] in intellectual culture, judged by the ordinary tests of instruction, he stood at a lower level; and the percentage of crime was said to be greater, as a rule, in agricultural than in manufacturing counties.[2] Enclosure had, in certain material respects, diminished his prospects and loosened his social ties. In this weakened condition there was nothing to resist disruptive influences which came from without. An education based on urban models played its part in hastening the catastrophe, and the rural exodus set in apace. The neglected state of rural labour in the middle of the century was among the most ominous features of English social life. The labourer might retrieve his

[1] Tuckett, *Past and Present State of the Labouring Population*, ii. 512.
[2] Kay-Shuttleworth, *Social Condition and Education of the People*, i. 391.

228

position, but the nation has been slow to recover the balance of its ideals.

A group which in the eighteenth century stood in the lowest rank had been meanwhile steadily advancing. The miners were less exposed than any other class to economic displacement; and their wages were relatively high.[1] The Tyne Valley in 1852 exhibited a state of material prosperity which was not easily rivalled. Housing accommodation in the newer collieries had distinctly improved; cottages were substantially furnished; and food was abundant.[2] In Cornwall, where earnings were at a lower rate, many of the miners had gardens and leisure to cultivate them, while others practised carpentry or fishing.[3] No part of the country had been more completely civilised by the Methodist Revival. It is as fair to lay stress on these examples as on the charges of gross feeding, roughness, and mental lethargy, which were commonly levelled at the mining population. A class which was still emerging from barbarism was an easy mark for censure; and the conditions of employment were fraught with innumerable abuses. But there were noted exceptions; the worst forms of intemperance and brutality were a survival from the past; crime in the Tyne Valley was considerably less than in the manufacturing districts; and everywhere religious

---

[1] Tuckett, *op. cit.*, ii. 535–41.

[2] *Our Coals and Coal Pits, etc.*, by a Traveller Underground (1853), 199. In parts of the agricultural districts precisely the reverse is noticed: ' a cottage erected in the last century will be generally found to be commodious and roomy; very different in the supply of comforts and conveniences from the hovels which are now ordinarily appropriated to the labouring class ' (Rev. H. Worsley, Easton, Suffolk)—Kay-Shuttleworth, i. 521. Cobbett notices ' in all the really agricultural villages . . . a great dilapidation and constant pulling down or falling down of houses '— *Rural Rides*, Oct. 31, 1822.

[3] *Cornwall, its Mines and Miners, etc.*, by the author of *Our Coals and Coal Pits*, 289 *sq.* (1855).

influences were at work refining manners and promoting education. The Commission of 1843[1] draws a broad distinction between coal and iron mines and other branches of the mining industry. In the lead mines of Alston Moor there were village libraries, and a superior system of elementary schools attended by children between the ages of six and eleven, and by boys in winter up to fourteen.[2] In Cornwall, most of the children were regularly at school until the age of employment, which was seldom lower than ten or twelve. Here juvenile labour was comparatively light; and distance, rather than fatigue, prevented attendance at evening classes.[3] Elementary education was less advanced in Northumberland and Durham, but not a few of the colliers had begun to develop the mental capacity which made this district, in later years, one of the most remarkable centres of University Extension.[4] It may be noticed that in 1847 the Miners' Association petitioned Parliament for a measure furthering education, after the manner of the Factory Acts.[5]

Meanwhile the mass of the population was collecting in the towns, and the general result was by no means clear. The great centres of commerce and transport at the present day differ socially from towns of a more purely industrial type; whilst the Metropolis stands almost in a class by itself. The same distinctions

---

[1] The Children's Employment Commission.
[2] *Ibid.*, Digest of Report, 193–5.   [3] *Ibid.*, 187–9.
[4] The author of *Cornwall, its Mines and Miners*, 228, notices that Cornwall produced relatively few students of science and mathematics, studies which were not uncommonly pursued in the North. See *Quarterly Review*, No. 220, p. 360—'Some (after the day's work) repair to the Methodist Meeting, some to the Club, some practise in the village band, some play upon melancholy instruments at home, and some study mathematical books picked up at stalls in the town. The mathematicians are most to our liking, and we find not a few here and there of very respectable attainments' (Northumberland and Durham).
[5] Nelson Boyd, *Coal Pits and Pitmen* (second edition), 130.

appeared in the middle of the last century. In Liverpool and Manchester there was a larger proportion of casual, ill-housed and sweated labour than in Birmingham and some of the manufacturing towns of the North; and the worst examples of congestion and sanitary abuse in the manufacturing districts were surpassed in the poorer parts of London.[1] What underlay these differences was only dimly perceived.

A treatise which appeared in 1846 classifies the workers directly dependent on manufactures into three groups. 'In an average state of trade, about one-third . . . are plunged in the most extreme misery, and hovering on the verge of actual starvation. Another third or perhaps a few more are earning an income scarcely better than that of the common agricultural labourer; but under circumstances directly injurious to health, morality and domestic comfort, being to a considerable extent dependent upon the exertions of their young children; and the mothers also contributing to produce this state of comparative independence. And the other third earning high wages, amply sufficient to support them in respectability and comfort.'[2] The factory operatives, who excited most attention, were not the worst situated. Below them were the hand-loom weavers; a class whose condition had steadily deteriorated, dwelling in cellars, bred to irregular habits, without power of combination, and, for the most part, beyond the reach of instruction. The impressions collected by Francis Place, which have been preserved in manuscript, deal more generally with social progress between 1790 and the passing of the Reform Bill. The barbarism which he remembered in his youth had

[1] Tuckett, *op. cit.*, ii. 489 *sqq.*; Kay-Shuttleworth, i. 454.
[2] Tuckett, *op. cit.*, ii. 495.

steadily declined ; and he notices a general improvement in habits, cleanliness and intelligence, extending downwards indefinitely in the social scale. But the force of his testimony is weakened by an undisguised and uncritical optimism. There is no pretence of distinguishing economic tendencies ; and many of his remarks are difficult to reconcile with other evidence which points to the growth of a labour-swamp in his immediate neighbourhood.[1] Two points, however, are clearly suggested : there had been a marked improvement in the higher grades of labour, and some of the cotton mills were abodes of vice.[2] What he proves is rather a gradual process of selection than a uniform advance.

Progress became more rapid during the next thirty years, and was especially noticeable in the manufacturing districts. The large towns established Boards of Health, and commenced a systematic treatment of sanitary abuses.[3] Free trade, accompanied by a return of commercial prosperity, lowered prices and increased employment. Lancashire became the centre of a remarkable temperance crusade which originated among the working class.[4] Co-operation diffused moral no less than material benefits ; and a shortening of the hours of labour was accompanied by a development of the means of recreation and instruction. Factory laws had begun to tell on the condition of the operatives. Formerly below the average in morals, intelligence and physique, they were becoming part of the aristocracy of labour.[5] Yet, in Manchester, between 1841 and

---

[1] Kay-Shuttleworth, *op. cit.*, i. 457 ; *cf.* 462.
[2] *Place MSS.* 27827, 192.
[3] Kay-Shuttleworth, *Four Periods of Education*, 42, 94 *sq.*
[4] Ludlow and Jones, *Progress of the Working Class*, 248 *sqq.*
[5] *Ibid.*, 110 *sqq.* In 1843, 19 per cent. factory children attended National, British and denominational schools, 45 per cent. dame and private schools ; in 1860, 70 per cent. attended public schools, 14 per cent.

1860, the rate of infant mortality had not diminished.[1] In the midst of an advancing society there was a residuum that did not improve.

A fresh light has been thrown on the situation by more recent inquiries which have investigated the problem at a later stage. In the Booth survey of London labour, completed in 1902, stress is laid on a process of selection which is creating a new middle class. The social groups extend in a continuous series, but the division between the lower middle and the upper working class is in a special sense indeterminate.[2] At

private (not dame) schools. Beneficial effect of factory legislation on the attitude of employers to social reform generally, *ibid.*, 112.

[1] Kay-Shuttleworth, *Four Periods of Education*, 148 *sq.* 1841, 11·189 per cent. ; 1851, 10·58 per cent. ; 1860, 11·34 per cent.

[2] ' Closely connected with the vitality and expansion of industry, we trace the advancement of the individual which in the aggregate is represented by the vitality and expansion of London. This it is that draws from the provinces their best blood, and amongst Londoners selects the most fit. Amongst such it is common for the children to aim at a higher position than their parents held ; and for the young people when they marry to move to a new house in a better district. A new middle class is thus forming which will, perhaps, hold the future in its grasp. Its advent seems to me the great social fact of to-day. Those who constitute this class are the especial product of the push of industry ; within their circle religion and education find the greatest response ; amongst them all popular movements take their rise, and from them draw their leaders. To them, in proportion as they have ideas, political power will pass ' —Booth, *Life and Labour in London*, final vol., 204. As to the composition of this class, he remarks that the ' organisation of modern industry finds room for much cheap clerk work for which the elementary schools ensure a copious supply, and requires also, on the practical side of the work, men of skill and character who earn higher wages than these clerks. Thus the financial distinction between clerk and working man tends to break down, and when for any purpose they consort together or make common cause, the social distinction is apt to break down too '— *ibid.* ser. 3, vol. 7, 400. It has been observed that in social and educational movements the term ' working man ' has to be liberally interpreted ; it must include the salaried clerk as well as the wage-earner. This does not necessarily imply, as it might have done in the earlier half of the last century, that labour movements are losing their hold on labour ; in a sense it means that the status of labour has advanced. In educational classes, at the present day, working men study on an equality with clerks and others, who are often members of working-class families, whereas in the Mechanics' Institutes the entrance of ' middle class ' students generally led to the withdrawal of the artisans.

the same time there is a distinction between the leaders
and the masses, and in certain respects a growing cleavage 'between the upper and lower grades of manual
labour.' [1] The Majority Report of the Poor Law Commission introduces a further set of distinctions. Labour
is classified provisionally into two groups, the skilled and
the unskilled, and the latter subdivided into a higher
and a lower grade—the criterion in this case being the
regularity of the wage rather than its amount. [2] This
distinction, which lays no claim to scientific accuracy,
finds a practical justification in the growth of casual
employment since the Poor Law Reform of 1834,
chiefly in dock centres but also in other branches of
industry. [3] The witnesses were agreed that the position
of skilled workers had improved, and the same opinion
was expressed, though with less confidence, of the
higher grade of unskilled labour; but there was
evidence, especially from London and other crowded
industrial centres, that the condition of labourers of
the lower grade had deteriorated. [4] In London the
number of unskilled labourers would seem to have
doubled within the past fifty years and to have 'increased at a greater rate than the population as a whole,'
whilst one half of them are described as living in an
'overcrowded condition,' and they have as a rule no
access to higher forms of employment. [5] Education is

---

[1] Booth, *op. cit.*, ser. 3, vol. 7, 400.
[2] *Poor Law Commission, Majority Report*, 361.
[3] *Ibid.*, 334 *sqq.*   [4] *Ibid.*, 361.
[5] *Ibid.*, 328. Mr. Sidney Webb asserts that the skilled grades in the
London building trade, the most typical London industry, are recruited
from the country ; the proportion of country-born workmen in breweries,
on railways, etc., is 50 per cent. or even 65 per cent. ; the London police
force, fire brigade, elementary teaching profession, city warehouses, etc.,
have a very small percentage of born Londoners. 'So far as we can make
out, the London industry in which there is the highest percentage of born
Londoners is that of unskilled general labour. This section must comprise

at once a measure and a cause of social characteristics. At one end of the scale is a class whose homes are well governed and whose children respond to the spirit of improvement. At the other is a submerged and disorganised group who lack the natural incentives to progress. The children, bred in an atmosphere of neglect, leave school at the earliest opportunity. Following the example, and impelled by the needs, of their parents they take to the least satisfactory occupations, and the vicious circle is complete.[1]

Before proceeding, it is necessary to repeat a word of caution which was suggested in the opening chapter. A classification of social groups which applies to the country as a whole requires to be supplemented by a classification of areas, having regard to the relative preponderance of different groups within the local community. Social conditions in London and other crowded centres differ not in degree, but in kind, from those prevailing in more purely industrial areas where

something like half a million of population in the Administrative County of London alone. Its social condition may be judged from the fact that not less than half of it lives in an overcrowded condition'— *Ibid.*, 328.

[1] 'The general features prevailing in the homes of these neglected or underfed school children are strikingly alike. . . . There is an absolute lack of organisation in the family life. It seems to be entirely absent under conditions where careful and minute organisation of the family resources is more essential than anything else. Existence drags along anyhow ; the hours of work, leisure and sleep are equally uncertain and irregular. . . . The underfeeding of the children is but a part of a more important feature in the life of this district. The children's health is affected by many different evils, overcrowding, want of sleep, dirt, and general irregularity of life' (Liverpool dock districts)—*Poor Law Commission, Minority Report*, 841. 'The elaborate investigation made by the London County Council into the circumstances of the families whose children need to be fed at school, brings to light not only that it is very largely the offspring of the under-employed casual labourers who are thus growing up stunted, under-nourished, and inadequately clothed ; but also that, in the vast majority of the cases, the children lack not food and clothing only, but even a low minimum of home care'—*Ibid.*, 1149. *Cf.* Reports of Board of Education on Medical Inspection.

the average of prosperity is higher and the level more
uniform. Well-to-do workers in the manufacturing
districts may earn less individually than the higher
grade of London artisans, but their proportion to the
rest of the population is greater ; they occupy a central
position in social life, and give a tone to the community.
As the ratio of such workers to the population diminishes,
their influence approaches a point at which it disappears
altogether. This conclusion lends support to a principle
which was deduced at an earlier stage of the inquiry.
Social characteristics depend less upon the amount of
income which a class enjoys, than upon its relation
to that of other classes. A class loses its morale, not
where its income is small in the aggregate, but where
it is small in relation to the accumulated wealth of
the neighbourhood. Where the workers are not overshadowed by a numerous and wealthier class, they are
more likely to develop initiative and self-confidence,
and to provide material for educational movements,
than in areas where distinctions in wealth and social
prestige are strongly marked.

Yet the evils which have been noticed as a tendency
of the age, though their incidence may vary with local
conditions, exert an influence more or less direct on
every type of industrial community. In the earlier
half of the last century large numbers of workers had
not been absorbed in the industrial system, and an old
race of domestic manufacturers was being squeezed
out of existence. To-day it is seen that industrial
changes result in a continuous rejection of the weak and
inefficient,[1] while a large part of the labouring class is

---

[1] ' As specialisation becomes more marked and definite, those who
have been . . . habituated to the processes that are superseded find it
more difficult to find occupation elsewhere. Trade unions and Employers'
Associations have . . . succeeded, the one in raising the standard of

permanently under-employed. Commerce has created numerous openings for casual and intermittent labour, and the number of those competing for this form of maintenance is periodically increased by a deflux from the ranks above them. Once out of the ranks of specialised industry, the position of the labourer is radically changed. Among the poor, a rise in nominal earnings does not add to their resources in the same proportion as a corresponding advance in the higher grades.[1] Competition for the means of subsistence increases, while occupation and environment bar the way to recovery.

The analysis may be carried back a stage further. The same forces have affected the lives of the rising generation ; and the magnitude of the evil is accentuated as we approach its source. ' We have,' says Mr. Sidney Webb, ' a great development of employments for boys of a thoroughly bad type, yielding high wages and no training,' and a positive decrease ' of places for boys in which they are trained to become competent men.'[2] The growth of commerce has developed forms of juvenile labour which afford no preparation for an after-career and are often physically and morally harmful. Specialisation has created openings for boys and girls in productive trades, in which there is no chance of their being absorbed in later life, but which retain their services until they are too old to seek regular employment.[3] The critical period occurs between

wages, the other the standard of industrial efficiency. Those who are not in the prime of life nor in possession of adequate physical strength or competency, are apt to fall out of an industrial system which is above their level'—*Poor Law Commission, Majority Report*, 359 ; *cf.* 334–41.

[1] *Ibid.*, 309.   [2] *Ibid.*, 327.

[3] ' The problem owes its rise in the main to the growth of cities as distributive centres—chiefly, and most disastrously, London—giving innumerable openings for errand boys, milk boys, office and shop boys, bookstall boys, van, lorry, and trace boys, street sellers, etc. In nearly all these

the time of leaving school and the age at which apprenticeship usually begins ; and it is said that between seventy
and eighty per cent. of the boys who pass through
elementary schools enter unskilled trades.[1] At the
same time the growth of large establishments and the
separation of processes which were formerly included
in a single craft have diminished the value of apprenticeship as a means of industrial, and still more of
moral, training.[2]

The tendency is one which has been noticed at
an earlier period. Economic change is continually
increasing the need of training and self-control, and
undermining influences which formerly controlled and
educated. The higher forms of manufacture suffer
from a dearth of competent artisans ;[3] and the decay
of craftsmanship is seen no less in agriculture than
in urban industry. Rural crafts cease to be trans-
mitted from father to son, and the farmer is generally
not in a position to instruct his labourers. The same
is true of the domestic arts. The home life of the poorest

occupations the training received leads to nothing ; and the occupations
themselves are in most cases destructive to healthy development, owing
to long hours, long periods of standing, walking or merely waiting, and,
morally, are wholly demoralising. . . . This particular problem, it will
be noticed, is not a problem of factory industry. But there is another
and even more serious form of the problem, where boys on leaving school
enter, without apprenticeship, into trades where there are no possible
openings for them when grown up ; loom-boys, doffers, shifters in the
cotton and woollen trades—where, it is said, there is little possibility of
more than one in ten being ultimately absorbed—rivet boys in shipbuilding,
drawers off in saw mills, packers in soap works, etc. In many of these
trades they are tempted by high wages to remain till they are too old to
enter any regular occupation. Here " the work performed by the boy,
instead of being in the nature of training, is a specialised compartment for
which his sole qualification is the fact that as an instrument of production
he is cheaper than a man " '—*ibid.*, 325 *sq.*

[1] *Ibid.*, 325.

[2] On the general question of apprenticeship and its decline, see *ibid.*,
349 *sqq.* ; Howell, *Contemporary Review*, Oct. 1877 ; Booth, *op. cit.*, ser.
2, i. 105, v. 127 ; Sadler, *Continuation Schools*, ch. 13.

[3] Sadler, *l.c.* ; Booth, *op. cit.*, v. 123 ; Shadwell, *Industrial Efficiency*, i. 148.

class is merely an extreme illustration of defects which extend indefinitely through the higher ranks. Physical degeneracy is due more often to bad feeding than to underfeeding, to an ill-prepared and monotonous diet than to lack of food.[1] Economic reactions, other than the strain of actual poverty, are dissolving the bonds of family union. The personal authority of the employer has almost vanished, and the sphere of parental influence is continually reduced. But the difficulty is not simply that an old form of training has deteriorated; its decay is a sign that old methods are inadequate to modern needs. The dangers which beset adolescence have extended beyond the reach of parental discipline. Household management and the care of children demand more knowledge than sufficed in simpler and more healthy surroundings. Something more is needed than a better system of workshop instruction, if the worker is to be capable of adapting himself to processes which continually change. His mental interests require to be enlarged, if he is to reap benefit and not detriment from a life which grows wider and more complex every decade. It is necessary not only to rebuild what has broken down, but to cover ground which has extended in the interval. Thus it is that the school has come to occupy a larger place in education than formerly. In schemes of physical care and domestic instruction, and in connection with industrial training and the choice of employments, it has invaded the province of the parent

---

[1] 'Nutrition does not improve. On the contrary, the proportion of children of sub-normal physique increases. . . . About half the children representing the healthy—or rather the normal—school population of the county are not up to a satisfactory level in this respect. This is due to . . . such removable causes as bad cooking, defective meal planning and monotony in diet'—Report of School Medical Officer for Durham County, 1912 (*Journal of Education*, September 1913).

and the employer, partly because their effective influence has diminished, partly because new demands have arisen and a higher standard is enforced.

Though it is not easy to define in precise terms the position reached at the close of the period with which this volume deals, it may be said broadly that somewhere in the middle of the nineteenth century a new stage commenced in the growth of educational movements. The first phase of the education controversy was concluded. Universal instruction had developed from an idea into a policy; and a decisive step had been taken in 1839 by the establishment of a Committee of Council to administer public grants. In 1850 Commissions were appointed to inquire into the management of the universities, which raised the question of educational endowments. In the following year the first International Exhibition aroused interest in technical training and started a movement which eventually played a part in the reorganisation of secondary schools. The division of periods is no less distinct in those spheres of endeavour, standing aside from the main currents of national education, of which a survey has been attempted in the preceding chapters. Two movements, whose relations to one another were not yet apparent, developed during the earlier half of the century; one consisting in an attempt to diffuse useful knowledge and to provide for the higher education of mechanics, the other connected with the growth of political and trade organisations which were a product of social unrest, and in which sections of the working class are found here and there struggling to evolve their own forms of instruction and to express their ideals. Both movements were experimental; and their breakdown, which became evident in the forties, formed the starting-point of a fresh series of developments which produced lasting results. A new phase of adult education commenced with the revival of co-operation at Rochdale in 1844, the appearance of an association formed by the Society of Friends in 1847 which became the pioneer of modern Adult Schools, the rise of Working Men's Colleges during the next decade which was followed by the Club and Institute Union of 1862, and the reform movement stimulated at the oldest seats of learning by the Commissions of 1850, which prepared the way, at least indirectly, for University Extension.

It does not fall within the scope of this volume to explore the undercurrents of opinion and sentiment which made the middle years of the century a critical period in the history not only of education, but of social thought ; but there is one issue of primary importance which has been kept in view at different stages of the inquiry, and round which the discussion has centred— the issue which turns on varying conceptions of social status.

As the Industrial Revolution developed, awakening latent energies and changing the forms of social life, the traditional classification of society into well-defined grades, arranged more or less in a regular series and duly subordinated one to anöther, was challenged with increasing force by a new doctrine which asserted the rights of the individual and discovered the basis of social order in freedom of individual enterprise. While the former conception had disposed men to identify intellectual with social distinctions, and resulted, as has been seen, in an attempt to confine popular instruction within narrow limits, the latter tended to lay stress on the capacities which different groups have in common and on the principle that they should start fair in the race of life. James Mill, in an educational treatise,[1] aimed frankly at a gradual approach to 'equality of instruction'; and the scheme for diffusing useful knowledge was designed to compensate individuals of every class whose opportunities of education had been curtailed. But the conception of equal opportunities had to be adapted to a social system which was based on inequality, and in which differences of acquired wealth produced gradations analogous to those derived from inheritance and social usage. Liberalism, in dealing with popular movements, relied in practice on middle-class leadership and introduced patronage in a new guise. Insistence on the capacities common to all classes resulted in the hypothesis of a standard type of humanity, represented for all practical purposes by the business man of the period, to whom education was a means to 'advancement in life.' It would seem almost to follow that the distinctive characteristics of particular social groups signified little more than differences in degree of mental development; and the defect of certain forms of education addressed to adult artisans in the first half of the century may be explained, in some measure, with reference to this assumption, which overlooked essential differences of outlook and experience.

The claim of labour to equality with the higher ranks in political and legal status was worked out during a period of middle-class ascendancy.[2] It was consistent with the principle entitling individuals to equal rights, and the support which it received did

[1] Supplement to the fourth, fifth, and sixth editions of the *Encyclopædia Britannica*, vol. iv. (1824).

[2] E.g. the Reform Act of 1867 which extended the franchise to artisans, and the Employers' and Workmen's Act of 1875 which altered the relation of master and servant into that of two ' equal parties to a civil contract.'

not involve sympathy with the solidarity of labour. Liberals of an earlier generation had assisted the repeal of the Combination Laws in deference to principle and in the hope that labour, when its right was admitted, would have the prudence not to combine. The reply came in the form of a movement which regarded equality between individuals as a step to equality between social groups, and which in its later phases has defined education as a public trust. The individual is to develop his talents, not that he may rise to a higher position, but that he may assist in raising the standard of his class.[1] The nucleus of this conception may be traced not only in the early socialist movement which failed, but also in small mutual improvement societies and discussion circles which were a permanent feature in the life of industrial communities, and which, in virtue of their spontaneous origin and the spirit of comradeship uniting their members, differed widely from the Mechanics' Institutes. After the collapse of Chartism in the forties, moderate counsels prevailed in the organisation of labour; but the maxim that knowledge is power was handed down as a legacy from earlier agitations, and the conception of education as a social lever reappeared in the programme of the new co-operative movement.

The Mechanics' Institutes were succeeded in the second half of the century by the formation of popular colleges and social clubs; a twofold movement which laid it down as a primary condition of success that working men had as much right as any other class to have their feelings considered, and renounced the notion that mental improvement was an avenue to a higher

---

[1] *Cf.* the aims of Ruskin College at Oxford (founded 1899): the student 'is taught to regard the education which he receives, not as a means of personal advancement, but as a trust for the good of others. He learns in order that he may raise, and not rise out of, the class to which he belongs.'

social career. The aim of education in the colleges was precisely the opposite—to secure for each individual, as one of a corporate body of fellow students, a status which he would not lightly abandon for selfish ends. It is useless to attempt reading into this premise any definite social theory. That a man might become a cultivated member of society regardless of his employment and economic position, was a postulate common to different schools of reform, while it showed a reaction from the commercial spirit of the age and an advance beyond earlier conceptions of status. The episode of the Working Men's Colleges, whose fellowship included both teachers and learners, is chiefly remarkable as an attempt to promote intercourse between individuals and social groups differing in class traditions and in their outlook on life ; and, in so far as the idea of a college came from the universities, as suggesting a link of connection between two spheres of corporate activity. Maurice spoke of a union between ' labour and learning ' ; and the phrase, which describes the inner life of a college for working men, gives also a clue to the significance of later developments. The history of higher popular education is not that of a single movement, but of the interaction between two main groups of organised effort, agreeing in certain social impulses but of independent origin and separated by the influence of historic antecedents ; one of them deriving its inspiration from the universities and aiming at the extension of university teaching, the other developing in a series of organisations which represent the intellectual side of an industrial movement.

Organisation is one of the chief factors differentiating modern developments of education in every sphere from the partial and often isolated experiments of an earlier epoch. By the close of the century the State had asserted in various ways its right of control, and a large measure of initiative fell within the domain of public authorities. New sources of financial aid were placed at the disposal of voluntary effort; and the claim of educational movements to public support was advanced on the general pretext that they contributed to the solution of a problem in which the interests of society as a whole were involved.

Yet the charge brought against organised education is that, so far from remedying, it has served to aggravate, social defects; that it has nourished a dislike for productive labour and, in stamping out barbarism, has weakened initiative; that it has challenged parental authority and emancipated the young before they have arrived at years of discretion, giving them a distaste for mental exertion; that for those who pursue education in later life the way of advance may be plainer and the path more secure, but there is not among adult students the same vigour and self-dependence that was characteristic of an earlier generation; and lastly, that in handing over responsibility to the State organised societies run the risk of forgetting their ideals.

It is much easier to draw logical inferences than to weigh the evidence of history. Yet a study of the past brings consolation; for many of the evils criticised are older than the causes alleged to explain them. For the past hundred years, a series of statements which suggest a growing desire for knowledge are balanced by an equal number to the opposite effect.[1] Parental

---

[1] ' Propose to a working man any great measure affecting the whole body, and he immediately asks himself the question, What am I to get by it ? meaning, what at this instant am I to have in my hand or in my pocket that I should like to have ? . . . There he sticks '—*Place MSS.* 27827, p. 194 (1835). ' Mechanics resist every novelty and shrink from every

apathy was lamented in the early reports of government inspectors ; and it was complained that education failed to reach those who were most in need of it.
On the other hand, there is evidence that the old attitude
of hostility is losing ground among a generation of
parents who have passed through the schools, and
that they are anxious that their children should appear

effort, unless it appear—and appear to their mode of comprehension—that
money will be made out of it on the spot '—Claxton, *Hints to Mechanics on
Self-Education and Mutual Instruction*, 89 (1838).   ' The great want of our
time I believe to be—a disposition on the part of our industrial population to obtain instruction.   This does not at present exist '—*Society of
Arts' Report on Industrial Instruction*, 122 *et passim* (1853).   ' I found the
towns [in Lancashire] vying with each other in the erection of new town
halls and in their superior style of erecting houses of business ; I found
also working men had bettered their physical condition considerably.
But I confess with pain, that I saw they had gone back, intellectually and
morally. . . .   In our old Chartist times, it is true, Lancashire working
men were in rags by thousands ; and many of them lacked food.   But
their intelligence was demonstrated wherever you went.   You would see
them in groups discussing the great doctrines of political justice . . . or
they were in earnest dispute respecting the teachings of socialism.   *Now*
you will see no such groups in Lancashire.   But you will hear well-dressed
working men talking, as they walk with their hands in their pockets, of
Co-ops . . . and their shares in them or in building societies.   And you
will see others, like idiots, leading small greyhound dogs, covered with
cloth, in a string !   They are about to race and they are betting money as
they go ! . . .   Except in Manchester and Liverpool, . . . I gathered no
large audiences in Lancashire.   Working men had ceased to think, and
wanted to hear no thoughtful talk ; at least, it was so with the greater
number.   From Lancashire I passed into Yorkshire, . . . and then . . .
began to lecture among the Northumberland colliers.   They heard me
eagerly '—*Life of Thomas Cooper*, by himself, 392 *sq.* (1869–70).   ' The
difficulty of persuading workmen to listen to anything which does not
concern pleasure or profit has long been acknowledged, and is, I think, even
stronger than it used to be '—Arnold Toynbee, Co-operative Congress,
1882.   ' The people have all been busy getting on, some too busy to think
of anything except their work, some too set on the pleasures now opened
to them to care for knowledge. . . .   It may be a stage in progress '—
Toynbee Hall Report, 1899–1900.
On the other hand, the correspondence in the *Mechanics' Magazine*
(1823–) throws some light on the attitude of intelligent workmen in the
early part of the last century ; we find genuine complaints of the difficulties in the way of self-culture, which have been repeated continually
ever since.   A citizen of Birmingham, writing to Hume in 1824, describes
the artisans of the town as ' rife with that sanguine and independent energy
which naturally results from partial and newly acquired knowledge

decently clad.[1] In this respect compulsion may exercise
the same stimulus as the pressure formerly used by
voluntary societies ; and, as instruction is better adapted
to vital needs, its appeal extends. Again, the success
of adult education in former years is liable to be
exaggerated, while its failure is overlooked. Institutions suffered from lack of resources and tried methods,
and from an isolation which made their position insecure. Much of the enthusiasm for knowledge arose
from inexperience, and failed when it was put to
a practical test. The heroic self-dependence of the
People's College at Sheffield belongs emphatically to
a stage of transition ; for it is seen that advanced study
cannot be self-supporting. The action of the State,
in promoting elementary education, has at any rate

untempered by experience. They are . . . enthusiastically excited with
the first undisciplined impulse of intellectual power . . . a set of intelligent, able and generally meritorious fellows '—*Place MSS.* 27827, p. 28.
Master engineers and others, examined before the Select Committee on
Machinery 1824, gave evidence of a general desire for scientific knowledge,
and an improvement in dress, habits and intelligence among the better
class artisans—*ibid.*, p. 70 *sq. Cf.* a typical passage in the opening number
of the *Flint Glass Makers' Magazine* (1850), advocating the education of
' every man in our trade beginning at the eldest and coming down to the
youngest. . . . If you do not wish to stand as you are and suffer more
oppression, we say to you, get knowledge, and in getting knowledge you
get power. . . . Let us earnestly advise you to educate ; get intelligence
instead of alcohol—it is sweeter and more lasting '—Webb, *TradeUnionism*,
179.   The first collective demand for education, so far as I can discover,
belongs to the year 1830, when 700 mechanics of Birmingham signed a
petition, on the reconstitution of King Edward's Grammar School, praying
that part of the endowment might be set apart for the benefit of the poorer
classes.

   [1] Booth, *Final Volume*, 202 *sq.* ' As regards the argument that by
allowing children to attend school at three years of age [instead of five]
the responsibility of the parent is weakened and their control over the
children diminished to the moral detriment both of parents and children,
the Committee are confident that in practice the general result is often the
other way. It is a common experience to find that children who are
attending school are cleaner and better clothed than those who remain
at home, and that there is a marked deterioration in the general appearance
of the children in any district on Saturdays and during the holidays '—
*Report of Consultative Committee (Board of Education) upon school attend-
ance of children below the age of five* (1908), 26.

multiplied the number of students who are competent to proceed to a higher level; while increased aid has reduced the financial difficulty which handicapped the poor. Whether the growth of opportunity will tend to weaken idealism and the impulse to self-sacrifice, remains to be seen. At present the conditions which the question presupposes do not exist. Difficulties which hinder systematic study have not ceased, and many of them are only beginning to attract attention. Economic hindrances are as numerous in years of prosperity as in a period of distress. Those who compare the history of recent movements with the efforts of individual students in the earlier half of the last century, will have little reason to lament a decay of enterprise. The amount of personal service rendered by artisans in the instruction of their own class has certainly increased. In this, as in other spheres, a study of history is the ' best cordial for drooping hearts.'

The demand for knowledge has been subject to fluctuations which are influenced by external circumstances and events. One is tempted to seek a connection between educational movements and the vicissitudes of trade. In some cases a depression of trade, reducing the hours of labour, has produced an increase in the attendance at places of instruction.[1] As the discipline of adversity has marked a turning point in the career of individual students, so a general displacement of labour may revive the feeling that knowledge is power, and that, if the people could understand the problem, they might effect a solution. Conversely, on the return of prosperity, idealism may yield to the pursuit of material interests and the most active minds

---

[1] Growth of night schools and adult classes in Lancashire during the depression caused by the American Civil War, 1861–5. Binns, *Century of Education*, 180 *n.*

may be absorbed in business routine. So it seemed to some of the Chartist leaders who had lived through the hungry forties ; and the same impression has been recorded in more recent times. But this theory does not account for all the facts. Commercial depression may remove the obstacle of 'overtime,' but it also breeds a deadening sense of insecurity. It may inspire heroism and self-sacrifice, but it diminishes financial resources and diverts energy from normal pursuits.[1] On the other hand, the rise of the Mechanics' Institutes and the success of University Extension among the miners of Durham are difficult to explain on the hypothesis which has been suggested ; and, if the impulse which created the Working Men's Colleges was derived from Chartist unrest, it was during the years of prosperity which followed that it produced plenteous results. It is safer to draw a general parallel between the periodic recurrence of educational movements and the revivals which occur in the sphere of commerce when trade is at its lowest ebb. The opportunity for awakening enthusiasm comes at the moment when previous efforts have most clearly failed.[2]

The demand is not constant, but it may be growing

[1] E.g. the collapse of a remarkably successful branch of the University Extension movement, in the Tyne district, owing to the Miners' strike in 1887.

[2] Complaints of indifference come mostly from persons who are engaged in awakening interest, and are generally a prelude to some new enterprise. ' Times change rapidly ; the spirit of the eighties, or even of the early nineties, has already passed away. . . . In education there has indeed been immense progress ; the machinery of schools has developed, and opportunities are at everyone's doors. But the enthusiasm for education has gone ; no one to-day would venture to raise the old cry of learning and culture for the masses with very much hope of an eager response '— *Toynbee Hall Report*, 1900–1 ; *cf.* account of a meeting at Toynbee Hall, in which reference was made to the enthusiasm aroused among working men in the North by University Extension in the early eighties, which, it seemed, no longer existed (*Co-operative News*, December 19, 1903). This was on the eve of the Tutorial class movement.

by degrees more stable and comprehensive. Every established institution has its remnant of serious students whose industry varies in direct proportion to the standard demanded of them.[1] Of this, the history of institutions so various as the Adult Schools, Ruskin College, and the College in Crowndale Road, contains ample evidence ; and the same class of artisans who frequented Huxley's lectures in Jermyn Street in the fifties[2] have attended in equal number and with the same regularity a course at Westminster in recent years. The spread of organisation in different forms among the working class has brought forward individuals keenly alive to the need of education, very often possessed of original ideas, and ready to assume the rôle of leadership. It is through the influence of such men that no movement has ceased without transmitting a heritage to later generations. Certain localities, again, occupy a central place in the history of adult education and have exercised a continuous influence. Thus it is that every new outburst of enthusiasm contains some of the force of earlier movements, and that influences which formerly flowed in separate channels gradually converge. The Workers'

[1] 'The history of the [University Extension] movement shows that the number of real students and the seriousness and value of their work has been in direct proportion to the extent of the demand made by the University Authority on the intellectual energy and industry of the student '—Dr. R. D. Roberts, *University Extension under the Old and the New Conditions* (an address at the Cambridge Summer Meeting, 1908), 17.

[2] Monday evening lectures on science and its applications at the Museum of Practical Geology, Jermyn Street, during the winter ; six courses of six lectures each by gentlemen connected with the Museum, fee 6*d.* Every man had to obtain a foreman's certificate, stating that he was a *bonâ fide* artisan. Accommodation for 600, applications usually reached 1000 ; 600 would drop to 450 or 420 as the days lengthened, but attendance generally regular. The students, chiefly superior artisans, attended carefully and asked questions at the close of the lecture. ' A more intelligent, more industrious or a more careful set of listeners . . . are rarely to be met with '—*Committee on Public Institutions, 1860*, QQ. 165–85, 547–67, 591–619, 1435, 1487.

Educational Association (1903) has drawn together a variety of movements, and a common impulse has elicited their latent powers. In another sense, forces which have strengthened the demand for knowledge may have introduced new limitations. The aims of study have been more clearly defined by industrial progress and by political changes which have opened to the industrial classes a larger share in public administration; and the demand has been encouraged through the application of science to new spheres of human activity. It is possible that this twofold development may exercise, at least temporarily, a narrowing influence. The interest formerly aroused by liberal culture may have yielded unduly to a demand for knowledge with a direct bearing on technical efficiency or political and economic aims. But the value of any form of study will depend ultimately on the spirit in which it is pursued. Where time is limited and specialisation is synonymous with thoroughness, method rather than subject-matter must be the test of a liberal education. It is found that technical or professional studies, pursued on scientific lines, possess a much greater educational value than was formerly admitted; and there are already signs that, as the idea of citizenship is more clearly appreciated, a broader type of human culture may be evolved from forms of instruction which have a reference to definite social needs.[1] It may be too soon to rely much on the experience of the Tutorial classes; but their history suggests that, where the spirit of learning has been awakened, the range of intellectual interests naturally extends.

It would be difficult, even with the aid of more

---

[1] Thus a Tutorial class in ' Civics ' was planned by Professor Geddes in Battersea (1907) with the definite object of broadening the study of social and economic questions.

accurate statistics than are generally available, to measure the extent to which an interest in serious study has found expression among different sections of the working class. The rolls of membership in Working Men's Colleges and Institutes, and the classification of attendances at Extension lectures and classes pursuing a continuous course of study, include individuals in every kind of employment, from miners and highly skilled artisans to factory hands and labourers. Except in the mining centres and a few industrial towns, the most regular and serious students appear to have belonged generally to the superior grade of artisans, to whom may be added about an equal number of school teachers, clerks, small tradesmen and assistants. There is, throughout, a tendency for movements to lose hold of the class to whom they originally appealed ; but working-class institutions during the past sixty years have not failed in this respect to the same extent as the Mechanics' Institutes in the earlier half of the last century.

INDEX